Women Going Backwards

Law and change in a family unfriendly society

SANDRA BERNS
Griffith University, Australia

ASHGATE

Published by
Ashgate Publishing Limited
Gower House
Croft Road
Aldershot
Hampshire GU11 3HR
England

Ashgate Publishing Limited
131 Main Street
Burlington, VT 05401-5600 USA

Ashgate website: http://www.ashgate.com

British Library Cataloguing in Publication Data
Berns, Sandra
    Women going backwards : law and change in a family
    unfriendly society. - (Applied legal philosophy)
    1.Sociological jurisprudence 2.Sex discrimination against
    women 3.Women - Legal status, laws, etc.
    I.Title
    340.1'15

Library of Congress Cataloging-in-Publication Data
Berns, Sandra.
    Women going backwards : law and change in a family unfriendly society / Sandra Berns.
        p. cm. -- (Applied legal philosophy)
    Includes bibliographical references and index.
    ISBN 0-7546-2303-3
        1. Women--Legal status, laws, etc. 2. Equality before the law. I. Title. II. Series.

    K644 .B47 2002
    342'.0878--dc21   2002066466

ISBN 0 7546 2303 3

Printed and bound in Great Britain by MPG Books Ltd, Bodmin, Cornwall

Contents

Preface

In most Western countries laws prohibiting discrimination against women, in employment and elsewhere, have been on the statute books for between 20 and 30 years. Despite this, the earnings gender gap persists and occupational segregation remains entrenched. Other depressing constants also remain entrenched, for example the over-representation of women and the children they nurture among the poor.

What follows is an exploration of the role of law in sustaining these inequalities. While some parts of this work focus on the particular structures embedded in the Australian legal system, the issues raised by these structures and the periodic 'moral panics' over apparently unfavourable demographic indicators are not unique to Australia. They are replicated in common law jurisdictions such as Canada, the UK and the USA and in civil law jurisdictions such as Sweden. For this reason, much of what follows will have a comparative focus.

Because law operates as a system, and because anti-discrimination law and equal opportunity law represent a minute fraction of that system, the legal focus will include family law, social welfare law, employment law and taxation law. All of these bodies of law have a profound impact upon gender relations and upon the opportunities available to men and women. Two key theoretical constructs will be introduced in our exploration of the relationship between the legal and the social: the notion of the unencumbered citizen and that of the breadwinner homemaker bargain. Together, it will be argued, these two constructs are both socially and legally embedded in liberal states. The interaction between the laws and policies which serve to reinforce them and changing social mores and expectations collectively produce the outcomes subsequently decried by politicians and policy makers and which, in turn, become the subject of media fuelled moral panics and further efforts at reform.

Acknowledgements

A Griffith University Research Grant funded research for this book. I should like to express my gratitude to Griffith University for the funding provided. I should also like to express my appreciation for the skill and diligence of my research assistant, Fiona Ring. Without her assistance and enthusiasm for the project it could not have been completed in as timely and effective a fashion.

Many colleagues have read portions of this manuscript during the time it was under preparation. I am deeply grateful for their time and for the valuable suggestions they have made. Particularly noteworthy are Professor Rosemary Hunter, Dr Bridget Cullen-Mandikos and Ms Paula Baron and I owe them my deepest gratitude for their assistance and suggestions. Without their help, this project could not have come to fruition. Responsibility for any errors or inconsistencies is of course mine alone.

List of Abbreviations

ABS	Australian Bureau of Statistics
ACAC	Australian Conciliation and Arbitration Commission
ACTU	Australian Council of Trade Unions
ADR	Alternative Dispute Resolution
AIFS	Australian Institute of Family Studies
AIRC	Australian Industrial Relations Commission
ALP	Australian Labor Party
ART	Assisted Reproductive Technology
AWA	Australian Workplace Agreement
AWIRS	Australian Workplace and Industrial Relations Survey
BCA	Business Council of Australia
BHP	BHP Steel Limited
CSA	Child Support Agency
EEO	Equal Employment Opportunity
EEON	Equal Employment Opportunity Network
FLA	Family Law Act 1975
GST	Goods and Services Tax
HREOC	Human Rights and Equal Opportunity Commission
ILO	International Labour Organisation
IWF	Independent Women's Forum
JET	Jobs, Education and Training
NESB	Non English Speaking Background
OECD	Organisation for Economic Cooperation and Development
PWPA	Professors World Peace Academy
SDA	Sex Discrimination Act 1984
WRA	Workplace Relations Act 1996

Chapter 1

The Persistence of Inequality

Framing Gender

Gender has become a culturally laden signifier. Sometimes used to differentiate the social from the biological, gender itself has become gendered. In common parlance, gender issues often slide inexorably into women's issues and are in that way designated as marginal, outside the concerns and lives of ordinary people. In this book, I hope to unpack signifiers such as gender, worker and family, and suggest ways in which the common readings of these signifiers reinforce existing practices and act as barriers to change. This chapter and those that follow are about the gendering of gender, and the impact of that gendering upon the lives of men and women. Inevitably, this book is also about change. Some of these changes are legal; others are social and still others are driven by political and policy agendas. While much of my focus will be Australian, the Australian story cannot be understood in isolation and the forces driving change transcend national boundaries. For this reason, substantial use will be made of comparative data from other jurisdictions, principally the United States, the United Kingdom, Canada and Sweden.

Because certain institutions are central to the ways in which gender is constructed within Australia and in nations with similar legal and political systems, I will concentrate on five areas: equal opportunity law,[1] family law, industrial relations law, social welfare law and taxation law. Together, law and policy in these realms shape the allocation of resources and opportunities within contemporary societies and have a significant impact upon the overall equality of men and women.[2] They also have a profound impact upon our understandings of work and the worker and upon the significance of family and the roles of family members. Four have, over the last three decades, undergone profound even radical change, while the fifth, taxation law, has, in Australia, proved relatively resistant to change and has often acted as a brake upon developments in other areas.[3] All are profoundly gendered, and the ways in which they are gendered are, increasingly, impacting upon the ways in which men and women see their roles and their choices and the ways in which these are related to the state. In this chapter I will begin to look at some of these institutions, chiefly those associated with work and family and sketch the areas of tension. This chapter will also introduce a key unifying conception, that of the 'unencumbered citizen', which will be explored in depth in chapter 2. I will argue that the unencumbered citizen, the unspoken given in political and economic theorising, continues to have a profound impact upon the ways in which our lives are constructed: as men and women, as workers, as parents and as citizens.

Of Workers and Women: The Role of Differential Gendering

In Australia, legislation requiring equal employment opportunity[4] and proscribing sex discrimination including sexual harassment[5] has been in place at the Commonwealth level since the mid-1980s. While the equal employment opportunity legislation is patchy, the extent of coverage depending upon the size of the employer,[6] its introduction suggested a commitment to changing workplace cultures and facilitating the participation of women. Sex discrimination legislation presents complications of its own. The coverage available depends upon whether particular workplaces are covered by Commonwealth legislation or by analogous legislation at state level, and many workplaces have remained uncovered until relatively recently, Queensland and Tasmania lagging well behind the other states in providing coverage for workers not covered by Commonwealth legislation. It is difficult to measure the impact of equal employment opportunity (EEO) law, both because it is limited to large employers and because it was phased in gradually, the largest workplaces being covered first. While some workplace cultures have begun to change, and there is some evidence that occupational segregation is beginning to diminish in covered workplaces,[7] progress has been glacial. The practical impact of sex discrimination legislation is more readily measured, however the continuing flow of discrimination complaints suggests that many employers (particularly small employers) disregard their obligations. In addition, because sex discrimination complaints must be initiated by the affected individual and are litigated only if conciliation fails, it has proved ineffective as an engine of cultural change.[8]

The most widely trumpeted development of the nineties, the 'family friendly' workplace, owes little to either sex discrimination or equal employment opportunity laws. Rather, talk of the family friendly workplace is linked to the increasing emphasis upon flexible practices, a development that the Liberal government wishes to portray as 'family friendly'. The evidence suggests that many flexible practices, such as the extension of the 'normal working day' from 6.00am to 10.00pm to enable the employer to make maximum use of resources, have made it difficult for many women to maintain their employment. Women are often unable to access childcare services before 7.00am or after 6.00pm and the extended hours also made it difficult for women to meet other family obligations. While some organisations, both large and small, are initiating progressive family friendly policies, these remain islands of progress in an otherwise bleak landscape.

Despite the fairly lengthy history of equal opportunity legislation in Australia, and the more recent fanfare about the family friendly workplace, two features of the Australian labour market have proved resistant to change. First, by world standards, the Australian labour market retains a significant degree of occupational segregation on the basis of gender, both horizontally in terms of occupational categories and hierarchically, high-level executive, managerial and professional roles remaining almost exclusively male.[9] Second, although the earnings gender gap has narrowed significantly since the equal pay decisions of the late 1960s and early 1970s, it remains a feature of the industrial relations landscape and is inextricably linked to the persistence of occupational segregation. Since the introduction of Commonwealth EEO and sex discrimination legislation, the decrease in the earnings gender gap has been negligible. More disturbingly, OECD data suggests that during the period between 1987 and 1997 the gender gap actually widened, largely due to a massive increase in the earnings gender gap for casual and part-time women. Information from the Australian Bureau of Statistics (ABS) confirms this and indicates that during the last decade not only has the gap between the earnings of male and female workers widened,[10] but also that between the top ten per cent and the bottom ten per cent of workers.[11]

Working women are losing ground in two ways. Not only is the gender gap increasing, women are also losing ground in terms of their distribution along the continuum of male wages as wages become more dispersed. According to the ABS, 'the gap between the lowest and highest decile for weekly total earnings was greater for males ($1014.70) than for females ($755.10)'.[12] Meritocratisation[13] is becoming entrenched in the Australian workforce, and women are not among its beneficiaries. Undoubtedly, many men will also be among the losers, both because of their concentration within the contracting manufacturing sector and because the remaining unskilled and labouring positions are clustered in the lowest decile.[14]

The disparity between wage outcomes for men and women and between the highest and lowest deciles seems likely to continue to increase. In 1996, in a major reform of the industrial relations framework, the arbitral regime that had been in place since Federation was abandoned. The award system was replaced by bargaining at the enterprise level, the remaining awards retaining only a 'safety net' function. The most recent ABS figures suggest that the increase in the earnings gender gap is largely due to significant pay increases in male dominated (and highly unionised) sectors, particularly among older male workers. Younger male workers are also losing ground, suggesting that the increase in gender equity between young female workers and young male workers may flow from falling wages among men in this age group and thus be a cause for concern rather than an encouraging development.

The new Commonwealth legislation[15] 'does not require the parties to an enterprise agreement to consider the equity implications of any agreement reached'.[16] While Part VI, Division 2[17] entrenches equal pay for work of equal value and proscribes discrimination there is also no legislative requirement for positive scrutiny of agreements prior to registration to ensure that they comply with sex discrimination and EEO law. Although Australian Workplace Agreements (AWAs) and enterprise agreements are subject to the no disadvantage test, the difference between AWAs in female dominated sectors and those in male dominated sectors is striking. In male dominated sectors, AWAs tend to incorporate productivity increases among their terms. These are largely absent in female dominated sectors, where AWAs are more likely to be concerned with work conditions and do not make provision for productivity increases.[18] Research into the changes to work hours since the advent of enterprise bargaining suggests that:

Employers in female dominated industries have been able to negotiate flexible hours provisions, such as span of hours, increases in part-time and casual positions, and reductions in penalty provisions, which are of greater benefit to employers than to employees. In male-dominated industries, on the other hand, the flexible hours provisions are more likely to include rostered days off, flexitime, and time off in lieu of overtime, which, while benefiting employers, also offer employees the opportunity to use flexible hours to their own benefit.[19]

Gender issues are thus relegated to the province of equal opportunity legislation and remain part of the periphery in an industrial relations framework from which the social has been displaced and the model of individuals bargaining at arm's length has attained hegemony.[20] A 1994 report from the Affirmative Action Agency suggested that less than two per cent of private sector employers saw any need to link enterprise bargaining outcomes with their affirmative action objectives, emphasising the marginality of affirmative action and its status as an externality.[21]

Another feature of conventional industrial relations analysis, its differentially gendered[22] character, is equally problematical. Analysis of work practices focuses upon job characteristics where the employees are male and upon personal and family characteristics where the employees are female.[23] When analysis is differentially gendered in this way, men as such disappear. The personal characteristics and family situations of male workers are obliterated and replaced by a quasi-universal image of the 'worker', reinforcing the dichotomy between workers and women. When the family wage was laid to rest in the late 1960s and early 1970s, the intention was to eliminate wages outcomes in which the male wage contained a component based upon presumed male responsibility for dependents. The current model acknowledges neither financial responsibility for dependents nor responsibility for carework. One reason it has proved so difficult to develop 'family friendly' policies is the pervasive assumption that taking account of family responsibilities is illicit. Workers are defined in terms of their relationship to other workers and to the workplace, women in terms of their family relationships and conventions concerning appropriate gender roles. The model of the worker that emerges is strikingly similar to the image of the 'unencumbered citizen'[24] that predominates in equality discourse generally. As with the citizen, its most important signifier is negative rather than positive, the apparent absence of gender.

The practice of differential gendering is not simply a feature of academic analysis, but deeply embedded in workplace cultures. Here, as elsewhere, language shapes reality in very specific ways. While these practices impact differently upon men and upon women, their impact is not limited by gender. When workers are defined without reference to their personal characteristics and family situations, it becomes entirely reasonable to presume that workers are available when and where required, an understanding that is profoundly compatible with the new model of workplace relations heralded by the legislation and the emphasis upon flexible workplaces. As the family wage became a thing of the past, the presumption that a worker had dependents to maintain lost its power as a bargaining chip. It was not replaced by any recognition that workers could not rely upon the unwaged labour of others to meet their domestic responsibilities. Instead, an awkward halfway house emerged. While the family wage was slowly vanishing, and the dual income household becoming normative, both workplaces and other infrastructures continued to be structured in traditional ways. Central to that tradition was the presumption that workers could rely upon the unwaged labour of others to meet their domestic responsibilities. Those workers who were unable to do so were largely concentrated in the casual and part-time sector at lower rates of pay. As benefits such as maternity and paternity leave began to appear in the public sector, and later in the private, they were typically seen, not as recognition that workers could no longer rely upon unwaged others for domestic labour and carework, but as special privileges for that hybrid creature, the female worker. Unlike the family wage, these benefits are seen as an imposition upon the market and some suggest that they are a form of discrimination against the childless.[25]

Both because the benefits that make up the family friendly workplace are understood as gendered, and because they are widely attributed to the pressure generated by equal opportunity measures, formally equal provisions produce inegalitarian outcomes. Should a man attempt to access his formally equal entitlement to paternity or carer's leave, or reject a proposed transfer because of the disruption it would cause to a partner's career, his behaviour can be seen as inappropriate. He has violated the norms associated with the status worker and adopted those associated with the 'female worker', and thus may be seen somewhat derisively to be following the 'mommy track'.[26] In this way, differential gendering both disadvantages those men who are seeking to reconcile their work and personal lives in progressive ways and acts as a barrier to change, particularly in times of high unemployment. The reluctance of many men to utilise available parenting and paternity leave provisions is one obvious outcome of differential gendering. A study of accountants in Ireland and the UK indicated that very few accountants took paid or unpaid paternity leave and those who did usually took it as annual leave or compassionate leave.[27]

Even in Sweden, with its long history of comparatively egalitarian relationships and with among the most progressive parental leave policies in the world, fathers utilise only around ten per cent of the available parental leave. Only 50 per cent utilise the 'daddy month', in part because they fear that to do so will damage them professionally.[28] Differential gendering reinforces the status of women as secondary workers[29] and, particularly in professional workplaces, suggests that those who seek to access legislative provisions guaranteeing maternity leave and carer's leave are not committed to their careers and have opted for the 'mommy track'. Conventional ways of ordering personal and working lives are thus buttressed against change despite the rhetorical affirmation of 'family friendly' work practices and workplaces.[30]

Differential gendering is not unique to industrial relations law and discourse. It is not destabilised by conventions requiring gender-neutral language because gender-neutral language tacitly reinforces differential gendering rather than destabilising it. Differential gendering is to be found in family law and policy, in taxation law and policy, in debates over the policy aspects of social welfare reform.

While it assumes different guises in different settings, its role is identical in all. Differential gendering implicitly figures 'woman' as the outsider: one who is not a worker, not a citizen. In this way, masculinity is simultaneously affirmed (as universal) and rendered invisible (and thus located beyond analysis).[31] If progress is to be made in narrowing the gender gap, and perhaps eradicating it, analysis must become fully gendered. Our battles are not with the men and women with whom we work, raise families and struggle for social justice, but with the hegemonic figures of the worker and the citizen and their private sphere counterparts, the breadwinner and the homemaker. The breadwinner and the homemaker are to the private sphere what the worker and citizen are to the public. They are the fulcrum upon which policy turns, as is clearly delineated by the increasing emphasis on government support for the single income family, family policy becoming a surrogate for policies designed to shore up the male breadwinner family.

The Equal Opportunity Paradox: From Women's Issues to Fathers' Rights

As the figures above emphasise, over the last decade it has become less likely that our lifetimes will see the gap between the wages of men and of women eliminated. We seem more willing to heed the voices decrying the changes that have already come about and the costs they impose,[32] sometimes even forgetting to ask why matters such as equal opportunity and childcare are still characterised as 'women's issues', and, by implication, relevant only to a special interest group.[33] An increasingly conservative political and social environment allied with a particular kind of economic rationalism has significantly altered the social landscape. Progressive forces spend much of their time defending the gains already made in a climate that seems hostile to claims of justice.[34]

As enthusiasm for equal opportunity wanes, new social movements are gaining significant ground. While these social movements are diverse, ranging from populist yearnings for a rural past decimated by the elimination of tariff protection and the vagaries of export demand for rural produce to an increasingly vocal fathers' rights movement, in many ways they collectively represent a politics of nostalgia. Their voices represent those who feel themselves marginalised, left with a repertoire of behaviours and responses that no longer produce desired results. This is hardly surprising.

Research in the United States suggests that the reforms of the Reagan era led to an increasing gap between the earnings of the best off segment of the community and those of the worst off and also suggests the following trends are critical:

> skill-based technological change, deindustrialization, industry deregulation, the decline of unions, lean production, winner-take-all labor markets, free trade, transnational capital mobility, immigration, and a persistent trade deficit.[35]

All of these trends are increasingly significant in Australia. Skill based technological change, deindustrialisation, industry deregulation, the decline of unions, immigration, transnational capital mobility and a persistent trade deficit have been structurally embedded in the Australian economy for more than a decade. Lean production, winner-take-all labour markets and free trade are more recent arrivals. While it is difficult to assess their impact in a fluid market setting, among those likely to have a significant impact in the Australian context are:

- the shift from an industrial economy to a service economy,
- the decline of unions,
- the impact of corporate and governmental downsizing,
- the replacement of permanent employees with a segmented labour force of relatively highly paid insiders and poorly paid outsiders, and
- the persistent current accounts deficit.

All are structurally embedded in the Australian economy and their effect has been augmented by the deregulation of the industrial relations framework. Bluestone notes:

> that while educational and occupational skill-wage differentials were growing rapidly in the United States and the United Kingdom during the 1980s, the experience elsewhere was quite different. Wage equality increased in the Netherlands; wage differentials did not change noticeably in France, Germany, and Italy; and wage dispersion increased modestly if at all in Australia, Canada, Japan and Sweden.[36]

He attributes these differences to the failure of most other jurisdictions to adopt the Reagan-Thatcher model of full deregulation and laissez-faire trade policies. Australia is adopting policies similar to those pursued in the US and UK in the 1980s and increasing wage dispersion and decreasing gender equity are already becoming apparent. Given this, it is likely that the gap between the wages outcomes of the highest decile (in which men are over-represented) and those of the lowest decile (in which women are over-represented) will continue to increase.[37] Against this background it is hardly surprising that many people perceive themselves to be economically disenfranchised, and that among them are the male casualties of deindustrialisation.[38]

The increasing public presence of the fathers' rights movement is a phenomenon of the nineties. While it emerged in Australia during the 1970s,[39] in the 1990s it has become an effective and vigorous pressure group and has succeeded in capturing the sympathy of government.[40] The burgeoning of the Internet has provided an environment in which fathers' rights groups can exchange information and ideas on a worldwide basis. Internationally at least, it is possible to distinguish between different 'official ideologies' which are deployed in different ways and interact with the wider men's movement. In Australia, many organisations allied with the fathers' rights movement, for example, the Gold Coast based Men's Rights Agency, and the Melbourne based Lone Fathers' Association, explicitly appropriate the rhetoric of equal opportunity in advancing their claims.[41]

The public rhetoric of these groups emphasises the formal equality women now enjoy in the workplace as beneficiaries of equal opportunity laws and contrasts that imagined ideal with the outcomes of Family Court decisions and with their self-description as 'disposable parents'.[42] The evidence suggests this is, in both cases, an oversimplification. The most dramatic economic progress made by women predated Commonwealth sex discrimination and equal employment opportunity legislation by more than a decade and was a consequence of feminist and trade union agitation for equal pay in the 1960s and early 1970s.[43] A few years later, in an equally decisive break with the past, the *Family Law Act* 1975 (*FLA*) abandoned the fault based system which had prevailed essentially unchanged since before Federation and replaced it with a no fault model. These two legal changes, one judicial and one parliamentary, redrew the legal landscape of gender relations in Australia.[44] What they did not change was the reality, either in the workplace or in the allocation of childcare and domestic labour.[45]

Progress towards closing the gender gap has stalled, and there is evidence it is widening once again.[46] OECD modelling suggests that the increase[47] is caused by a substantial increase for part-time and casual workers in female dominated sectors.[48] These are significant areas of employment for women with caring responsibilities; indeed they are often the only jobs open to women seeking part-time work with 'family friendly' hours. Because women remain responsible for most of the caring labour in Australian homes, some prefer to work hours that allow them to be available to their children outside school hours and to perform household duties.[49] Yet choice, as such, is only one factor pushing women into the 'peripheral workforce'. A significant proportion of women in the part-time workforce would prefer more hours, and women are more likely than men to hold two or more jobs. This suggests that for many women 'part-time status is less a matter of choice than an artefact of women's employment opportunities in an occupationally and industrially segregated workforce'.[50] Because the historic primacy given full time (male) workers by trade unions and the difficulties in organising casual and part-time employees, these are sectors where the rates of union membership are extremely low. Such workers have little clout in enterprise bargaining and in negotiating favourable AWAs and often must take what they are given or lose out entirely. As Fastenau notes:

> Occupational and industrial segregation appear to be the products of structural/systemic discriminations arising from historical socio-cultural forces, and the lesser benefits experienced by women in employment in these segregated occupations and industries are likely to be the products of their weaker social and political as well as industrial power.[51]

Within family law, the market's negative becomes a developed print. Following separation, most couples replicate pre-separation gender roles in parenting arrangements; either by consent order or through a parenting plan. In the minority of cases that proceed to litigation, social realities model decision-making.[52] While in recent reported cases Family Court judges have largely avoided obvious forms of gender bias, when relationships fail, the Family Court is confronted by evidence concerning the division of household labour and the earning capacities of the parties. Pre-divorce, parenting practices usually track conventional gender roles. The Family Court recognises those realities in its decisions, effectively reinstating breadwinner homemaker contract following dissolution.[53] That same allocation of caring labour embeds:

> The separation of men from children/child care within the economic provider discourse, a separation which in turn informs the gendered strategies of men and women in negotiating divorce and separation and, for many divorced fathers, their sense of a need to 'be a man' in coping with separation.[54]

Despite their construction of a profoundly gendered reality, a reality overtly and self-consciously opposed to that inhabited by their proclaimed archenemy, the 'feminists',[55] arguments put by fathers' rights groups provide a wedge allowing discourse to be opened up in a significant way. Both because their arguments are deeply rooted in rights discourse and because they span family and market, these arguments invite us to be much more open about the links between family roles and market roles and the ways in which they interact. Their appropriation of rights discourse provides an odd counterpoint to the absence of a constitutionally entrenched 'Bill of Rights'. In Australia there is an additional irony in this appropriation, given that the new parenting provisions are explicitly couched in the language of responsibilities rather than rights. Claims of rights are empowering; responsibilities are often burdensome. 'Rights' have long been the prerogative of white, middle class, heterosexual males, constructed to exclude those who are not white, not middle class, not heterosexual.[56] To do rights is specifically to do a particular way of claiming masculinity, of situating oneself as a masculine subject.[57]

One prominent strand of fathers' rights discourse explicitly argues that equal opportunity ought to operate within the family exactly as it does within the market. Thus, arguments are put that just as women are now able to compete for employment on an equal footing, so too men ought to be seen as equally able to engage in primary parenting and equally appropriate as custodial parents when a relationship breaks down.[58] It is easy to see the attraction of this model. Operating within an intellectual framework which suggests that 'equal opportunity laws' allowed women to insinuate themselves within the 'masculine' domain of the market, they argue that these laws 'ought' to be extended to the family. The subtext is that equal opportunity deprives men of jobs and privileges women by disallowing criteria that traditionally favoured men; the last-on, first-off rule is a good example.[59] Transplanted to the family law context the argument is that current practices deny men equal opportunity in family law by giving weight to factors such as who has been the primary parent during the relationship and who is better able to provide evidence of parenting skills.[60] Some argue that the default position ought to be father custody, thus restoring the incentive men need to be productive providers and curbing women's 'destructive sexuality'![61] While these arguments are interesting, as framed they are limited, reductive and self-serving. In their typical form they suggest that because women now have equal opportunity in the market,[62] having displaced men, so too men should be entitled to equal opportunity in the home (at least after the end of a relationship).[63] The argument put by Malcolm Mathias, President of the Victorian Branch of the Lone Fathers' Association, is typical of this genre:

> Males seem to be penalised for earning the family income by denying them equal opportunity to become the custodial parent after family breakdown. The Family Court expectation is that they should go on earning the income for two households after divorce, irrespective of who chose divorce.[64]

Here, as elsewhere, the rhetoric of equal opportunity stops short of making gender visible. Although women have gained significant economic ground since the 1970s, and men, at least in some occupational categories, have lost some ground, economic parity remains out of reach. While both discrimination and occupational segregation are significant factors, both are exacerbated by the fact that women continue to be responsible for a majority of domestic labour and childcare and either choose occupations that facilitate a dual role or are believed to do so.[65] It remains accurate, therefore, to describe women as economically disadvantaged and affectively advantaged. The rhetoric of fathers' rights groups reminds us that the converse is also true. If women remain economically disadvantaged by their continuing responsibility for childcare and for domestic labour,[66] it is also possible to see men as economically advantaged and affectively disadvantaged. In both cases, moreover, it is possible to characterise the relevant disadvantage as 'chosen'.

The statistical information concerning men's relative economic advantages is relatively well known. The background data upon which I base my claim of affective disadvantage is less well understood, although many of its elements are commonplace. Because men are relatively unlikely to assume equal responsibility for childcare and for domestic labour, they are frequently less involved in the day-to-day lives of their children than are women. Their gendered entitlement to disassociate themselves from the minutiae of family life leaves them vulnerable, not least because they are less aware of the fragility of relationships than are their partners and, as a consequence, frequently unaware of impending breakdown. While these disadvantages are submerged while relationships subsist, both are sheeted home when separation occurs.

On dissolution two things happen. First, because conventional roles remain strong and the former wife has usually been the primary parent, in a majority of cases she is likely to be the residential parent most often by a 'consent order', or, more recently, as the outcome of a negotiated parenting plan.[67] Second, because of the disparity between male and female wages and because of her role as primary parent she is often unable to support herself and the children fully.[68] At this point, the Child Support formula comes into play, transferring resources from the former husband to the former wife in order that she may provide for the children with minimal reliance on the public purse.[69] In this way, the legal order reinstates conventional roles upon separation, effectively sustaining the breadwinner homemaker bargain following family breakdown.[70] In this context, it is important that two points be made. First, given the extent to which conventional roles remain entrenched within the wider community and the extent to which powerful institutional forces operate to reinforce them, it is difficult to see what other options are available, particularly if family law is considered on its own. Second, while the rhetoric of the fathers' rights movement is often extreme, it is important to understand the source of their grievances. It is, however, much more difficult to understand how those grievances can be addressed, in fact they cannot be addressed unless we begin to modify the background conditions that foster them. These conditions are a consequence of the radical separation of home and workplace that is our legacy from the industrial revolution and the regulatory frameworks that developed during the nineteenth and twentieth centuries. Before suggesting avenues for change, it is important to explore the ways in which the state has shaped both home and workplace and the consequences of that shaping, both in jurisdictions where it is relatively covert, such as Australia, and in jurisdictions where it is overt, such as Sweden.

Family and Market: An Unholy Alliance – The Australian Story

At the heart of that shaping in Australia has been the use of wage regulation as an instrument of social policy, a practice that has shaped work practices and social practices. Until the late 1960s, the 'family wage' was the norm.[71] Ardently fought for by trade unionists at the dawn of the twentieth century,[72] it was defined as a wage that permitted a working man to support a wife and two or three children at an adequate level. In this way, the worker officially became the breadwinner, what Patricia Mann has termed the incorporated male family self.[73] Female workers were defined by the absence of such responsibilities, the presumption being they were responsible only for their own keep.[74] The family wage was entrenched by decisions of the Conciliation and Arbitration Court that set the minimum wage for women at 50-55 per cent of male earnings except where they worked in exclusively female occupations.[75] Many occupations were closed to women as a consequence of trade union pressure.[76] In the public service, women were compelled to resign upon marriage or, if they were allowed to continue working, were denied permanent status.[77]

This wage structure remained intact until the Women's Employment Board drafted women into essential war work at significantly higher rates of pay during World War II.[78] Following demobilisation, women were once again excluded from male jobs and the minimum wage reinstated. Undoubtedly the pressure generated by the reduction post-war was one factor in the 1950 decision of the Federal Arbitration Court that set the female basic wage at 75 per cent of male wages. This policy has had two lasting effects. First, the combination of modest female wages and the widespread exclusion of married women from the workforce denied most women independent access to resources, reinforcing their dependence on men.[79] Second, it artificially depressed wages in female sectors and entrenched high levels of occupational segregation. High rates of occupational segregation and depressed wages in 'female occupations' remain key features of the Australian industrial landscape.[80]

Frances Castles suggests wages were a cornerstone of Australian social policy from Federation onwards and remained so until the concept of a 'family wage' began to collapse in the 1960s and that one consequence was the extraordinarily low rate of female employment.[81] Not until the National Wage Cases in 1969 and 1972 was the principle of a 'family wage' replaced by two very different principles, 'equal pay for equal work' (1969) and 'equal pay for work of equal value' (1972).[82] If social policy and trade union agitation were the engines that drove the concept of the 'family wage' and institutionalised particular family and economic structures by radically reducing alternatives, the family wage was only one thread in a complex tapestry.[83]

At much the same time as the family wage was entrenched as a key element in social policy, the Commonwealth parliament enacted a maternity allowance. The legislation provided for a payment of five pounds to the mother in respect of each occasion on which a child is either born alive or is viable.[84] One critical limitation was imposed. Section 6(1) provided that:

> The maternity allowance shall be payable only to women who are inhabitants of the Commonwealth or who intend to settle therein [while section 6(2) provided that] Women who are Asiatics, or are aboriginal natives of Australia, Papua, or the islands of the Pacific, shall not be paid a maternity allowance.[85]

Eligibility for the maternity allowance did not depend upon legal marriage, although the omission had been hotly debated in the Parliament, as it was feared that this feature would encourage women to become mothers before they became wives. While first-wave feminists argued for the maternity allowance as payment for services rendered to the state through the production of future citizens, it is perhaps better seen as a strategic response by government to falling birth rates and increasing reliance upon contraception.[86] Other elements of social policy also reinforced dependence. While entitlement to benefits was not generally differentially distributed by gender, only women qualified as 'dependent spouses' and a 'widow's pension' later became available in case of death or desertion, although it was terminated by remarriage.

Until the 1970s the legal regimes governing marriage and divorce largely followed those in the United Kingdom, although some Australian states liberalised access to divorce requirements well before similar moves in the UK. The real work of entrenching dependence in the context of a particular family form occurred at the intersection of industrial policy, social welfare policy and family law. The enthronement of the family wage as official state policy and the pervasive bars on the employment of married women proved effective and lasting as regulatory protocols, as did the absence of benefits for single mothers and the absence of supports for mothers who engaged in waged labour. Even where they remained unspoken, underlying such policies were a range of assumptions concerning distribution within families and appropriate family roles. These have remained strong despite legal changes.

Following the abandonment of the family wage as the centrepiece of Australian social policy, other regulatory mechanisms have reinforced relationships of dependence. De facto relationships are assimilated to legal relationships and governed by parallel regimes where heterosexual couples are concerned.[87] This kind of regulation is direct. It is obvious, lacking in subtlety. Much subtler regulatory paradigms are also at work. Taxation law, social security law and all of the hundreds of government policies that confer or withhold benefits according to policy decisions to encourage certain kinds of conduct and discourage others also function as regulatory systems.[88]

Despite the radical separation of family and market deemed axiomatic by our culture and institutions, this pattern of overt and covert regulation is remarkably similar to the mechanisms by which market relationships are regulated. Laws that protect consumers from the power of large corporations and seek to inhibit the development of anti-competitive pressures are commonplace. Increasingly they regulate the relationship between market actors (even those of apparently equal power), deem particular sorts of legal agreements improper or unenforceable.[89] Just as a family relationship renders contracts between family members unenforceable, an unequal power relationship between the parties to a commercial transaction may render unconscionable conduct that would otherwise pass unnoticed.[90] In this way, the law structures, reinforces and legitimates relationships within the market in much the same way in which it structures, reinforces and legitimates relationships within the family.[91]

None of this is remarkable, and that is my point. Our fantasy of separate spheres means that we have been reluctant to recognise that the regulatory paradigms influencing the conduct of market players and the regulatory paradigms influencing the conduct of family members are not independent self-referential systems. What happens in the market creates possibilities within the family as well as the market and what happens in the family creates possibilities within the market as well as the family. During much of Australia's history, three discrete policies united to produce a powerful impetus towards particular social structures. A generally protectionist stance towards local industry, radical restrictions on female workplace participation and a social welfare policy predicated upon the family wage united to produce particular sorts of outcomes.

Today, the policy picture is much more ambiguous. The protectionist stance has largely been abandoned and Australia is rapidly shifting from an industrial economy to a service economy. The impact of more than a decade of anti-discrimination laws and policies has altered the marketplace, although debate continues over the depth of the changes. While anti-discrimination law has had some impact, the impact of affirmative action has been limited. Peetz et al suggest that occupational segregation is beginning to diminish in covered workplaces and there is also some evidence that productivity is enhanced.[92] On the other hand, covered workplaces appear not to use their affirmative action strategies in setting their enterprise bargaining agendas, suggesting that affirmative action is firmly situated on the margins and is largely irrelevant to the organisation's relationship with its employees.[93] This suggests that the cultural changes wrought by affirmative action are not even 'skin deep'. Affirmative action is simply a matter of reporting and planning, often involving solely those whose responsibility it is to ensure that legislative requirements are met. As yet, little progress has been made in altering institutional cultures and the legacy of sex segregation in the workplace remains deeply entrenched.

Family law continues to play out the consequences of the reforms of the 1970s, including an apparent upsurge in female instigated dissolution.[94] Apparently in response to the increasing prominence of the fathers' rights movement and the hostility of its members towards the child support regime introduced in the late 1980s, recent reforms to the *FLA* have entrenched joint parental responsibility and introduced 'parenting plans' and specific issues orders to facilitate negotiation regarding the details of parenting following divorce. The most recent reforms amend the child support scheme, reducing the payments by the liable parent where the child spends as little as ten per cent of his or her time on overnight contact visits, ostensibly to encourage fathers to maintain contact with their children. At the same time, a conservative government pursues a family policy with roots in nostalgia for the 1950s, repackaged under slogans emphasising choice, and designed to shore up the viability of the male breadwinner family. Policies to facilitate combining waged work with care work such as paid maternity leave and adequate subsidised childcare facilities remain largely unattainable.

In industrial policy, despite public rhetoric suggesting that the abandonment of the 'rigid' award system and its replacement with the 'flexibility' of enterprise bargaining[95] would yield a 'family friendly' workplace; much flexibility benefits employers rather than employees. Describing a recent agreement at Heinz, Belinda Probert notes that:

> In the food processing industry ... a recent agreement ... involves a totally new category of worker known as a 'flexible part-time worker' and replacing casuals. These new part-time positions are to be permanent, with guaranteed minimum hours per week, and full access to training and all the award provisions for permanent staff ... However the flexibility clause means that extra hours may be needed in any week ...

> The advantages to the employer are obvious. They want a permanent workforce because with increased investment in training, high turnover is extremely costly ... At the same time the employer wants far greater numerical flexibility than can be achieved with a full-time workforce. For the employees there is the very significant advantage, particularly in a recession, of permanence ... [T]he flexibility of hours is very much an employer-oriented flexibility. While provision exists for consultation, the driving force is the employers' requirements to which employees must adapt. Since the major reason given by women for working part-time is to be able to take care of their children, it is essential to see the fundamental contradiction here.[96]

Where, as presently seems to be the case, the imperatives driving economic policy and the regulation of market actors and the imperatives driving family policy are potentially in conflict, the outcomes of both policies are often compromised. The forms of economic rationalism currently fashionable: the withdrawal of tariff protection for local industry, the replacement of a centralised wage-fixing system with enterprise bargaining and individualised workplace agreements,[97] and the collapse of the manufacturing sector make the 'traditional family' unattainable for most Australians. These changes have had a second effect, one that is not yet widely recognised in Australia, that of destabilising our understandings of masculinity and what it means to be a man.[98] Yet the same forces that make many traditional families economically marginal, the gradual withdrawal of social services and the emphasis upon the voluntary sector and the decline in support for childcare,[99] are, increasingly, forcing many families back towards variants of the traditional model.[100]

Sara Charlesworth suggests that:

> The drive towards increasing working-time flexibility is taking place in what many workers, particularly women workers, experience as an inflexible world. These 'inflexibilities' include the double load many women carry in respect to paid work and domestic responsibilities. A related inflexibility is the limited hours of formal and informal child-care, which makes it difficult for workers who work changing shifts or have to unexpectedly work additional hours ... In addition, there is increasing evidence that in the retail and finance industries part-time workers are having their hours reduced and/or spread across more days. As a result the 'flexible' part-time worker faces additional travel time and costs.[101]

While it is easy to see the immediate impact of these changes on women, particularly those in the part-time workforce, the real impact will bite much deeper, entrenching traditional roles and exacerbating family fragility. Laura Bennett comments that:

> The current move towards hours flexibility involves ... an attack on the concept of 'ordinary hours' ... A recent study of agreements in New South Wales found that hours provisions commonly featured an increased span of hours in the day as well as increased variability of shifts, annualized hours, reduced public holidays and reduced rates of pay for overtime and shiftwork.[102]

I am not commenting on the 'necessity' or otherwise for these changes viewed from the perspective of the individual enterprise or government policy makers. Rather, my concern is with intersection of economic policy and family policy. If these trends are fully realised, one of the probable outcomes is a reduced space for families more generally. As the notion of social and unsocial working hours collapses, pressure on relationships increases. While unsocial working hours are nothing new, particularly in traditionally male dominated sectors of the economy where lengthy overtime and excessive hours have long been a reality, the change in background conditions suggests that these are increasingly carrying costs. Where the male breadwinner family is beyond question, the 'sexual contract' involves the acceptance by men of these hours as part of the 'breadwinner bargain' and an acceptance by their wives and children of separate spheres and separate lives as part of the 'homemaker bargain'. As notions of marriage and family life change, this 'sexual contract' is losing its appeal. Many women, already de facto sole parents, may, given the availability of divorce and social welfare benefits enabling an independent, if economically marginal existence, elect to become de jure sole parents. From their perspective, little if anything will have changed, a marginal loss of economic resources compensated for, at least in part, by an increase in autonomy and control. In those families where, given the cost and often inadequacy of childcare, parents work different shifts to enable an adequate income while minimising child care costs, the lack of space for relationships, both between parents and between parents and children, is likely to impose similar costs.

The distribution of 'unsocial hours' is itself gendered. Belinda Probert comments that:

> Preserving the distinction between social and unsocial hours in ways which differentiate on a gender basis between those who are supposed to work the social and unsocial hours is, however, equally disturbing. The Hotel Intercontinental rejected the need for any new forms of flexibly rostered hours on the grounds that:

> Sufficient flexibility was already available through the current 24 hour rostering system. For example, women employees were able to work the evening shift whilst their partners worked day shift in their company, alleviating the need for expensive child care arrangements.[103]

From one perspective, it is possible to see such arrangements as advantageous, allowing women to sustain labour force participation and some economic independence while avoiding reliance on increasingly unaffordable and inaccessible child care services. On another level, for many families, it seems likely that in an era in which relationships are increasingly fragile such arrangements will threaten them further, if only because little space remains in which interaction can take place. Against the background of the collapse of the distinction between social and unsocial hours, and quite radical alterations in traditional patterns of work, 'family space' is likely to come increasingly under threat.

The Unencumbered Citizen

As 'family space' shrinks, perhaps to the vanishing point, the winners and losers in these changes become clearer. I have already suggested that women struggling to balance employment and family responsibilities are likely to be significant losers. They are not alone. As unsocial hours become the norm, men are also losers. Often the hours they are expected to work distance them from their partners and their children, leaving little space for meaningful interaction. In this context, the UK evidence that one of the most significant reasons given for a woman's decision to end her marriage was the lack of emotional and practical support from her partner is telling. Relationships take both work and shared time to sustain if they are no longer predetermined by gender roles and entrenched by the absence of viable alternatives, and as work pressures increase and time diminishes, neither is likely to be freely available.

In this section, I want to talk a little about some of the reasons why this has happened before moving on to some of the consequences of our cultural reluctance to understand the interrelationships between family and market. One of the most deeply embedded of these reasons is to be found in the model of citizenship that emerged from the simplifications embedded in classical and neo-classical economic theory and in liberal political theory. I call the person at the centre of this model the 'unencumbered citizen'.

My understanding of the unencumbered citizen is derived from the model of radical simplification characteristic of economic theory. Because economic theory operates on a scientific model, it is essential for it to eliminate as many variables as possible before testing its key assumptions. Unsurprisingly, given that much such theorising is largely concerned with market interactions and represents these interactions as one off encounters between abstract market actors, it characterises market actors in highly abstract terms and is concerned solely with their economic interactions. Because market actors are understood wholly in terms of the preferences they exercise in terms of work, leisure and consumption, the model of 'rational choice' has become a kind of talisman.[104]

The pervasiveness of this construct has encouraged the belief that it has a kind of empirical reality, rather than serving as a simplifying assumption for economic analysis and investigation. When it is understood, not as a simplifying assumption, but as a representation of social and legal reality, it encourages us to flatten concepts such as choice and intention, render one-dimensional what is inherently poly-dimensional. I will return to this flattening subsequently and argue that it has deformed our understanding in very specific ways.

Rights discourse has become a second talisman. As with the model of rational choice, rights discourse has played a critical role in the shaping of the 'unencumbered citizen'. One consequence of this is manifested in the increasing politicisation of the fathers' rights movement. Bertoia and Drakich suggest that in Canada, 'the groups have constructed a public rhetoric based on equality and gender neutral models to underscore their rights and to influence law reform'.[105] In Australia, despite a legislative shift from rights to responsibilities in the recent reforms to the *FLA*[106] the discourse of fathers' rights organisations focuses upon rights, specifically rights to contact and to maintain oversight over a former partner's parenting and expenditure of child support funds.[107] Research done in the Brisbane registry of the Family Court suggests that the legislative shift from rights to responsibilities appeared not to have had the desired effect. One court counsellor interviewed put the matter thus:

> I think we have a fundamental problem. If I had a dollar for every time someone on the phone asked 'What are my rights?', I'd be rich. I cannot remember the last time someone said to me 'What are my responsibilities?' ... Sadly, the fact is that clients do not ask about their responsibilities. They ask about 'How can I have control? How can I be empowered to make decisions?' – not what their responsibilities are.[108]

Our language of relationships becomes, in this way, a language of rights claims. Often this encourages us to understand loss, not in emotional terms, but in terms of the deprivation of rights. Given the pervasiveness of rights talk, it is hardly surprising that the rhetoric of equal opportunity has become the common currency of diverse groups and individuals. Almost invariably, what is sought is equality within particular spheres. The focus is on particular advantages and disadvantages. As rhetoric, rights talk facilitates insistence upon compartmentalisation and a reluctance to confront the connections between different spheres and the ways in which the opportunities available in one sphere may constrict those available in others. Much of this is traditional, a product both of a particular understanding about the relationship between public and private and a particular way of understanding the social world and our rights and obligations within it. This understanding is deeply embedded in our cultural and political conventions.

When the citizen is understood as a free and equal moral person capable of being self supporting over a complete life[109] embedded in that description is an understanding what a person is and the proper way for that person to live. Underlying it is the assumption that market participation is the norm, that the individual is unencumbered by responsibility for domestic labour and parenting and that inequality, properly understood, arises from 'morally arbitrary' characteristics. Choices, such as the choice to withdraw from waged labour to fulfil family responsibilities, become mere preferences, like preferences for peaches rather than plums. Inequality that arises because of choices of this kind, those made 'voluntarily' by individuals, becomes irrelevant. The family becomes a 'black box', akin to the firm in conventional economic analysis. Family members vanish and all that remains is the head of household, the family embodied.

From the perspective of women, this analysis is not particularly helpful. As household labour and childcare dissolve into leisure activities[110] the earnings gender gap can also be seen as a product of choice and thus 'invisible' to egalitarian concerns.[111] Other things become invisible as well. We accept certain forms of occupational segregation almost without question, realising perhaps that so long as women, and only women, are likely to move in and out of the workforce to meet family commitments these positions provide a kind of safety net and allow women a degree of economic independence. What they do not do, of course, is encourage change, either in patterns of domestic labour or in patterns of occupational choice.

Consider the measures necessary to ensure that women like men would be capable of being self-supporting (as that phrase is presently understood) over the whole of their lives. Adequate paid maternity leave, paid parenting leave for both men and women[112] and adequate and affordable child care facilities represent *minimal* public commitments to equality of fair opportunity.[113] Increased flexibility in both workplace and schooling hours and in the social allocation of leisure would enable reconciliation of parenting responsibilities with employment and advancement options to a far greater extent than is presently possible, as would the expansion of workplace based child care facilities. Even more important would be a cultural shift enabling both men and women to alternate periods of full and part time employment and periods out of the workforce without the attendant loss of benefits and opportunities for advancement.[114] In the United States, a national study on corporate attitudes towards parental leave found that:

> Corporations take a far more negative view of unpaid leaves for men than they do unpaid leaves for women. Almost two-thirds of total respondents did not consider it reasonable for men to take any parental leave whatsoever ...

> Even among companies that currently offer unpaid leaves to men, many thought it unreasonable for men to take them. Fully 41% of companies with unpaid leave policies for men did not sanction their using the policy.[115]

Australian attitudes are similar. While the *Workplace Relations Act* 1996[116] treats maternal and paternal leave in formally identical terms, formally identical treatment does not necessarily lead to identical outcomes. If attitudes towards paternal and maternal leave are different, and if that difference suggests that taking advantage of parenting leave will disproportionately disadvantage those men who take it, traditional roles are powerfully reinforced. When, as is frequently the case today, such attitudes are combined with persistent wage differentials, even between men and women with apparently equivalent training and experience, they create an environment in which it is almost impossible to break free of conventional practices. The economic penalty is too high, the rewards too distant and hard to grasp.

If we are to bridge the gender gap, the social revolution required is substantial. Fair equality of opportunity, faithfully implemented, would require that both men and women perceive themselves as equally committed to domestic labour and parenting. It would also require that both perceive themselves as equally committed to market activities. A social change of this magnitude requires a revolution in prevailing values and attitudes. It is in no sense a value neutral exercise but one which must, if it is successful, impact profoundly upon beliefs concerning appropriate roles for men and women, both within the family and within the public sphere. While gender equality would not require the abolition of the family, it would require its re-imagination and restructuring upon an egalitarian basis, with both the benefits and burdens of cooperation fairly shared in all spheres. Already, many argue that enhanced employment participation by women has contributed to the destruction of the family, that protection for women and children against violence in the home is an attack upon family values. Likewise, arguments are mounted with renewed vigour that the increasing prevalence of working mothers is destructive of the stability of the social fabric and leads to increased anti-social activity by young people and the breakdown of stable family relationships. Similarly, arguments on economic grounds can be and are being mounted against measures essential to facilitate workplace access by women. It remains easier (although not necessarily more 'efficient') for business to structure opportunities along conventional lines, particularly where government policies are profoundly ambivalent.

The chapters that follow will argue that this ambivalence carries a high price. Put simply, the demographic indicators often cited as cause for concern – falling fertility rates, high divorce rates, high levels of welfare dependence among sole parents – are precisely what should have been expected from the policies pursued over the last 30 years in social welfare law, in taxation law, in family law and in industrial relations law. The interaction of these legal regimes with the sexual contract and with the ideological backdrop of the unencumbered citizen has shaped the society in which we live. In succeeding chapters, we will explore the manner of this shaping and the extent to which it persists.

Notes

1   I use the term equal opportunity law as an umbrella to incorporate both equal employment opportunity and sex discrimination law.
2   See Daly, Mary, *The Gender Division of Welfare: The Impact of the British and German Welfare States*, Cambridge, UK, Cambridge Univ. Press, 2000. While Daly's analysis is primarily concerned with England and Germany, her theoretical framework emphasises law's role in the allocation of resources and opportunities.
3   A broadly based Goods and Services Tax (GST) was introduced in July 2000.
4   *Affirmative Action (Equal Opportunity for Women) Act* 1986, now known as the *Equal Opportunity for Women in the Workplace Act* 1999.
5   *Sex Discrimination Act* 1984 (Cth), *Anti-Discrimination Act* 1977 (NSW), *Sex Discrimination Act* 1975 (SA), *Equal Opportunity Act* 1977 (Vic) replaced by *Equal Opportunity Act* 1995 (Vic), *Equal Opportunity Act* 1984 (WA).
6   Workplaces with under 100 employees are exempted from the reporting requirements.
7   The 1995 AWIRS study suggests that in workplaces covered by EEO legislation the proportion of all male or all female workplaces has declined significantly while it has remained essentially unchanged in uncovered workplaces. When this is coupled with the incidence of complaints under sex discrimination legislation from workplaces too small to be covered by EEO legislation, it is clear that many small enterprises either remain unaware of their legal obligations under sex discrimination laws or have chosen to ignore them. See Peetz, David, Margaret Gardner, Kerry Brown & Sandra Berns, 'Gender Equity, Affirmative Action Legislation and the Workplace', Centre for Research in Employment and Work, Griffith University, Report to the Review of the Affirmative Action Act May 1998, 30.
8   See Thornton, Margaret, *The Liberal Promise: Anti-discrimination Legislation in Australia*, Melbourne, OUP, 1990.
9   High levels of occupational segregation are characteristic, not only of Australia, but also of Canada, the USA, the UK and Sweden. Occupational segregation is gradually decreasing in other jurisdictions but has remained stable in Australia. While Sweden's overall occupational segregation is similar to that in Australia, the wage differential between male and female work is much smaller and most Swedish women in 'female occupations' are either full time employees or permanent part-time employees in career track positions. In Australia women are concentrated in casual and non-career track part-time work in gender-segregated workplaces, an area of the workforce where the gender gap has widened during the last decade.
10 Figures taken from ABS Cat. 6302.0 suggest that, calculated on the basis of average weekly adult full-time ordinary earnings, the gender gap has increased marginally in education and property and business services (by 2%) and markedly in hospitality (4%+). Women make up 56% of the workforce in the hospitality industry, 68% of the

workforce in education and 42% of the workforce in property and business services. Together, these industries employ 28% of the full-time female workforce. The only industry in which the gender gap narrowed significantly was health, employing 17% of women, where it narrowed by 1.3%. The figures are for 1996 and 1998 respectively. ABS figures for average weekly total earnings suggest only marginal changes (less than 1%) except in hospitality where the decrease was 12%. These figures mirror OECD figures suggesting that while the gender gap for full time women overall decreased marginally between 1987 and 1997, the gender gap for casual and part time women increased significantly, leading to an increase in the gender gap overall.

11   Henderson, Ian, 'For women the gender gap doesn't pay', *The Australian*, 26 March 1999. Official government statistics suggest that the average weekly earnings of women employed on a full time basis are approximately 79% of the average weekly earnings of males employed full time. While a large part of this differential comes from the greater access of men to overtime and over award payments and corrected figures suggest that the ratio when these are disregarded is about 89%, the figures are disturbing. Data released by ABS on 4 July 2000 (ABS Cat. 4102) accessed on line at http://www.abs.gov.au/ on 5 July 2000 suggest that the earnings gender gap has increased by 2% since 1994, largely because of wage increases in male dominated industries and increases in managerial salaries where men far outstripped women at the higher levels. Statistics for non-managerial employees reveals that the ratio of female to male pay fell during this period from 94% to 91% where only base pay is considered. Where total weekly wage is considered for full-time employees, the ratio fell from 85% to 83%. Comparable statistics for other jurisdictions are as follows: USA 75%, Sweden 84%, France & Spain 83%, Canada, 65%, UK 64%. Australian data are sourced from 'Frequently Asked Questions' http://www.austemb.org/faqs.htm; EEC data from 'Still a Big Pay Gap Between Men and Women' http://europa.eu.int/en/comm/eurostat/ and US data from 'Explaining Trends in the Gender Wage Gap' http://www.whitehouse.gov/. Canadian data was from Scott, Katherine & Clarence Lochhead, 'Are Women Catching up in the Earnings Race?' http://www.ccsd.ca/insite6.htm. Interestingly, the Canadian data also suggested that while about 18% of full time male employees had earnings in the highest decile, only about 4% of women fell in that decile. About 13% of women and 5% of men had earnings in the lowest decile. All on-line data was accessed on 11 November 1999. Comprehensive US data, broken down by ethnic group as well as gender may be found at US Department of Labor, Women's Bureau, 'Facts on Working Women' at http://www.dol.gov/dol/wb/.

12   See Henderson, above. The earnings gender gap is almost exactly replicated by the wealth gap. See 'Women's Economic Status – Equal Wealth, Output 4', a report prepared for the Australian Commonwealth/State and New Zealand Standing Committee for Advisors on the Status of Women, May 1999, accessed 2 October 1999, http://www.dpmc.gov.au/osw/.

13   I use meritocratisation to refer to increasing wage differentiation within the workplace, including the development of an extremely highly paid cadre of workers in managerial positions. In Australia, as elsewhere, this has been accompanied by decreasing wage parity for unskilled and semi-skilled workers. As the gap between the best off 10% and the worst off 10% widens in terms, the workforce becomes increasingly meritocratised.

14   This is not, of course, unique to Australia as the case studies in Faludi, Susan, *Stiffed: The Betrayal of the Modern Man*, London, Chatto & Windus Ltd, 1999 emphasise.

15   *Workplace Relations and Other Legislation Amendment Act* 1996.

16   MacDermott, Therese, 'Industrial Legislation in 1996: The Reform Agenda' (1997) 39(1) *Journal of Industrial Relations* 52, 62-3.

17 *Workplace Relations Act* s 143(1C) applies to awards, s 170LU(5) applies to enterprise agreements and s 170VG(1) applies to AWAs. These provisions give the AIRC power to ensure that awards, enterprise agreements and AWAs do not discriminate on the basis of sex.

18 This difference may be related to the over-representation of women in the services sector where productivity is notoriously difficult to measure accurately.

19 Fastenau, Maureen, 'Women's Employment in Australia, 1986-1996: A Period of Glacial Change' (1997) 3 *International Employment Relations Review* 61, 65 citing research done by Sara Charlesworth and reported in *Stretching flexibility: enterprise bargaining, women workers and changes to working hours*, Sydney, Human Rights and Equal Opportunity Commission, 1996.

20 Margaret Gardner suggests that institutionally Australia has shifted from an integrative model to an aggregative model. See Gardner, Margaret, 'Industrial Relations Reform and Strategy: If enterprise bargaining is the answer what was the question?' Professorial Lecture delivered on 23 March 1999, 18-19. In Sweden, equal opportunity, child care and parental leave policies are within the labour market policy portfolio rather than being fragmented between EEO, sex discrimination and family policy.

21 Fastenau, 65-6.

22 Differential gendering is a linguistic and social practice by which quasi-universal figures such as the worker and the citizen are analysed without reference to gender, class or other defining characteristics. As a consequence, when analysts seek to explore the impact of workplace practices upon a subset of workers, for example, women, their personal characteristics assume primacy and job characteristics are relegated to the background.

23 Pocock, Barbara, 'Gender and Australian Industrial Relations Theory' (1997) 8(1) *Labour & Industry* 1, 6.

24 While I shall elaborate upon the 'unencumbered' citizen in chapter 2, a brief introduction to the concept is useful here. The 'unencumbered citizen' is the name I give to the quasi-universal figure that predominates in political theory. The 'unencumbered citizen' is classless, raceless, devoid of ethnicity and of social signifiers denoting particular and partial allegiances. The 'unencumbered citizen' is also ungendered, without relationships and the obligations that often attend relationships, such as responsibility for child care, elder care and domestic labour. While the 'unencumbered citizen' is devoid of all defining characteristics, the absence of those characteristics does not, as might be expected, render it a bare cipher. Rather, it is understood as white, middle-class, heterosexual and male.

25 Burkett, Elinor, *The Baby Boon: How Family-Friendly America Cheats the Childless*, New York, The Free Press, 2000.

26 The term 'mommy track' is used derisively in professional workplaces to refer to the career paths of female professionals who access maternity leave or seek career track part time work. Whatever their capabilities such workers are tacitly understood to have sacrificed their career aspirations in order to maintain a balance between work and family, foregoing opportunities for partnership, for example. While such practices legally constitute indirect discrimination within the terms of the *Sex Discrimination Act* 1984 (Cth), they have proved resilient and it is only quite recently that the impact of such practices have been litigated in Australia. See *Hickie v Hunt & Hunt* [1998] HREOCA 8 (9 March 1998).

27 Monks, Kathy & Patricia Barker, 'The Glass Ceiling: Cracked but not Broken? Evidence from a Study of Chartered Accountants', DCUBS Research Papers 1995-6 No. 1 accessed at http://www.dcu.ie/business/ on 10 November 1999.

28   Swedish law provides leave of absence with parental benefit in connection with childbirth for 450 days, half the time for the mother and half for the father, although either parent is entitled to declare in writing that entitlement is ceded to the other parent. One month of this benefit is exclusively reserved for the father (the 'daddy month') and one-month for the mother and the specified parent must use this period or it is forfeited. Three hundred and sixty working days of this benefit is at 80% of gross income while the balance is compensated at a fixed daily rate of SEK 60. See Swedish Institute, 'Equality Between Men and Women' accessed on http://www.si.se/eng/ on 22 December 1999. Other noteworthy provisions include a temporary parental benefit for the care of a sick child where the father takes about 31% of available days. According to UN data, in the manufacturing sector, in 1995 women earned about 90% of male wages in Sweden and about 81% in Australia. In both countries, women comprised about 14% of the total workforce in that sector. See 'Statistics and Indicators on the World's Women' accessed at http://www.un.org/Depts/unsd/gender/ on 3 December 1999. Gunilla Furst suggests that there is 'a widespread belief that men who stay at home are punished by their superiors at work, damaging both their career prospects and their wage growth. Current research shows ... that in financial terms men do lose more than women by interrupting their careers, which may be a contributory factor in their unwillingness to take parental leave or reduce their working hours'. Furst, Gunilla, *Sweden – The Equal Way*, trans. by Stephen Croall, Stockholm, Swedish Institute, 1999, 36.

29   Men are assumed to be career oriented, committed to stable employment and advancement while women are assumed to give priority to family concerns over commitment to career and advancement. This factor has been significant in maintaining high levels of occupational segregation, women often being concentrated in areas of the workforce where career paths are negligible and where casual and part-time work predominates.

30   Research done on management attitudes towards and usage of the FMLA (Family and Medical Leave Act) in the United States notes the strong positive correlation between usage and the attitudes of top management. Where management is supportive, leave is more likely to be accessed; where management is neutral or negative, leave is less likely to be accessed. See Thomson, Holly B & Jon M Werner, 'The Family and Medical Leave Act: Assessing the Costs and Benefits of Use', 146 accessed at http://www.kentlaw.edu/ on 10 November 1999. Survey findings by the Federal Court 8th Circuit Gender Fairness Task Force Report http://www.wulaw.wustl.edu/8th.cir/ accessed on 10 November 1999 suggested reluctance to access family leave for fear of a punitive response. Paternity leave was not generally available. Where available it was unpaid and discretionary, supervisors being free to reject applications if inconvenient. According to the survey: 'Nearly one in five employees, women more often than men, indicated that they had decided against taking leave for family reasons due to concerns about the reactions of supervisors or coworkers'.

31   Richard Collier suggests that the new men's movement 'in shoring up a masculine identity based on the twin pillars of male authority and economic responsibility' is giving expression to a set of middle class grievances circling the unreality of the male breadwinner family under existing conditions. In this context what is critical is the way in which worker elides into breadwinner, and breadwinner equates to father. When these relationships are destabilised, masculinity loses its centre of gravity. See Collier, Richard, '"Coming Together?" Post-Heterosexuality, Masculine Crisis and the New Men's Movement' (1996) 4 *Feminist Legal Studies* 3, 26. The case studies in Faludi, *Stiffed*, make much the same point. See also Levit, Nancy, *The Gender Line: Men,*

Women and the Law, New York, NYU Press, 1998 and Mann, Patricia S, *Micro-Politics: Agency in a Post-Feminist Era*, Minneapolis, Univ. of Minnesota Press, 1994.

32   The popular press routinely highlights debates over the harm done by long day childcare. See, for example, 'Children ignored as martyrs go to war', The *Weekend Australian Review*, 4-5 July 1998; 'Social engineering aside, mum is not a dirty word', The *Australian*, 25 August 1998; Cook, Peter, 'Home truths absent in early childcare debate' The *Australian*, 24 March 1999.

33   For a recent embodiment of this argument see Patrick, Vincent & Antonia Feitz, 'Is a mismatch between family choices and government policy hurting children?' being a paper presented at the National Social Policy Conference, UNSW, 21-23 July 1999. Essentially, the authors attack current EEO policy on the basis that by depriving men of the wages that are 'rightfully' theirs, EEO harms children.

34   The proposed amendments to the *Sex Discrimination Act* 1984 allowing states to discriminate on the basis of marital status in the provision of assisted reproduction technologies (ARTs) is an example of the vulnerability of apparently progressive legislation. While the government has introduced this legislation in response to a decision holding that Victorian legislation restricting ARTs to women who are either married or living in a de facto relationship conflicted with the *SDA* and was therefore struck down, its willingness to do so demonstrates the vulnerability of sex discrimination legislation where powerful interests seek to challenge it.

35   Bluestone, Barry, 'The Inequality Express' 20 (Winter '95) *American Prospect* 5. This was downloaded from http://www.prospect.org/ on 8 November 1999.

36   Bluestone, above, 9.

37   In this context it is worth noting that the P10P50 ratio declined by 11.4% for men and 10.3% for women between 1994-1998 while the P90P50 ration increased by 8% for men and 3.3% for women. While wage dispersion is increasing for both men and women, it is increasing more rapidly for men. In simple terms, the gap between the bottom 10% of wage earners and the average wage earner is widening substantially while the gap between the top 10% of wage earners and the average wage earner is also widening, although not as rapidly. ABS 4102 at http://www.abs.gov.au/ accessed on 5 July 2000.

38   Generally see Faludi. She writes tellingly of the way in which these displaced men see themselves as unmoored, their masculinity called into question by the collapse of their economic roles.

39   World wide, fathers' rights groups emerged as a consequence of male resentment following the introduction of no fault divorce and the freedom of many women to terminate unsatisfying marriages.

40   See Kaye, Miranda & Julia Tolmie, 'Fathers' Rights Groups in Australia and Their Engagement with Issues in Family Law' (1998) 12 *Australian Journal of Family Law* 19. The authors suggest that this is the case and that the lobbying activities of fathers' rights groups played a significant role in recent changes to the *Family Law Act* 1975. It seems likely that the 1998 'Men's Forum' was another form of response to their engagement with family law issues and the 'crisis of masculinity' that they aver.

41   The Lone Fathers' Association is part of the first wave of fathers' rights groups, having emerged in the 1970s following the introduction of no fault divorce. The Men's Rights Agency is apparently of much more recent origin. Both have been prominent in campaigns for changes to the *Family Law Act* 1975 and the child support arrangements.

42   Given that the impact of equal opportunity laws began to bite in the mid to late 1980s, it seems likely that other changes, such as the overall fall in real wages during 1987-1990 and the emphasis upon productivity trade offs for wage increases are responsible for the

decline in male employment and wages. According to Fieldes, 'Between 1990 and 1993 the number of full time jobs held by women decreased by 4.4 per cent. For men the reduction was 6 per cent. In the same period the number of part-time jobs increased at a much greater rate – by 5.5 per cent for women, and 24.4 per cent for men, in the context of an overall reduction in the size of the workforce'. Fieldes, Diane, 'Women's Wages and Decentralised Wage Fixing: The Australian Experience' in Bramble, Tom, Bill Harvey, Richard Hall & Gillian Whitehouse, eds, Current Research in Industrial Relations, *Proceedings of the 11th AIRAANZ Conference*, Brisbane, Queensland, Australia 30 January-1 February 1997, hosted by the graduate School of Management and Department of Government, The University of Queensland.

43   In NSW the *Industrial Arbitration (Female Rates) Amendment Act* 1958 provided that, upon application, the Industrial Commission (NSW) could include provision for equal pay in awards and industrial agreements and that, where applicable, this was to be phased in by 1963. In 1969 the Conciliation and Arbitration Commission (Cth) affirmed equal pay for equal work, to be phased in by 1972 and a second decision in 1972 provided for equal pay for work of equal value, to be implemented by the end of June 1975. Two major changes occurred. First, within a decade, Australia moved from having one of the highest gaps between male and female wages in the OECD (and one of the lowest female participation rates) to having one of the lowest and a participation rate in the upper quartile. See Castles, Francis G, 'The Institutional Design of the Australian Welfare State' (1997) 50 *International Social Security Review* 25, 35-36.

44   The relationship between equal pay for equal work and a family law regime which oscillates uneasily between the ideal of a clean break and the legislative insistence upon the need to support a woman who wishes only to continue in her role as 'homemaker' is still being worked through on a practical level.

45   Recent research suggests that 'three out of every 10 male undergraduates whom a university woman meets probably expect that, after marriage, their wives will confine themselves to caring for them and their children. In fact, it is likely that even more men who publicly endorse equitable relationships secretly wish for a more traditional life style'. The same research indicates that only about 19% of female undergraduates share this vision. Kerr, Barbara, 'The Dating Game', The *Australian*, 31 March 1999.

46   Grimshaw, Damian & Jill Rubery, Labour Market and Social Policy – Occasional Papers No. 26, 'The Concentration of Women's Employment and Relative Occupational Pay: A Statistical Framework for Comparative Analysis', Paris, OECD, 1997, 17.

47   About 2% overall. See Grimshaw & Rubery, above.

48   About 10% overall. See Grimshaw & Rubery, above.

49   While women have moved into the workplace in increasing numbers, there is little evidence that men have assumed greater responsibility for household labour although there is some evidence that they are playing a more active role in parenting.

50   Fastenau, 67 citing ABS statistics from 1997. See also ABS Underemployed Workers, Australia (6265.0) accessed at http://www.abs.gov.au/ on 18 July 2000.

51   Fastenau, 73.

52   There is little evidence that working mothers are disadvantaged in parenting cases, a position that contrasts with that in Canada and the US. Similarly, at least at appellate level, there is also little evidence that men who wish to be full time parents and rely upon the parenting payment for support are disadvantaged, unlike those in the UK.

53   While an overwhelming majority of residential parents are female, this is typically by consent order, or, more recently the terms of a parenting plan. Empirical research into the impact of Part VII *FLA* (which, inter alia, introduced the concept of a parenting

plan) suggests that parenting plans were unlikely to be widely used in the long term. First, they were not significantly different from consent orders in impact, and second, consent orders were easier and cheaper to obtain. See Dewar, John & Stephen Parker, 'Parenting, planning and partnership: The impact of the new Part VII of the *Family Law Act* 1975', Family Law Research Unit Working Paper No. 3, 26, 33-35 available on line at http://www.gu.edu.au/centre/flru/. Where residence is litigated, outcomes are more evenly balanced.

54   Collier, 46.

55   One might suggest that if there were not a feminist movement, it would have been necessary to invent one, and the documentation on many fathers' rights web sites suggests that is precisely what is being done.

56   The left 'critique of rights', a critique which suggested that rights claims were both alienating and destructive of community, was itself critiqued by critical race theorists and by some feminist scholars, who pointed out that such critiques began to appear only when women and people of colour claimed rights as their own. See Delgado, Richard, 'The Ethereal Scholar: Does Critical Legal Studies have What Minorities Want?' (1987) 22 *Harv CR-CL LR* 301 and Minow, Martha, 'Rights and Relations: Families and Children' in *Making All the Difference: Inclusion, Exclusion, and American Law*, Ithaca, NY, Cornell Univ. Press, 1990, 267 and 'Interpreting Rights: An Essay for Robert Cover' (1987) 96 *Yale LJ* 1860.

57   See Gabel, Peter, 'The Phenomenology of Rights Consciousness and the Pact of the Withdrawn Selves' (1984) 62 *Texas LR* 1563.

58   A 2-year study of Canadian fathers' rights groups suggests that while the rhetoric of such groups is egalitarian, the reality is very different. See Bertoia, Carl & Janice Drakich, 'The Fathers' Rights Movement: Contradictions in Rhetoric and Practice' (1993) 14 *Journal of Family Issues* 592 especially 612.

59   Because the last on first off rule explicitly privileges length of service, it disadvantages women who have only recently gained access to particular occupations and those whose service is broken, for example by family responsibilities. Paradoxically, of course, given the extent of gender segregation in the workforce, many of the jobs taken by women are in female sectors, sectors that historically have had little attraction for men.

60   The US web site FATHERS (http://fathers.denninger.net/) accessed on 3 April 1999 defines equality in these terms: 'Equality means, in this context: No person shall be disabused of their civil rights to raise, cherish, love and parent their children without first being adjudicated to be an unfit parent under the criminal standard of proof.
     No person shall have their parenting time interfered with, nor be able to parent their children for less than approximately half of the time, unless they have either been found unfit as above or have voluntarily relinquished their parental rights.
     No person shall be forced to support another under false pretense, and as such child support may never exceed one half of the actual, documentable, and proven financial needs of the children involved, measured by the standard of non-discretionary and necessary expense, and then only when a parent has constructively abandoned or been adjudicated unfit for joint parental responsibility. No law recognizing "special rights" in the area of parental rights, divorce, domestic violence and abuse, or other family-related matters may be passed or enforced where the language of the law, its implementation, or its enforcement is documentably biased towards or against for or against a specific gender'.

61   Amneus' 'argument' was accessed at http://www.fathermag.com/news/ on 18 July 2000.

62 The gap between perception and reality is significant. If one reads the literature on websites such as those of the Lone Fathers' Association and the Men's Rights Organisation, the image is of full female equality in the market. During the boom years of the 1980s, women filled 56% of the 1.5 million new jobs created and female participation in the waged labour force grew by about 10% while male participation declined slightly, particularly for older men. On the other hand, the Australian workforce remains highly segregated by gender and even after correcting for part-time employment and overtime; average female earnings were only 83% of average male earnings in 1989. Brennan, Deborah, *The Politics of Australian Child Care: Philanthropy to Feminism and Beyond*, Cambridge, CUP, 1998 (rev ed), 169-170. Barbara Pocock suggests that an early effect of the abandonment of the centralised wage fixing regime and the introduction of enterprise bargaining was a widening of the gender gap. Pocock, B, 'Better the Devil You Know: Prospects for Women under Labor and Coalition Industrial Relations Policies' in Bryce, Marilyn, ed, *Industrial Relations Policy under the Microscope*, ACIRRT Working Paper No. 40, April 1996. Another measure of the 'gender gap' and its persistence may be found in recent amendments to child support assessment procedures. Until amendments last year, the threshold figure used to calculate child support obligations of residential parents was the average male weekly wage, about $39,000 pa. Average ordinary weekly earnings were substituted, with the consequence that the threshold dropped to about $30,000. Effectively the changes mean that the child support owing to many employed residential mothers has been significantly reduced.

63 Despite the rhetorical affirmation by many segments of the fathers' rights movement of the importance of fathers to the development and well being of children, these arguments are firmly rooted in the economic interests of the members of such organisations.

64 See Mathias, Malcolm, 'Family Breakdown in Australia: An attempt to get at the truth about the magnitude of the problem', at http://www.netspace.net.au/~lfaavic/ on 9 February 1999.

65 The ILO suggests that about one third of the remaining gender gap is a consequence of discriminatory practices. Much of the balance is a consequence of occupational segregation and of the propensity of women to pursue occupations that facilitate part-time work. In this context it is significant that United Nations statistics suggest that in Australia 82% of women are employed in the services sector, while only 58% of men are so employed. Those working in the services sector are particularly vulnerable to some of the consequences of deregulation: the abandonment of standard hours, pressures towards flexibility, and high proportions of casual and part time employees. US research suggests that the shift from an industrial economy to a services economy is one of the factors contributing to the widening gap between the highest and lowest paid segments of the economy. Significantly, Swedish research shows that the choices men and women make in allocating the balance of paid and unpaid work, choices which are rational financially, have the social effect of consolidating the subordination of women in economic life and sustaining the gender gap. See Furst, 36-37.

66 Indirect support for this statement comes from the fact that the earnings of young women are essentially equal to those of young men. As women reach the peak years of family formation and childcare, inequality increases.

67 In Canada, the United States and Australia fathers' rights rhetoric increasingly insists that 'consent orders' are not truly consensual. Rather, they follow legal advice suggesting that, unless the mother is demonstrably unfit, any challenge is likely to fail. In the Brisbane registry of the Family Court one judge suggested that consent orders

were likely to remain widely used despite the introduction of parenting plans. The legislative regime prescribes detailed scrutiny in the case of parenting plans, whereas the scrutiny of consent orders (at least where the parties are both legally represented) is likely to be confined to the formal aspects and to detection of obvious breaches. Generally see Dewar & Parker, above. Bertoia & Drakich suggest at 602 that despite this rhetoric, they found no evidence that fathers' rights group members actually sought to participate equally in the care of children. Rather what was sought 'was the right to exercise the level of parenting that went on prior to the divorce'.

68   While the services of the Child Support Agency are available to all residential parents, their use is compulsory where the residential parent relies upon government benefits for all or part of her income.

69   Where there are substantial assets property distribution may be used to redress the imbalance in the relative economic resources of the parties.

70   Nancy Dowd suggests that sole parenting is the norm, both during marriage and following divorce. While many men are 'economic fathers', most are not social fathers. See Dowd, Nancy E, *Redefining Fatherhood*, New York, NYU Press, 2000.

71   The 'family wage' was not eradicated from federal industrial awards until 1974 although the evidence suggests that it began to break down well before that time. The first peacetime hint of coming change was the NSW *Industrial Arbitration (Female Rates) Amendment Act* 1958 which provided for equal pay, although during WWII the Women's Employment Board had been formed to draft women into essential war work at higher rates of pay.

72   Carmel Shute suggests that the Australian trade union movement had its origins in a 'crisis of masculinity' in which 'unions restored men's self-esteem by establishing a "self-respecting accommodation with capitalism" and by attempting to exclude women (and non-whites) from the ranks of labour'. Shute, Carmel, 'Unequal Partners: Women, Power and the Trade Union Movement' in Grieve, Norma & Ailsa Burns, eds, *Australian Women: Contemporary Feminist Thought'* Melbourne, OUP, 1994, 166, 167.

73   See Mann, 131-141.

74   This presumption never reflected reality. Working class women have always engaged in waged labour and some were the sole support for their families.

75   *Ex parte HV McKay* (the Harvester Case) (1907) 2 CAR 1 entrenched the family wage; *Union v Mildura Branch of the Australian Dried Fruits Association* (the Fruitpicker's Case) (1912) 6 CAR 62, 71-72) limited its application to fields where men and women worked at the same occupation. This encouraged the segregation of women into separate occupations, a feature that remains characteristic of the Australian labour market.

76   Arbitration Reports of the time show that during the period 1909 to 1912, women in New South Wales alone were prohibited from taking apprenticeships in more than twenty trades, including those of baker, butcher, pastrycook, and bootmaker. Some bans were industry-wide, for example in the iron trade. See Bryson, Lois, 'Women, Paid Work, and Social Policy' in Norma Grieve and Ailsa Burns, eds, *Australian Women: Contemporary Feminist Thought*, Melbourne, OUP, 1994, 179, 181. See also Grimshaw, Patricia, Marilyn Lake, Ann Mcgrath & Marian Quartly, *Creating a Nation 1788-1990*, Melbourne, McPhee Gribble, 177-203.

77   The Commonwealth public service bar on permanent status for married women was not abolished until 1966.

78   The Women's Employment Board was created in 1942.

79   Historically, this was reinforced by spending patterns, female earnings typically going towards 'extras' including schooling expenses, children's clothing and holidays, male earnings typically going towards the acquisition of tangible assets.

80   While attempts were made to address these features in the 1980s, the Arbitration and Conciliation Commission resisted them. The first crack in this wall, ironically, has come in 2000 in the New South Wales Industrial Relations Commission in the Equal Remuneration and Other Conditions of Employment Test Case. The decision was handed down on Friday 30 June 2000. It allows for fresh consideration of the value of work in some occupations may have been undervalued for historical reasons. Comparators are not required; comparisons may be made across dissimilar work and across enterprises. While the decision is not limited to 'female' occupations, it is likely that many of the cases will concern such occupations. The decision applies only to awards and in NSW to enterprise awards. There is a certain irony in the fact that the award system is finally prepared to consider equal value as its importance and influence is waning.

81   Castles, 35.

82   Castles, 36. See Fieldes, 119 who suggests that the family wage was finally put to rest by a combination of exceptionally low unemployment and a more general upsurge in radicalism accompanying the Vietnam War.

83   Much the same result was attained in the United States and Canada through trade union activism. Ironically, while it began to break down much earlier in the United States and Canada, as equal pay for equal work began to make inroads, the pattern of legal entrenchment followed by legal abandonment meant that the gender gap closed much more rapidly in Australia, although its legacy of occupational segregation has proved difficult to shift.

84   *Maternity Allowance Act* 1912 ss 4-5. The maternity allowance was roughly equivalent to four weeks wages, a relatively generous payment for its era.

85   *Maternity Allowance Act* 1912 ss 6(1) & (2).

86   See Grimshaw, Lake, et al, 206. The authors note that when it was introduced the Prime Minister celebrated the maternity allowance for its power to encourage the birth of more young Australians. It is significant that the two decades prior to its introduction saw a marked decline in the Australian fertility rate.

87   Regulations of this sort were incorporated in the *Social Security Act* 1947 and its successor. Guidelines were provided to assist in determining when a man and a woman sharing housing might be deemed to have a de facto relationship.

88   For an extended discussion of these regulatory paradigms, see Berns, Sandra S, 'Regulation of the Family: Whose Interests does it Serve?' (1992) 1 *Griffith LR* 152.

89   See, for example, *Accounting Systems 2000 (Developments) Pty Ltd v CCH Aust Ltd* (1993) 114 ALR 355.

90   Tension becomes acute where commercial entities are dealing with consumers who are disadvantaged in some way as in *Commercial Bank of Australia Ltd v Amadio* (1983) 151 CLR 447, or where emotionally contracted debt is involved as in the rebirth of *Yerkey v Jones* (1939) 63 CLR 649 in *Garcia v National Australia Bank Limited* [1998] HCA 48.

91   For an extended discussion of the parallels between market regulation and family regulation see Olsen, Frances E, 'The Family and the Market: A Study of Ideology and Legal Reform' (1983) 96 *Harvard LR* 1497.

92   Peetz, et al, above.

93   Reports to the Affirmative Action Agency suggested that in 1996 only 52 organisations linked affirmative action and industrial issues in enterprise bargaining. See

'Submission: Affirmative Action Agency' to the Regulatory Review of the *Affirmative Action (Equal Employment Opportunity for Women) Act* 1986, n 386.

94 This should not have been wholly unexpected. Emile Durkheim, writing in the late 1950s, argued that marriage was essential to male emotional and social stability but disadvantageous to women's emotional well-being. See Durkheim, Emile, *Suicide: a study in sociology*, trans. by John A Spaulding and George Simpson, ed. with an introduction by George Simpson, Glencoe, Ill, The Free Press, Routledge, (1951), 1970. Effectively, the legal changes of the 1970s and the increasing acceptability of divorce enable significant numbers of women to vote with their feet. This is particularly likely where, as in Australia, safety net provisions enable women to devote the majority of their time to parenting following dissolution.

95 Also available under the new regime are Australian Workplace Agreements, essentially individual contracts between workers and their employers. AWAs override any existing enterprise agreements and awards.

96 Probert, Belinda, *Part-time Work and Managerial Strategy: Flexibility in the New Industrial Relations Framework*, Canberra, AGPS, 1995, 41-42.

97 While these are often said to enhance 'family friendly' practices, Sara Charlesworth argues that 'flexibility' involves substantial perils for women workers. Charlesworth, Sara, 'Enterprise Bargaining and Women Workers: The Seven Perils of Flexibility' (1997) 2 *Labour & Industry* 101, especially 104-108.

98 Patricia Mann describes this image of the family as 'the incorporated male family self'. See Mann, 136-141. Generally see Faludi for an account of the dislocation felt by those socialised into gender roles that are increasingly unattainable.

99 Brennan, 205-227, summarises the changes to childcare funding and regulation since the Coalition assumed government in 1996. She particularly notes the influence of the Lyons forum upon government policy and its traditional hostility to women in the workforce.

100 For all but wealthy families, the abandonment of the 'family wage' rendered the traditional family untenable. Bettina Cass reminds us, however, that even before these changes the groups most likely to be impoverished were those theoretically protected by the family wage: large low income families, sole parent families, the aged, families with an unemployed or disabled breadwinner and indigenous families. See Cass, Bettina, 'Towards a New Australian Model: Social Protection and Social Participation Through Market Wage and Social Wage', ACIRRT Working Paper No. 40, April 1996 in Bryce, Merilyn, ed, *Industrial Relations Policy Under the Microscope*, Proceedings from the Conference, 'Industrial Relations Under the Microscope: A Critical Assessment and Outlook' held at Holiday Inn, Menzies, Sydney, 7 December, 1995, 71, 73.

101 Charlesworth, 112. Footnotes omitted. While the government is clearly well aware of these pressures, and the Prime Minister has proposed a radically extended school day to assist working parents, the proposal provoked howls of outrage from teachers and has not resurfaced.

102 Bennett, Laura, 'Women and Enterprise Bargaining: The Legal and Institutional Framework' (1994) 36(2) *Journal of Industrial Relations* 191, 198.

103 Probert, 34.

104 While this model is most frequently encountered in accounts of market relationships, it has played a significant role in some forms of economic analysis of the family.

105 Bertoia & Drakich, 595.

106 See *Family Law Act* 1975, Division 2, ss 61A-E. The amendments provide that children have a right to contact with both their parents.

107 In Australia Miranda Kaye and Julia Tolmie have analysed the discourse of fathers' rights groups. Their analysis suggests that the surface discourse of rights masks an underlying discourse of power and control. See Kaye, Miranda & Julia Tolmie, 'Fathers' Rights Groups in Australia and Their Engagement with Issues in Family Law' (1998) 12 *Australian Journal of Family Law* 19. The key grievance of many of those in such groups seems to be the inclusion of a sum designed to partly compensate the residential parent for the economic loss inherent in carework in child support calculations. They argue that this surreptitiously reinstates spousal maintenance under the child support provisions and that this is unjust.

108 Dewar & Parker, 43.

109 In his recent work John Rawls describes the liberal citizen in precisely those terms. See Rawls, John, *Political Liberalism*, New York, Columbia Univ. Press, 1993.

110 In economic analysis, leisure is frequently defined as useful uses of time for purposes other than wage earning and consumption. Often women face a double bind in this area as well. Those women who seek to maintain market roles frequently find that not only do they experience the 'gender gap' in wages; they experience a gender gap in terms of leisure time as they understand it, time which is available for personal pursuits and forms of enjoyment. This second gender gap, which is well documented, disappears when leisure is defined as a useful use of time for purposes other than consumption and income generation.

111 Obviously, this is an oversimplification. Nonetheless, girls and women continue to prefer careers that accommodate broken employment patterns relatively easily and those that allow for relatively unimpeded re-entry after a period out of the workforce and periods of part-time and/or casual participation. OECD research suggests that about one-third of the remaining gender gap is attributable to occupational segregation, one-third stems from direct or indirect discrimination and one-third is directly attributable to differences in human capital such as those noted above. Legal intervention is potentially able to eliminate that attributable to direct or indirect discrimination. The remaining two-thirds is much more difficult to combat. To the extent that girls and women make differential investments in human capital based upon their expectations of the kinds of employment which are most compatible with existing opportunities and family responsibilities, their choices tend to perpetuate occupational segregation and a residual gap in human capital, given that men traditionally have made occupational choices based on security of tenure and the potential for advancement and have invested in their human capital accordingly.

112 The *Workplace Relations Act* 1996 provides for unpaid parental leave in Division 5 and Schedule 14. The person taking parental leave must be the primary caretaker of the child, and the legislation provides for cancellation of the leave if the person ceases to be primary caretaker. Overlap between maternal and paternal leave is only permitted during a 1-week period immediately following childbirth. Paid maternity leave is confined to larger enterprises and to the public sector.

113 The Swedish model is instructive. Paid leave pegged at 80% of salary is available to either parent for 360 days and may be used either following the birth of a child or at any time during the next eight years. Thirty days of this leave are reserved for each parent; the balance may be transferred according to individual preferences.

114 While progress has been made, too often these options are seen as accommodating the needs of women rather than the needs of parents.

115 'Catalyst, Report on A National Study Of Parental Leaves' 65-66 (1986), reprinted in 'The Parental and Medical Leave Act of 1986: Joint Hearing on HR 4300' before the

Subcomm on Labor-Management relations and the Subcomm on Labor Standards of the House Comm on Education & Labor, 99 Cong, 2d Sess 151-228 (1986).

116 The relevant provisions are intended to give effect to the *Family Responsibilities Convention* and the *Workers with Family Responsibilities Recommendation* 1981, which the General Conference of the International Labour Organisation adopted on 23 June 1981 and which is known as Recommendation 165.

Chapter 2

The Unencumbered Citizen

The Subject of Citizenship

Citizenship means different things in different contexts. To the lawyer citizenship is embedded in notions of domicile, residence, suffrage – possession of the appropriate documents.[1] Margaret Thornton suggests that:

> Citizenship is the status determining membership of a legally cognisable political community, although it involves more than a passive belonging. First, it includes abstract rights that are legally recognised and that apply equally to all citizens, at least in a formal sense. Second, the concept includes a more subtle layer of meaning that operates to qualify the first, relating to the degree of participation within the community of citizens ... It is apparent that variables such as gender, race, ethnicity and class are significant determinants of the extent of active participation within a particular polity ... 'Equality between and among citizens was assumed from the beginning on the part of liberals and democrats; indeed, the citizen was, by definition, equal to any other *qua* citizen'.[2]

In this chapter, I want to explore that equality of status that Thornton identifies as the hallmark of liberal citizenship and to suggest that this understanding of citizenship has costs as well as benefits. I think it is important to be clear at the outset about what I am not arguing. I am not arguing that we have any alternative to the kind of formal equality that defines liberal citizenship. While the variables Thornton flags as determinative of participation within a liberal polity are critical, they are critical against the background of a formal equality that can be shamed into allowing access, however grudging, to what Rawls terms basic social goods and Marshall describes as social citizenship.

I am interested in the rhetoric of formal equality and particularly in the notion that citizens remain equal, as citizens, however unequal they may be as workers and as private individuals. The rhetoric of formal equality isolates theoretical understandings of the citizen and prevents contamination by a parallel 'social' in which individuals are classified by difference: differences in class, race, religion, gender and sexuality representing variables which locate individual men and women within homes, workplaces and communities. Because this rhetoric and the assumptions that accompany it are deeply embedded in liberal traditions we often fail to recognise the ways in which they have contributed to the shaping of those traditions.

Formal equality is a given. It is no longer contentious. In most western nation states, voting rights for all citizens are taken for granted even while debate continues regarding peripheral practices, for example whether formal equality requires that votes be of 'equal value' or whether universal adult suffrage is sufficient on its own.[3] Other debates also flourish. In a confrontation between traditional cultural practices and contemporary values, French parents have been threatened with imprisonment for continuing the traditional practice of infibulation.[4] More benignly, on the boundary of the social and the political dress codes remind us of the limits of formal equality. Military rules governing the attire of serving members are challenged on the one hand by the kippah of the religious Jew and on the other by Rastafarian dreadlocks.[5] At stake, or so it seems, is military discipline with its demand for absolute obedience and the submission of the individual to the collective. In other spheres as well, dress codes are potent sites of conflict. Whether the flashpoint is the conflict between the turban of a young Sikh boy and the dress regulations of a British school[6] or that between the braids of a Native American youth and the regulations of an American school,[7] they remind us of the limits of formal equality.[8] These skirmishes are of interest both because they highlight the ongoing tension between the universalist values affirmed by the modern nation state and the values and traditions of the diverse communities within it and because the hegemony of the universal over the local and particular is reaffirmed.[9] In nation states such as Australia, Canada and the United States, the relationship between indigenous communities and the wider community delineates another site of tension as demands for self-determination and sovereignty proliferate.

The Unencumbered Citizen

Choice and Difference: Fragmenting the Self

In the conflicts between the universal and particular characteristic of late modernity we find the genesis of the unencumbered citizen, the rights bearing subject. What I find interesting about the particular flashpoints sketched above is a feature they share with many of the reasons sketched in the first chapter for women's continuing economic equality. They can be understood as choices made by the individual. The religious Jew could, after all, have complied with military dress regulations, thereby setting his particularity aside. Similarly, the Sikh turban and Pawnee braids could have been foresworn and the dress code of the dominant group adhered to. The rights bearing subject, despite attempted legal interventions, is neither the Sikh nor the orthodox Jew nor the Pawnee initiate. While it would violate formal equality to proscribe the practice of the Sikh religion or of Judaism, overt evidence of cultural and religious particularity ought to remain private, a matter between the individual and his or her deity. Where, as with the Pawnee initiate, the particular practice and associated cultural traditions are difficult to reconcile with Western understandings of religion, the matter is even more tendentious. Indigenous understandings of religion and the associated cultural practices sit uneasily within a political tradition whose defining characteristic is a sharp distinction between the sacred and the secular.[10] Against the claim that all of life is sacred, the institutional response is that while that may be the case, no rights are necessarily associated with the outward manifestations of that belief.[11] While freedom of religion may entitle the Amish to withdraw their children from the state educational system at the end of primary schooling,[12] if the individual wishes to participate in wider institutions he or she does so on their terms, that is, as a citizen, a bearer of rights. The Amish youth who elects to leave the insular community and join the wider community must, ultimately, set aside the dress and customs of his or her community of origin and adopt those of the majority. An Amish upbringing is no answer to employment criteria identifying a high school education as a minimum qualification.

While the particular examples I have given are male, the marks of their difference are both visible and 'chosen'. If the Sikh, the orthodox Jew or the Pawnee were denied institutional access simply because of their racial or religious background, their rights would have been violated on contemporary understandings, although this was not always the case.[13] Stripped of the particularities imposed by their religious and cultural heritage, they become unencumbered citizens, and their participatory entitlement is formally beyond question.[14]

The position of women is simultaneously similar and different. In this chapter I will argue that the barriers to equal participation by women are more like those depending upon cultural and religious particularity than like those depending upon racial difference as a matter of biological fact. Like the barriers imposed by religious and cultural traditions they are conventionally understood as 'chosen'. The economic and participatory disadvantages consequential upon women's responsibility for care work and for household labour seem, within the liberal paradigm, more like the barriers faced by the Sikh, the orthodox Jew and the Pawnee than like those consequential upon the brute fact of racial difference. That this is not hard and fast should be obvious. Inevitably, the biological indicia of racial difference are invested with cultural significance. Where the biological indicia are present, cultural stigmata are presumed as well.[15] What I am arguing, however, is that legal challenge has, in such cases, a reasonable chance of success. Shelini Neallani speaks of adopting a raceless persona in order to function effectively within law school and within the legal profession. Implicit in the notion of a raceless persona is the distinction between the cultural indicia of group membership, whether it is found in speech patterns, in dress, or in the behaviours characteristic of a particular group, and the biological indicia of race.[16] As Neallani notes:

> As a Woman of Colour, I believe that racelessness is produced by the understanding that our success depends not only on our abilities, but also on White Mainstream People feeling comfortable with us, by perceiving a 'likeness' with us. While it is one way of diminishing our oppression, the strategy of racelessness can be seen as accommodating behaviour which has its own costs.[17]

Abandonment of these cultural indicia becomes a tacit precondition to access, an option that is only available to a very few.[18] In a similar vein, Mari Matsuda notes that in professional contexts she abandons the Creole patois of her Hawaiian upbringing for her best Anglo diction.[19] In both cases, the distinction is between the biological and the social, a distinction that, I would argue, parallels that between the sacred and the profane and is of equal significance. In both cases, the cultural and social indicia of difference are consciously eradicated, permitting assimilation to the Anglo norm.

Something else is highlighted as well. The distinction between the rights bearing subject (or citizen) and the fully encumbered individual of the social is culturally and historically determined. Thomas Hobbes wrote *Leviathan*[20] against the background of the English wars of religion. The distinction between a civil society in which life, liberty and property were secured and a state of nature in which life was nasty, brutish and short is precisely the distinction between the formal equality of the state and the particularity of local allegiances. Leviathan offered peace and prosperity because local particularities were vanquished by submission to an absolute sovereign. In the *Social Contract*[21] Rousseau put the matter even more strongly, arguing that if the political, the home of the rights bearing subject, was to survive, particular associations within the state must be eradicated.[22] Asher Horowitz reminds us that the

> historical predicament that makes the social contract both possible and necessary is the existence of civil society. The existence of absolutely independent individuals, for whom the only grounds of obligation lie in their private wills, makes the contract necessary, because such individuals have an absolute need for protection from their equals ... Yet the contract is possible because these same individuals recognize their antagonists as their equals – none claims any **a priori** right to rule, but only to fight. Under these conditions social existence must assume the form of a contract. It must be a contract since an act of exchange is the only relation among absolutely independent individuals that is legitimate.[23]

The liberal state demands the eradication of the particularities of the social and the substitution of the rights bearing subject or citizen. When Horowitz speaks of the relationship between absolutely independent individuals that he describes as civil society, he speaks of the equally critical fact that the only ground of obligation is to be found in their own private wills. Understanding the liberal order in this way alerts us to a further dimension. All the ties and obligations constitutive of the social, the indicia of difference, must be left behind if people are to meet as equals in the public sphere. The kippah of the Orthodox Jew, the dreadlocks of the Rastafarian, the turban of the Sikh belong, not to the realm of the liberal state with its equal citizens bound by contractual agreements, but to the individual (and private) domestic enclaves within it. Because they speak of an obligation that is taken as given, one that is constitutive of what it means to be an Orthodox Jew, a Rastafarian, or a Sikh, they are a threat to the liberal vision of equal citizens. Little wonder then that when protection is claimed for these indicia of difference the answer often comes back; they are your choice. They have nothing to do with the liberal polity. You have chosen inequality and it is nothing to do with the laws of the state.

The Political and the Social: Possibilities and Dangers

While the biological differences between the sexes can be read as equivalent to the biological differences associated with race and ethnicity, it is more difficult still to isolate the biological from the social. The battle between those who believe that gender roles are biologically determined and those who believe that they are socially constructed remains live in liberal nation states. Powerful religious and cultural traditions cling to biological determinism and their voices are increasingly dominant in sexual politics. Against the feminist insistence that the personal is the political, the forces of the religious right and a newly powerful men's rights movement collectively insist that the biological is the social.[24] For both, what is at stake is male authority within the family and the reinforcement of conventional gender roles. Against the background of the social, political and economic changes outlined in the first chapter, they argue that the social fabric has been fatally eroded by the changes of the last three decades and that the push for gender equality has gone too far. Very often, their arguments demand the reinstatement of conventional religious and social values as legal rules and the abolition of the secular and universal norms characteristic of the legal regimes of liberal nation states.[25]

Contemporary legal and political flashpoints: no-fault divorce,[26] abortion rights,[27] social benefits to single parent families,[28] the notion of a family tax[29] are subtle re-workings of one open textured narrative. That narrative can be conceptualised in a variety of ways. One genre resonates around the separation of church and state and the meaning of that separation. A second, related, genre takes as its theme traditional family values. Marshalled against the hegemony of the traditional family we find contemporary variants: female headed households, gay and lesbian families, dual career couples, all emblematic of moral decay and the fraying of the social fabric. Increasingly the discourse is one of moral panic.

The increasing vehemence with which neo-conservative forces pursue the reinstatement of the values of the social into the political ought not to be underestimated. It is possible to read it as an ongoing attempt to break down the legal barriers isolating the political from the social and to reinscribe one set of values characteristic of the social as political norms. While some communitarian scholars[30] would welcome such a reinscription, it offers perils as well as possibilities. One of the great achievements of late modernity has been the progress made over the last century towards isolating the political from the social. The great battles over liberation are the sign and symbol of this progress. We ought not to forget that two centuries ago beliefs and attitudes that are today repugnant to many were the accepted subtexts of government and political life. In the late eighteenth century Thomas Jefferson[31] drafted a Declaration of Independence that affirmed the equality of all men while founding a union in which slavery was accepted and Native Americans were, in one area after another, driven from their traditional lands. Woman suffrage was, of course, unthinkable. Michael Walzer suggests that liberalism is one way of mapping the political and the social:

> Think of liberalism as a certain way of drawing the map of the social and political world. The … preliberal map showed a largely undifferentiated land mass, with

> rivers and mountains, cities and towns, but no borders ... Society was conceived
> as an organic and integrated whole ... Confronting this world, liberal theorists
> preached and practiced the art of separation. They drew lines, marked off different
> realms, and created the socio-political map with which we are still familiar ...
> Liberalism is a world of walls, and each one creates a new liberty.[32]

While the isolation of the political from the social has not yet been fully
realised and hard won gains are being lost on many fronts, without it the
identification of characteristics that ought to be irrelevant to political equality
would have been almost impossible. Scholars describe these characteristics in
different ways. Michael Walzer suggests that different standards apply within
different spheres, allowing the continuation of traditional life-worlds within the
social in the context of an overarching egalitarianism.[33] John Rawls insists upon
the isolation of the political and the social, arguing that the egalitarianism he
espouses is political equality merely.[34] Inherent in the Rawlsian project is a sharp
distinction between the political and the affective or associational domains. Justice
belongs, or so he argues, to the former, other values to the latter. Within the
political, he identifies differences that are morally irrelevant, differences such as
race, religious affiliation[35] and disability. Individuals do not choose these
differences and it follows that they ought not to be considered in the distribution of
basic social goods. Within the social, difference is chosen and it follows that it is
irrelevant to equality. Rawls is largely silent on differences associated with gender
and gender roles perhaps because the distinction between biological sex and
particular gender roles is regularly challenged[36] in a way that the distinction
between race and culture is not.[37]

Scholars such as Walzer and Rawls are silent for another reason as well. The
distinction between the political and the social is critical to their theoretical
framework. Concrete practices such as domestic labour and care work seem firmly
social in a way that racial difference does not, at least to liberal eyes. For Walzer,
those practices belong to a separate sphere, one in which different standards of
justice apply. For Rawls, the distinction between the affective and the political is
fixed. Nowhere does he acknowledge the possibility that the social inevitably
contaminates the political and the political the social and that relative equality in
one is not possible without relative equality in the other.

Neo-classical theorist Alastair MacIntyre identifies this barrier as fundamental.
He argues that

> the liberal claim was to provide a political, legal, and economic framework in
> which assent to the same set of rationally justifiable principles would enable those
> who espouse widely different and incompatible conceptions of the good life for
> human beings to live together peaceably within the same society, enjoying the
> same political status and engaging in the same economic relationships.[38]

In the public arena, all that may be permitted is the expression of preferences, and
it is for this reason that the ability to bargain has become crucial. For MacIntyre to
be a liberal is to believe that there can be no overriding good, but only a range of

goods pursued in compartmentalised spheres – political, economic, familial, artistic, athletic, scientific – the list is his. According to MacIntyre:

> the liberal self is one that moves from sphere to sphere, compartmentalizing its attitudes. The claims of any one sphere to attention or to resources are once again to be determined by the summing of individual preferences and by bargaining.[39]

I believe that this is largely true, and true in a way that highlights many of the reasons for the persistence of the gender gap. Feminist scholarship characterises the distinction between the political and the social as that between public and private, but this is, I believe, an oversimplification. The social is much broader than what is conventionally conceptualised as the private. Already substantial pressure exists to collapse the barrier between the political and the social and to embed the values characteristic of the social within public discourse. Typically, this pressure is regressive rather than progressive. While collapsing this barrier might create space for the recognition of domestic and caring labour and enable the kinds of social changes outlined in the first chapter, it might have very different consequences. It might, for example, encourage those who advocate 'traditional family values' to increase their pressure for the kinds of social and political changes needed to reinstate the 'family wage', implement taxation changes to facilitate income splitting within families,[40] and curtail still further the availability of the sole parent's benefit.[41] Already, Australian government policy has significantly reduced the social supports for working parents including access to affordable childcare.[42]

Today there is significant social and political pressure to halt the proliferation of alternative family forms.[43] Grassroots social movements have long targeted gay and lesbian households and female-headed households as socially undesirable and unsuitable for rearing children.[44] Pressure groups such as these seek neither more nor less than the implementation of values rooted in the social within the political. Only a perilous naivety allows us to believe that those who hold these views are marginal and unrepresentative or that their impact would be limited. As conservative politicians pre-empt the rhetoric of choice,[45] reminding us that the purpose of policy changes is to allow women to 'choose' the lifestyle they prefer, it is easy to forget that behind the rhetoric of choice is a shift in the values of the political. The rhetoric of small government, the rolling back of social protection and the open advocacy of local autonomy threaten to enlarge the power of the social at the expense of the political. The rhetoric of community responsibility and empowerment bespeaks a critical shift in the balance of power between them.[46] As Madame Justice Rosalie Silberman Abella reminds us:

> What we appear to have done, having watched the dazzling success of so many individuals in so many of the groups we had previously excluded, is concluded that the battle with discrimination has been won and that we can, as victors, remove our human rights weapons from the social battlefield. Having seen women elected, appointed, promoted and educated in droves; having seen the winds of progress blow away segregation and apartheid; having permitted parades to demonstrate gay and lesbian pride; having constructed hundreds of ramps for

persons with disabilities; and having invited aboriginal people to participate in constitutional discussions we had started to protect distinct cultures, many were no longer persuaded that the diversity theory of rights was any longer relevant, and sought to return to the simpler rights theory in which everyone was treated the same. We became nostalgic for the conformity of the civil liberties approach, and frightened by the way human rights had dramatically changed every institution in society – from the family to the legislature.[47]

As the social is enlarged, we need to recall precisely why classical liberals feared such a development and affirmed the autonomous individual. Rawls' search for an overlapping consensus between the various social groups comprising the modern nation state was at least in part motivated by his fear of a resurgent social seeking to impose sectarian values upon a diminished (even vestigial) nation state. If the values of liberalism seem hostile to many of the changes essential if the gender gap is to be further diminished, the values of a newly resurgent social are even more so.

Women, Rights and the Possibility of a Genderless Persona

Even at the margins, as with the battle over maternity leave and the eradication of discrimination based on pregnancy,[48] the social configures the biological in unexpected ways. In both the United States and Australia exemptions developed which made it possible to argue that the fact that women might become pregnant ought to entitle employers to exclude them from certain workplaces on the basis of potential harm to the foetus.[49] The image of the woman as permanently potentially pregnant, which for a time predominated in equal opportunity law, inadvertently focused attention upon a further difficulty. The discourse of the rights bearing individual (or citizen), both absolutely independent and formally equal, does not offer any vocabulary apt to address the relationship between the pregnant woman and the foetus.[50] The battle over the availability of abortion, which continues unabated in the United States and which surfaces from time to time in Australia illustrates the perils of 'rights talk' in this context. Separateness often seems a precondition for the status of rights bearing individual, and it is a condition which neither pregnant woman nor foetus can meet.

Gender issues remain difficult for many of the same historical reasons that Horowitz describes as making the social contract both possible and necessary. Because the liberal state came to understand itself as a realm of formally equal individuals (in precisely the way economists understand a market as constituted by formally equal individuals), particularity was banished to the social. The social came to signify not merely the affective space of the family, but also the communal enclaves in which cultural and religious traditions might be performatively enacted.[51] If status had become formally irrelevant within the political, it flourished unchecked within the social. Social existence was ordered and hierarchical in ways similar to those deemed essential by social contract theorists such as Hobbes and Rousseau. Here was to be found the sphere of necessity, where women's nurturing and caring labour constituted the substratum which made communal life possible and enabled unencumbered participation in civil society and political institutions. As Robin West notes:

> Women's duties, rights, and responsibilities as citizens also suffer from "second shift" duties. Simply put, so long as there is laundry to wash, diapers to change, children to feed, and houses to clean, and so long as women more than men are disposed to do them – for *whatever reason* – there is that much less time for women to engage in public debate, run for office, form citizen or community groups, serve on juries, or even just vote ... Someone must tend to the body's very real, earthbound, and contingent needs if the mind is to be freed for transcendental and political deliberations. So long as women disproportionately tend to those earthly, bodily needs, they are that much less equipped for the duties of citizenship – as citizenship is traditionally understood.[52]

The gender gap persists because women's participation in the institutions of civil society and, *a fortiori*, in the domain of the political, is simultaneously conditioned and constrained by their role in the sphere of necessity. While repeated attempts have been made to level the playing field, one needs only to think of contemporary interventions such as EEO policies and arguments for a 'family friendly' workplace, the gender gap remains a fixture of the contemporary landscape.[53] Interventions designed to ameliorate the gender gap arouse substantial ire, both among traditionalist forces and among those who argue that such interventions give women an unwarranted competitive advantage.[54] Whether within the social, in civil society, or in the domain of the political, biology is often read as destiny.

Perhaps we do not ask often enough what it might mean to adopt a 'genderless persona'. Earlier I noted that both Mari Matsuda[55] and Shelini Neallani[56] alluded to the necessity to adopt a raceless persona in order to participate as an equal in the institutions of late modernity. The adoption of a raceless persona implicitly suggests that the biological indicia of race can be isolated from the socially acquired indicia of racial and social difference, leaving skin colour and physical features as the sole emblems of racial difference. The cultural differences might, on some level, be described as chosen. The biological differences were apparently immutable. Significantly, Neallani suggested that the adoption of a raceless persona significantly enhanced the comfort level of the Anglos which whom she dealt.[57] Neither Matsuda nor Neallani spoke of adopting a genderless persona because for them the barriers imposed by racial difference overshadowed those imposed by gender.

I want to explore what it might mean to adopt a genderless persona within academia, because that is the sphere with which I have greatest familiarity. It is also one in which, in Australia at least, concerted efforts have been made to implement equal opportunity policies along with a modest degree of affirmative action. Perhaps the first critical indicator is that of career path. Australian research[58] suggests that the single most important determinant of promotion prospects in academia is the possession of a PhD and that junior male academics are significantly more likely to hold a PhD than are junior female academics. Other critical indicators include the development of a substantial publication profile, and increasingly, a demonstrated ability to secure national competitive research grants. The critical period in an academic career is likely to be the first ten or so years in academia. During this period it becomes clear who is likely to advance rapidly up the hierarchy, ultimately becoming eligible for promotion to Associate Professor and Professor, and who will progress more slowly, ultimately peaking at senior lecturer. While such performance indicators are 'objective', they are also predicated upon a relatively uninterrupted career path. Married women, particularly those with caring responsibilities, are less likely to be among those securing rapid advancement. This stratifies female academics in two ways. On the one hand, ambitious young women may seek to delay child bearing until they are close to realising their career goals and can afford the services of a full time nanny. Those who elect to have families in their twenties or early thirties may encounter difficulty establishing a track record which qualifies them for promotion. Unless promotion committees are sensitive to gender issues, periods of maternity leave and fractional appointment are likely to be ignored in evaluating performance. Where promotion to higher levels is sought, one of the indicators that distinguishes the 'high flyer' from the academic who is unlikely to advance beyond the career grade rank of senior lecturer is the rate of progress through the ranks.

A further difference is also critical. While promotion committees are increasingly sensitive to gender issues, student attitudes are not. In an environment in which students are overtly encouraged to position themselves as consumers, their expectations of male and female academics are very different.[59] As a consequence, female academics are often expected (both by students and by their superiors) to adopt a 'nurturing' role towards their students and this leads to an inequitable division of the 'pastoral care' dimension of the academic role. Here, very often, gender socialisation and student expectations interact to ensure that female academics spend a greater part of their working time in pastoral care than do their male counterparts, with the predictable effect upon research and measurable output. To adopt a genderless persona would, in these circumstances, mean to eschew child bearing and domestic responsibility, to reject student (and administrative) expectations regarding pastoral care, and to focus single-mindedly upon career goals. Unsurprisingly, just as adopting a 'raceless' persona means adopting the behaviour and speech patterns of the dominant race, adopting a 'genderless' persona means enacting the life choices associated with middle class white males. Even if this is done, however, because behaviours are filtered through complex reference systems a truly genderless persona may remain tantalisingly out of reach.[60] One critical difference may be found in a commonplace phrase. It remains (lamentably) common to describe a person who has successfully adopted a raceless persona as a credit to his or her race. Culturally, it remains unacceptable to describe a woman who has adopted a genderless persona as a credit to her sex. For those of us who are born female, there is no closet.

The rhetoric of choice is seductive. Margaret Thornton reminds us that 'women have been expected to tend to housework, nurturing and caring concerns in order to leave men free to engage in war, work, sport, leisure and civic life'.[61]

War, work, sport, leisure and civic life are the domain of the citizen. Household labour, care work, and nurturing activity belong to the sphere of necessity. Because these activities do not constitute work, as public sphere institutions understand work, because within the sphere of necessity there is no clear distinction between work and leisure, necessary labour vanishes into leisure or consumption. Women become part of the 'infrastructure underpinning public and social life'.[62] To participate as a citizen, as a rights bearing individual is to participate in the activities of the public sphere, to eschew those of the sphere of necessity. Throughout much of recorded history, those who were part of the infrastructure were not fully citizens and did not count as rights bearing individuals.[63]

The Unencumbered Citizen

Who, then, is the unencumbered citizen, the bearer of rights? The unencumbered citizen is devoid of markers denoting particularity. The social indicia that accompany racial, ethnic and religious background have nothing to do with the subject of rights. In theory, the brute facts of race, ethnicity and religion neither facilitate nor inhibit participation. The unencumbered citizen is neither black nor white, neither Catholic nor Muslim nor Jew. Those facts are irrelevant to her status as the subject of rights. The unencumbered citizen is able to access the 'infrastructure' required to participate fully and as an equal in the public sphere. Thus, the unencumbered citizen has a wife, or behaves as if she does. If she has religious beliefs, she wears them lightly and is prepared to subordinate them to the requirements of public sphere participation. If she has a family, she relies upon others for care work and all of the other services that facilitate single-minded concentration upon the tasks at hand. She is, in short, 'unencumbered': by interpersonal obligations, by responsibilities, by beliefs.

Her world is the world of civil society, of workplaces and contracts, and overarching all, at least for some, the world of citizenship. Here, law imposes rights and obligations, not role, belief or custom. Here, as Robert Cover reminds us, obligations are enforced rather than internalised.[64] Emotional commitment is unnecessary precisely because the threat of force of state imposed violence is always present. In a critical and chilling phrase, Cover describes the courts of the imperial state as jurispathic, law-killing. For the thicket of binding normative obligations and prescriptive rules characteristic of the social, the court substitutes one binding law authoritatively interpreted and enforced by violence.[65] Yet, and it is well to remember this, the boundary between the social and the political is neither natural nor fixed. Rather, it is socially, politically and legally constructed, and for this reason, always open to further interventions, new ways of reading the citizen, the worker, even, dare I say it, new ways of reading the family.

Encumbering the Citizen

Transfixed at a crossroads, we can neither allow the social to reclaim the political nor abandon efforts to redraw the boundary in ways more sympathetic to women's interests. One appealing possibility is to 'encumber the citizen', to reimagine the citizen and the worker in ways which acknowledge the human necessity of care work and household labour. In this way, we potentially transform both the political and the economic. Yet encumbering the citizen in this way can be perilous. Others wish to encumber the citizen in different ways. On the one hand we have the patriarchal head of household entitled as of right to represent all within it.[66] Elsewhere we find the *'ubermenchen'* entitled as of right to eradicate otherness in his quest for racial and ethnic cleansing[67] and the representative of the 'official religion' marginalising and sometimes killing those who fail to conform to religious dictates.[68] We need a vocabulary and a set of concrete practices which both enable us to encumber the citizen and to challenge those who 'value ideological conformity over intellectual pluralism' and seek to turn 'our marketplace of ideas ... into the marketplace of idea'.[69]

Arguments are needed, arguments that suggest that participation in care work and household labour is somehow different from other choices, is essential rather than contingent. If participation in care work and household labour is essential rather than contingent, it becomes possible to argue that they should properly be understood to be universal, a human given rather than a particular and individual choice. Even here, caution is needed. While, given the prolonged neoteny of the human race, care work can be seen as a given, as essential for the survival of the species,[70] it is not difficult to question whether household labour, at least beyond the minimum necessary for health and safety, is such a given. For this reason, the arguments that follow will largely be centred on care work. I would insist, however, that within our culture care work itself entails a certain amount of household labour, that necessary to ensure a relatively safe and clean environment, to provide adequate meals, and to maintain culturally appropriate attire. Beyond this minimum, I think it is best to accept that household labour is contingent rather than universal and can, therefore, be characterised as chosen.[71] Nancy Fraser has suggested that in post-industrial welfare states such as Australia:

> the key to achieving gender equity ... is to make women's current life patterns the norm for everyone. Women today often combine breadwinning and caregiving, albeit with great difficulty and strain. A postindustrial welfare state must ensure that men do the same, while redesigning institutions so as to eliminate the difficulty and strain.
>
> We might call this vision *universal caregiver.*
>
> What, then, might such a welfare state look like? ... [I]ts employment sector would not be divided into two different tracks, all jobs would assume workers who are caregivers, too; all would have a shorter work week than full-time jobs have now; and all would have employment-enabling services. Unlike universal breadwinner, however, employees would not be assumed to shift all care-work to social services. Some informal care-work would be publicly supported and integrated on a par with paid work in a single social-insurance system. Some would be performed in households by relatives and friends, but such households would not necessarily be heterosexual nuclear families. Other supported care work would be located outside households altogether – in civil society. In state-funded

but locally organised institutions, childless adults, older people and others without kin-based responsibilities would join parents and others in democratic, self-managed carework activities.[72]

Even if we are successful in encumbering our understanding of the citizen and the worker, so that those roles incorporate the assumption that all will share responsibility for care work and for the minimum of household labour required for maintaining basic standards, we are immediately confronted by other difficulties. The bright line distinction between the political and the social is only one cornerstone of the procedural republic.

Rights Discourse at the Intersection of Culture and Gender

Rights discourse is another cornerstone of the procedural republic. Rights discourse makes a number of assumptions about people and about the ways in which people relate to one another. Like the rhetoric of choice, the rhetoric of rights is fundamental to the liberal understanding of law, of citizenship and of market relations. Conventionally rights are conceptualised as negative, as the right to be free from particular kinds of legal intervention. Rights thus restrict the capacity of governments to enact laws of particular kinds. For example, our implied right to freedom of political speech[73] limits the power of government to restrict political speech. Constitutionally entrenched bills of rights such as the US Bill of Rights and the Canadian Charter of Rights and Freedoms operate in this way, limiting the power of the state to enact certain kinds of legislation. Rights discourse is often employed in ways that suggest that rights are essential to preserve the boundary between self and other.[74] Madam Justice Abella reminds us that:

> Because not all people are, should be, or can be the same, it is hard to see how the objective measure of equality or human rights can be assimilation. What *is* easy to see, however, is the seductive appeal that assimilation offers. Its carrot is the mainstream, and membership is premised on homogenisation.
>
> If this means conformity to values of civility and tolerance, assimilation is devoutly to be wished. But if it means, as it usually does, obliterating racial, cultural, linguistic, religious or gender differences, let alone pride in any of them, then it is neither realistic nor equitable. Access to the mainstream must be *based* on those differences; and integration, not assimilation, must be seen as the social goal.[75]

While, in Canada and elsewhere, the notion of group rights is being explored in the context of a multi-cultural and multi-national society, very little in the jurisprudence of rights claims inspires any confidence that group rights are actually compatible with gender equality. Culture has become a slippery signifier. Not that long ago, culture was variously an artefact (something to be studied in Anthropology courses), something to be admired (as in 'I am going overseas to learn about other cultures'), or even something to be celebrated (as our 'cultural heritage'). As an idea, it was straightforward and uncomplicated. In those days, too, some spoke easily and without conscious concern of assimilation and of melting pots. Less long ago than we might like to think it was commonplace to speak of 'the white man's burden' and of the 'white slave traffic'[76] with all the complex understandings comprised in those discourses.

Today, these images are relics of a vanished naivete. 'Culture' slides uneasily into ethnicity, into race, into all of the different originalisms that are staking claims for both authority and authenticity. Patricia Williams begins *The Alchemy of Race and Rights* by insisting that 'subject position is everything in my analysis of law'.[77] The rest of her book seeks to convey something of the fragility and complexity of that phrase, 'subject position' and the tension between one's own understanding of one's subject position and the understandings of others. Central among the signifiers which constitute our subject positions, culture has become a witches' brew of banal but emotionally critical customs such as those associated with food, with forms of dress and with music and dance and deeply embedded familial, religious, and ceremonial traditions. The 'trope' woman plays a central role in these traditions. Sometimes it seems that it is because of these traditions that alterations in her role are seen as profoundly threatening, even destructive.

Frequently, women are deemed the key to cultural transmission and preservation. If this is the case her fidelity to tradition becomes essential to cultural survival.[78] Often, culture is perceived as immutable, so that any change becomes a threat of unbearable potency. In nation states such as Australia, Canada and the USA, governments confront culturally driven imperatives in which familial and gender roles have become lightening rods for social and cultural decay. Will Kymlicka draws a distinction between two kinds of collective rights:

> The first involves the right of a group against its own members; the second involves the right of a group against the larger society. Both kinds of collective rights can be seen as protecting the stability of national, ethnic, or religious groups. However, they respond to different sources of instability. The first kind is intended to protect the groups from the destabilizing impact of *internal* dissent (e.g., the decision of individual members not to follow traditional practices or customs), whereas the second is intended to protect the groups from the impact of *external* pressures (e.g., the economic or political decisions of the larger society)
> ...[79]

While Kymlicka adopts a relatively optimistic stance, it is difficult to know whether to share his optimism. Walzer challenges Kymlicka's analysis and suggests that while it may be possible for the Québecois to sustain their community within the framework of an overarching liberal regime the case of the First Nations peoples is much more difficult and comments:

> [I]t isn't at all clear that their way of life can be sustained, even under conditions of autonomy, within liberal limits: it isn't historically a liberal way of life. Internally intolerant and illiberal groups (like most churches, say) can be tolerated in a liberal society insofar as they take the form of voluntary associations. But can

they be tolerated as autonomous communities with coercive authority over their members? ...

Because of their conquest and long subordination, the Aboriginal peoples are given, and should be given, more legal and political room to organize and enact their ancient culture. But the room still has windows and doors; it can't be closed off from the larger society, so long as its inhabitants are also citizens. Any of them can decide to leave and live outside or to campaign inside against established leaders and practices ... Aboriginal nations are tolerated as nations, but their members are, at the same time, tolerated as individuals who can revise or reject their national way of life.[80]

Within these cultural enclaves, the role of woman as cultural signifier and reproducer remains as a potential flashpoint. Sometimes the issue is the 'right' of a Native American or First Nations woman with a non-native spouse to be recognised as a member of her community in the same way a Native American or First Nations man with a non-native spouse is recognised as member of his community.[81] At other times it involves the right of Native American or Australian indigenous women to be free from domestic violence within their own communities.[82] Sometimes, the matter is 'off the agenda' from the perspective of some members of the indigenous community, and a 'local matter' from the perspective of the wider society.[83] Either way, tolerance seems inadequate. In such cases, and in others which are not quite so clear cut, we need to ask how we can ensure that individual agency is respected, both within insular communities and outside of them while at the same time respecting difference and group solidarity.[84]

If what I have written above suggests scepticism about the value of rights that is only partially true. So long as rights remain negative, there are limits to what they can accomplish and surely the notion of a constitutionally embedded bill of rights has dangers as well as attraction. On the other hand, as Richard Delgado has noted:

members of the majority race will generally prefer informality, minorities formality. Whites will want community. We will want the safety that comes from structure, rights and rules.[85]

Rights discourse provides a mechanism for staking and defending claims to personhood and recognition, however limited. Jodie Dean argues that formal equality has limited the effectiveness of rights discourse for women because experiences unique to women are automatically relegated to the status of 'exceptions' to a masculine norm. In place of the formally defined juridical subject she argues for the elaboration of that concept to 'refer to the embodied person as a bearer of discursive rights'.[86] Through the notion of discursive rights, she seeks to protect the potential for participation within the relationships of civil society. According to Dean:

Attributing discursive rights to embodied persons, then, allows us to view selves as in progress in that it does not require us to limit or fix the content of these selves. The definitions generated in law are themselves up for democratic interpretation and negotiation. Designed to capture the insight that in certain contexts rights secure the protection of basic liberties, the notion of the embodied person as a bearer of discursive rights is premised on the idea that self-determination presupposes the psychological integrity of embodied persons.

The concept of discursive rights emphasises the continued questioning and confrontation of cultural interpretations that cheapen the value of these rights for particular groups in civil society. To this end, it focuses on the forum and context in which rights claims are made ... By recognising the right of each to challenge and contest exclusionary meanings, they provide spaces for the inclusion of different voices. The stress on the context in which right claims are made draws attention to the situatedness of those others, those hypothetical thirds, who continue to remain outside the boundaries of given articulations of rights.[87]

Dean suggests that it is possible to disrupt the self-referential nature of rights discourse by acknowledging its situated character and making space for narratives that disclose the social and embodied meaning of rights. How might the kind of discursive and argumentative process Dean advocates create spaces for new understandings of rights within law? As she acknowledges:

Laws do not regulate interactions among persons as concrete and irreplaceable members of specific communities; rather, they govern interactions among actors who recognise themselves as members of an abstract community produced by law. Just as legal norms are abstract, so are legal persons. Because they embody the organised expectations of a legal community, legal persons are generalised others. Similarly, their mutual recognition is also abstract. Legal persons respect each other as equal participants in a collective debate regarding the character of the legally constituted community. This equality of respect embodies the intersubjective sense of rights, the way they express a relationship of recognition as well as a social practice rooted in social and political commitment.[88]

The legal notion of reasonableness can, she argues, be understood as requiring a positioning that is simultaneously hypothetical and concrete: the perspective of the situated hypothetical third person. If law is to acknowledge and respond to difference what is needed is greater indeterminacy. The meaning of legal concepts such as the reasonable person and privacy are conceptually over-determined, not indeterminate. Making space for difference entails breaking up the entrenched and determinate images embedded in seemingly indeterminate conceptions such as the reasonable person and making space for alternative conceptions of reasonableness.

The Encumbered Citizen and the Procedural Republic

Within the procedural republic that is our legal system is such a vision possible? In criminal law,[89] in torts,[90] in contract,[91] in jurisdiction after jurisdiction, conventional legal conceptions of reasonableness are under challenge. Some of these innovations seem, initially at least, hopeful and promising, others deeply disturbing. In *Malcolm Thomas Green v The Queen*[92] the High Court of Australia by a 4-1 majority held that, given the appellant's history, an unsolicited homosexual advance was capable of constituting provocation at law. In dissent Kirby J noted:

> In my view, the "ordinary person" in Australian society today is not so homophobic as to respond to a non-violent sexual advance by a homosexual person as to form an intent to kill or to inflict grievous bodily harm ... But the notion that the ordinary 22 year-old male (the age of the accused) in Australia today would so lose self-control as to form an intent to kill or grievously injure the deceased because of a non-violent sexual advance by a homosexual person is unconvincing. It should not be accepted by this Court as an objective standard applicable in contemporary Australia. [He continued:]

> If every woman who was the subject of a "gentle", "non-aggressive" although persistent sexual advance, in a comparable situation to that described in the evidence in this case could respond with brutal violence rising to an intention to kill or inflict grievous bodily harm on the male importuning her, and then claim provocation after a homicide, the law of provocation would be sorely tested and undesirably extended.[93]

We seem further than we might have hoped from a legal and political system capable of taking difference seriously. *Green v The Queen*[94] suggests that we are still a long way from recognising that what is required is a background understanding of a multiplicity of situated hypothetical others and an honest, if not always successful attempt to understand what an objective standard of reasonableness might mean for those others. It illustrates the dangers as well. If standards proliferate so that there is one standard for a homophobic late adolescent male, another for one outraged at a wife's infidelity and yet another for a woman charged with the murder of an abusive partner, we are further away from this goal than we might have hoped.[95] Surely the question must be how we are to establish an objective standard of reasonableness able to acknowledge difference. In the wider context, ultimately, it must be how we are to develop an encumbered subject of rights, a way of acknowledging within rights claims, the hypothetical situated subject and the objective reality of that subject. Drucilla Cornell reminds us that:

> Justice is not something to be achieved, it is something to be struggled for. Substituting subjective for universal standards does not make the law more just; if anything, it turns the law away from the struggle for justice by embroiling the law in a myriad of formal and doctrinal disputes about the reasonable woman, the reasonable black woman, the reasonable lesbian, etc. Instead of focusing on the essential injustice of, and the need to continually transform the significance of, general normative standards, feminists have fostered debate about what *is* the reasonable woman or what *is* the reasonable black lesbian. Law, when it retreats from the universal concern of equivalent evaluation ceases to struggle for justice and instead becomes an administrative institution charged with debating, constructing, and enforcing an exploding matrix of norms that purport to define reasonableness for increasingly narrow categories of individuals.[96]

Cornell reminds us of the dangers the politics of identity foreshadow for our understandings of law and of justice. The question is not simply how our understandings of the citizen can be encumbered, but how, when they are, we can reimagine critical normative standards such as tolerance and reasonableness in a world of encumbered individuals. As Madame Justice Abella notes:

> As groups and the individuals in them spoke with increasing confidence of their rights … more and more people *outside* these groups started asserting their right to be free *from* pluralism. People we used to call "biased" now felt free to raise insensitivity and intolerance to the level of a constitutionally protected right on the same plateau with the rights of minorities, or women, or aboriginal people. We started to think that all rights are created equal, even the right to discriminate.[97]

Very often, those who advance rights claims see them as weapons, not against an excess of government authority, but against those who are different, whose claims threaten their image of an imagined polity in which their chosen way of life is beyond challenge. What is often forgotten, both by those who seek the security of a vanished past and by those who tenaciously advance the cause of an imagined future, is the contingency of all possible social arrangements and of the role played by law in making and unmaking prevailing institutional arrangements. If, as Mann suggests, the unencumbered citizen is simply the incorporated male family self writ large, we need to remember that the unencumbered citizen of political theory, like the reasonable person of law is already profoundly encumbered. Existing social and institutional relationships, enforced and inscribed by existing legal norms, are invariably partial, reflect a set of assumptions which often seem unchangeable precisely because they have been allowed to remain unarticulated.

In the next chapter, and in those that follow, we will begin to look at some of these institutional arrangements in more detail: in equal opportunity law, in family law, in labour law, in taxation law among others. As we begin this investigation, we need to think very carefully about the ways in which these institutional arrangements reflect particular and inevitably partial assumptions about work and the worker, about family and the relationships that constitute it, and about social and political understandings of equality.

Notes

1   See Berns, Sandra, 'Law, Citizenship and the Politics of Identity: Sketching the Limits of Citizenship' (1998) 7 *Griffith LR* 1.

2   Thornton, Margaret, 'Embodying the Citizen' in Thornton, Margaret, ed., *Public and Private: Feminist Legal Debates*, Melbourne, OUP, 1995, 198, 200-201.

3   Different jurisdictions answer this in different ways. In the United States, the notion of 'equal value' prevails. In Australia, the High Court has held that this is not a requirement, while in Canada forms of guaranteed representation for national and linguistic minorities are being explored.

4   See Winter, Bronwyn, 'Women, the Law, and Cultural Relativism in France: The Case of Excision' 19 *Signs* 939. In France, under Article 312, *Alinéa* 3, *Code Pénal*, 1983-

84, 184, there have been a series of actions dating back to 1979. Some of these actions have been against the *exciseuse*, others against the parents. Several of these actions have followed the death of the child as a result of the excision.

5   *Goldman v Weinberger, Secretary of Defence et al* 475 US 503 (1985) held, in a split decision, that the First Amendment did not exempt the petitioner from conforming to military dress regulations. It therefore disallowed the wearing of the yarmulke while on duty. Stevens J, concurring noted that the critical issue was uniformity for all religious faiths. If a yarmulke were allowed, it would be necessary to allow the Sikh turban, the saffron robe of a Yogi and Rastafarian dreadlocks. The only safe course was to disallow all.

6   See *Mandla v Dowell Lee and anor* [1982] 3 All ER 1108 (CA). Lord Denning held that denying Gurinder the right to wear his turban did not constitute racial or ethnic discrimination. When the matter went before the House of Lords in *Mandla and anor v Dowell Lee and anor* [1983] 1 All ER 1063 Mandla's appeal was upheld.

7   *New Rider v Board of Education of Independent School District No. 1, Pawnee County, Oklahoma* 414 US 1097, 38 L Ed 2d 556, 94 S Ct 733(1973). The US Supreme Court, by a majority, denied certiorari. When the appeal was rejected by the 10th Circuit Court of Appeals, Chief Judge Lewis, concurring noted at 700 that: 'The Pawnee are near-pantheists, their every act having religious significance in their basic desire to live in harmony with the Universe'. *New Rider v Board of Education of Independent School District No. 1, Pawnee County Oklahoma* 480 F 2d 693 (1973).

8   See the discussion of some of these issues in Walzer, Michael, *On Toleration*, Princeton, NJ, Yale Univ. Press, 1997, 60-76.

9   On the importance of some of these traditions see Caldwell, Paulette M, 'A Hair Piece: Perspectives on the Intersection of Race and Gender' in Delgado, Richard, ed, *Critical Race Theory: The Cutting Edge*, Philadelphia, Temple Univ. Press, 1995, 267. In *Teterud v Burns* 522 F 2d 357 (1975), which involved a prison inmate who challenged a prison regulation prohibiting the wearing of long braided hair, the 8th Circuit Court of Appeal upheld the prisoner's appeal and held that institutional aims could be achieved by less restrictive means.

10   Ongoing religio-ethnic battles in the former Yugoslavia, in Israel, and in Northern Ireland remind us that the distinction between the sacred and the secular is hard won and precarious. The liberal state depends, fundamentally, upon securing that distinction and upon giving the secular priority over the sacred. While we who live in western democratic states may deem that battle won, the victory is precarious, as the current battles over abortion and pornography ought to remind us.

11   The US Supreme Court has considered claims involving Native American sacred sites on a number of occasions. Three different standards are applied in determining whether government action constitutes a burden on free exercise: 'the centrality standard, the coercive effect standard, and the indispensability standard'. If the challenged action is held to constitute a burden, the Court will then go on to balance Native American interests in free exercise against government interests. In a series of cases, the claims failed. See the discussion in Note, 'The First Amendment and the American Indian Religious Freedom Act: An Approach to Protecting Native American Religion' 71 *Iowa Law Review* 869 (1986), 879, and more generally, 879-885.

12   *Wisconsin v Yoder* 406 US 205, 32 L Ed 574 (1972).

13   The battles over racial and religious equality are largely won on the level of formal equality. That they remain live as a matter of cultural practice may tell us something about the entrenchment of religious and racial prejudice and about the magnitude of the victory represented by the entrenchment of formal equality in our institutional fabric.

14 I am not suggesting that prejudice does not exist at the level of the social. I am
    suggesting that where the only evidence of particularity is to be found in the biological
    indicia of racial or ethnic background the remedies afforded by formal equality are
    largely efficacious.

15 The operation of stereotypes provides an excellent example. Stereotypes enable neutral
    characteristics to be invested with cultural and ethical significance.

16 Cf López, Ian F Haney, 'The Social Construction of Race' in Delgado, Richard,
    Critical Race Theory, 191. López concludes at 200: 'Nevertheless, race is not an
    inescapable physical fact. Rather, it is a social construction that, however, perilously,
    remains subject to contestation at the hands of individuals and communities alike'.
    Perhaps, in this way, race is more fluid than biological sex, although as with race the
    social meaning of biological sex is contested.

17 Neallani, Shelina, 'Women of Colour in the Legal Profession: Facing the Familiar
    Barriers of Race and Sex' (1992) 5 *Canadian Journal of Women & the Law* 148, 158-
    159.

18 See, for example, Bell, Derrick, *Race, Racism and American Law*, 2nd ed, Boston, Little
    & Brown, 1992, 657 where Bell suggests that:
    1. Employment discrimination laws will not eliminate employment
        discrimination.
    2. Employment discrimination laws will not help millions of non-whites.
    3. Employment discrimination laws could divide those blacks who can from
        those who can not benefit from its protection.

19 Matsuda, Mari J, 'Voices of America: Accent, Anti-Discrimination Law, and a
    Jurisprudence for the Last Reconstruction', 100 *Yale LJ* 1334, 1405 (1991).

20 Hobbes, Thomas, *Leviathan*, ed by CB MacPherson, Harmondsworth, Middlesex,
    England, Penguin Books, 1968.

21 Rousseau, Jean Jacques, *The Social Contract and Discourses*, trans. with an
    introduction by GDH Cole, London, JM Dent & Sons, 1913.

22 In their place, Rousseau proposed a 'civil religion'. See Rousseau, *The Social Contract*,
    27.

23 Horowitz, Asher, *Rousseau, Nature, and History*, Toronto, Univ. of Toronto Press,
    1987, 183. More generally, see pp. 168-193.

24 The US based organisation, Promise Keepers, provides an excellent example. See
    http://www2.promisekeepers.org/. While the Cheltenham Group of the UK Men's
    Movement is secularly based, the perspectives put forward are strikingly similar. See
    http://www.ukmm.org.uk/ accessed on 1 July 1999.

25 See the 'Men's Manifesto' at http://www.coeffic.demon.co.uk/manifest.htm, the site of
    the UK Men's Movement. For a similar document, this time from the US Men's
    Defence Association see http://www.mensdefense.org/manif0.html. Both were accessed
    on 1 July 1999.

26 In US jurisdictions there is an increasing trend towards 'covenant marriage', which
    allows couples to contract in to a fully fault based regime with significant restrictions
    on dissolution. See Covenant Marriage Links http://www.divorcereform.org/cov.html.

27 For an excellent discussion of abortion rights in the US context see Colker, Ruth,
    Pregnant Men: Practice, Theory, and the Law, Bloomington, Indiana University Press,
    1994, chs 4 & 5, 89-127.

28 See, for example, Trainor, Brian T, 'The Forgotten Children', *IPA Review*, Melbourne,
    1995; Woods, Mary Helen, 'Difficulties Faced in Sole Parent Families' (1987) 18 (3)
    The Australian Family: Journal of the Family Association 26; cf Robson, Ruthann,
    'Resisting the Family: Repositioning Lesbians in Legal Theory' (1994) 19 *Signs* 975.

At 981, Robson notes that 'the contest over the terrain of family occurs within a legal and political regime hostile to feminism and lesbianism. This point is worth stressing because it is so obvious as to be ignored. In conservative political rhetoric, the phrase "family values" is generally understood to connote an opposition to lesbianism and other "deviations."'

29 See Cooper, Tony, 'Taxing the Family Unit: Income Splitting for All?' (1995) 5 *Revenue LJ* 82; Lambert, Simon, Gillian Beer & Julie Smith, 'Taxing the Individual or the Couple: A Distributional Analysis' Discussion Paper 15, National Centre for Social and Economic Modelling, University of Canberra, 1996.

30 See, for example, Sandel, Michael, *Liberalism and the Limits of Justice*, Cambridge, Cambridge Univ. Press, 1982. Others, such as Michael Walzer, suggest that 'we can never be consistent defenders of multiculturalism or individualism; we can never be simply communitarians or liberals, or modernists or postmodernists, but must be now one, now the other, as the balance requires'. See Walzer, *On Toleration*, 112.

31 Private citizen Jefferson, himself a slaveholder, was conscious of the compromise and the inconsistency, writing somewhat later 'Indeed I tremble for my country when I reflect that God is just'. *Notes on the State of Virginia* 1781-1785.

32 Walzer, Michael, 'Liberalism and the Art of Separation' (1984) 12 (3) *Political Theory*, 315.

33 Walzer, Michael, *Spheres of Justice: A Defence of Pluralism and Equality*, Oxford, Martin Robertson, 1983.

34 Rawls, *Political Liberalism*, above.

35 This is undeniably difficult, but classically liberal. I understand it in this way. Religious differences ought to be irrelevant to participation and access to goods. That is the core liberal settlement. Access to the burdens and benefits of social cooperation ought not depend upon the fact of religious preference. Where, however, religious preference cannot be isolated in any straightforward way from concrete practices that impinge upon participation the rhetoric of choice predominates. While the balance between core and periphery is not stable, the distinction persists.

36 I noted the challenges by the religious right and the fathers' rights movement earlier. Other challenges come from some elements of the feminist movement who argue that women speak in a different voice and that nurture and caring are somehow 'hard-wired' into women. Walzer offers a moderate and thoughtful account of what is at stake in *On Toleration*, 60-71.

37 Racial difference is also socially constructed, in the sense that it has a biological ground and social meaning. One has only to think of the recurrent 'definitional skirmishes' over the racial classification of those of mixed racial background and today even more pointed in the context of membership in some indigenous communities, both in Australia and elsewhere. As in the case of religious preference, where the distinction is made between affiliation as social fact and the concrete practices associated with believers, a tacit distinction is made between a biological fact and associated cultural practices.

38 MacIntyre, Alastair, *Whose Justice? Which Rationality?*, Notre Dame, Univ. of Notre Dame Press, 1988, 335-336.

39 MacIntyre, 337.

40 Cooper, above, 87 notes that 'income splitting between spouses has been advocated by John Howard, the Leader of the Opposition. Mr Howard argued for elective family income splitting only in the case of a family with dependent children which relies on a single income ... [I]t is arguable that such reasoning represents a conservative populist approach to what should really be achieved by dependant tax rebates, which by their

nature are of greater value to lower income earners'. He notes at 88 that while the populist view suggests that a tax system which makes a single income family pay more than a dual income family on the same taxable income is unjust, the debate frequently ignores the increase in work related expenses and child care costs and the loss of the economic value of a full time homemaker. Cooper also notes the difficulty posed by definitional issues, for example, what constitutes a family.

41   In Canada and the United States a clear majority of sole parents are employed full time, in some cases in more than one job, whereas in Australia a majority are either unemployed or in part time positions. See Baker, Maureen, 'Poverty, Ideology and Employability: Canadian and Australian Policies for Low-Income Mothers' (1998) 33 *Australian Journal of Social Issues* 355. See also Shaver, Sheila 'Poverty, Gender and Sole Parenthood' in Fincher, Ruth and John Nieuwenhuysen, eds, *Australian Poverty: Then and Now*, Melbourne, Melbourne Univ. Press, 1998, 276. She notes at 287 that recent changes in the social security system have 'removed provision in social security for sole parents to maintain a distinctive female life-cycle pattern shaped by wifehood and motherhood'.

42   Lee, Julie and Glenda Strachan, 'Who's Minding the Baby Now? Child Care Under the Howard Government' (1998) 9 (2) *Labour and Industry* 81, 99 suggest that the net effects of changes to child care policy under Howard 'are likely to increase inequities between families where women in full time and/or professional occupations who can afford formal child care services will continue to use them but women in less advantaged labour market positions will be compelled to resort to informal services and/or withdraw from the labour force'.

43   The most recent symptom of this regressive shift is the ongoing attempt by the present government to amend the *Sex Discrimination Act* 1984 to permit ART providers to discriminate against women who are not legally married.

44   Compare Muehlenberg, Bill, 'What is a Family?' (1995) 16 *The Australian Family* 3 with its assumption that marriage is critical and that 'the attempt to redefine the family … ignores the historical and social record, and indicates that society has lost its ethical and intellectual moorings' at 6 with Nicholson, Alastair AO RFD (Chief Justice of the Family Court), 'The Changing Concept of Family – the Significance of Recognition and Protection' (1997) 11 *Australian Journal of Family Law* 13. In this context Silverstein, Louise B & Carl F Auerbach, 'Deconstructing the Essential Father' (1999) 54(6) *American Psychologist* 397 is exceptionally interesting. It explores the role of the father and suggests that 'parenting roles are interchangeable, that neither mothers nor fathers are unique or essential, and that the significant variables in predicting father involvement are economic, rather than marital' at 398.

45   See the following Liberal Party policy documents circulated during the 1998 election campaign: 'Status of Women: Opportunity and Choice' Authorised by L. Crosby, Liberal Party of Australia, Corner Blackwell & Macquarie St, Bardon, ACT 2600 accessed at http://www.liberal.org.au/ARCHIVES/ on 5 July 1999.

46   For a thoughtful and insightful analysis of some of these pressures, see Walzer, *On Toleration*, 52-82.

47   Abella, Madam Justice Rosalie Silverman, *Human Rights and the Judicial Role*, Ninth AIJA Oration in Judicial Administration, delivered at School of Electrical Engineering and Computer Science, The University of Melbourne, Friday, 23 October 1998, 9-10.

48   In *Geduldig v Aiello* 417 US 484, 496 (1974) and *General Electric Co v Gilbert* 429 US 125, 138 (1976) the Supreme Court steadfastly maintained that excluding pregnancy from health insurance and disability benefits did not constitute discrimination based on gender. Congress disagreed and amended Title VII to prohibit discrimination based on

pregnancy. In Australia, discrimination based on pregnancy is prohibited under sex discrimination legislation and is frequently litigated.

49 The sorry history of *International Union UAW v Johnson Controls* 499 US 187, 211 (1991) is an excellent illustration. The case concerned a Title VII challenge to an employment policy that excluded fertile women from working with lead on the grounds of potential foetal harm. Both the trial judge and the Seventh Circuit Court of Appeals upheld the exclusion, thus treating female sterility as a bona fide occupational qualification. In 1991 the US Supreme court unanimously held that the policy was discriminatory. In an interesting discussion of *Johnson Controls*, Nancy Levit points out that the Supreme Court viewed the matter exclusively as a woman's issue, despite the fact that one of the appellants was male. See Levit, 74-77. In Australia BHP enjoyed a similar exemption from the requirements of the EEO legislation.

50 US case law is littered with curious interventions into the conduct of pregnant women. Sometimes these interventions take the form of court ordered caesareans against the will of the mother. Under other circumstances they represent attempts to convict a drug-addicted mother of 'dealing' where her addiction is transmitted to her unborn child through the umbilical cord immediately after birth. For a sophisticated exploration of these issues see Ikemoto, Lisa C, 'The Code of Perfect Pregnancy: At the Intersection of the Ideology of Motherhood, the Practice of Defaulting to Science, and the Interventionist Mindset of Law' 53 *Ohio St LJ* 1205 (1992). Ikemoto notes the rise of the 'two patient' model of pregnancy, commenting that 'This cultural understanding prescribes the perception that in a woman-fetus relationship, the woman is in a position of power relative to the fetus, which in turn must be protected in order to prevent harm caused by the woman's abuse of that power'.

51 For some insular communities, of course, the social constitutes the entire life-world of their members. For such communities, excursions into the civil society remain largely minor and on their terms. For others and particularly for those communities that lack the infrastructure and the resources to permit relative withdrawal the tension between the communal life-world and the need to participate in wider institutions is acute. See Walzer, *On Toleration*, 76-82.

52 West, Robin L, *Caring for Justice*, New York, NYU Press, 1997, 112.

53 See Chapter 1 for an extended discussion of these issues.

54 In this context, one has only to think of the ire of the fathers' rights movement that the formal equality of the economic and the political is not replicated in the family, at least in the context of dissolution of marriage and arrangements concerning children. In this context Nancy Levit's comment about the source of male resentment is perspicacious. 'Men are rightfully resentful about being locked into the social roles of breadwinner, protector, and provider. It is no coincidence that men's rights groups seek custody, evangelical groups seek to form closer relations with their family and faith groups, and profeminist groups actively want to assume more child care responsibilities. The thematic complaint resonates with empirical experience: social forces have excluded men from the arena of nurturing'. Levit, 182-183.

55 Matsuda, 1405.

56 Neallani, 158-159.

57 Neallani, 158-159.

58 Baron, Paula and Elizabeth Barber, *An Evaluation of Australian Academic Performance Measurements*, Report to DETYA, Evaluations and Investigations Program, 1998.

59 Both male and female students hold these expectations.

60 It goes without saying that a raceless persona may remain out of reach for many of the same reasons. See, for example, Russell, Jennifer M, 'On Being a Gorilla in Your

Midst, or, The Life of One Blackwoman in the Legal Academy' in Delgado, Richard, ed, *Critical Race Theory: The Cutting Edge*, Philadelphia, Temple Univ. Press, 1995, 498.

61   Thornton, 'Embodying the Citizen', above, 213.

62   Thornton, 'Embodying the Citizen', above, 213.

63   I think here of the slaves, metics and wives of the Greek polis, and more recently the African slaves of the Americas. I think also of the men and women of the working classes in an era, not so long ago, when property ownership was a precondition for suffrage. Immanuel Kant identified women and all those who worked for a living as 'passive citizens'. They were part of the infrastructure supporting citizens and enabling them to participate in law giving.

64   Cover, Robert, 'Nomos and Narrative' in Minow, Martha, Michael Ryan, and Austin Sarat, *Narrative, Violence, and the Law*, Ann Arbor, University of Michigan Press, 1992, 95, 106. Cover describes imperial community as one in which 'norms are universal and enforced by institutions'.

65   From a very different frame of reference political theorist Jane Mansbridge suggests that: 'All real democracies ... produce outcomes that are substantively unjust. But workers, women, subordinated races, lower classes, and other disadvantaged groups fare far better in those democracies than they would in most cases if the democracies began to fall apart. Raw power, unmitigated by democratic values, usually hurts the disadvantaged far more than does democratic power. The disadvantaged need the relatively just coercion that democracies produce'. Mansbridge, Jane, 'Using Power/Fighting Power: The Polity' in Benhabib, Seyla, ed, *Democracy and Difference: Contesting the Boundaries of the Political*, Princeton, NJ, Princeton University Press, 1996, 46, 56.

66   Those who call for the resurgence of the male-headed nuclear family (and in some cases, the elimination of female suffrage) represent a contemporary instantiation of the patriarchal household.

67   The brutal battle for the Balkans reminds us that racial and religious purity remains a potent flash point and reminds us as well of the brutality that accompanies these skirmishes, particularly where conquest by rape has become the norm.

68   This battle continues to rage in states, such as Israel and Afganistan, which are trapped between the secular and the sacred.

69   Abella, 13.

70   To say that carework is a given, is not, of course, to suggest who should be responsible. The way in which carework is organised is culturally and historically determined. It is only to say that every human society will find it necessary to make arrangements for carework, whether those arrangements are made by nuclear families, kinship groupings, or various forms of social provision.

71   This does not mean that the present allocation of household labour ought to be understood as either natural or fixed. Rather, it suggests that preferences and bargaining have a significant role to play.

72   Fraser, Nancy, 'Gender Equity and the Welfare State: A Postindustrial Thought Experiment' in Benhabib, Seyla, ed, *Democracy and Difference: Contesting the Boundaries of the Political*, Princeton, NJ, Princeton University Press, 1996, 218, 235.

73   *Theophanous v Herald & Weekly Times Ltd* (1994) 182 CLR 104.

74   See, for example, Gabel, above and West, Robin L, 'Foreword: Taking Freedom Seriously' 104 *Harv LR* 43 (1990).

75   Abella, 11.

76 Kipling's 'white man's burden' and the threatening and equally legendary 'white slave traffic' are historical contemporaries. If white English males (in India) saw themselves as 'civilising the natives' and bestowing upon them the dubious benefits of English culture, fantasies concerning the sexual prowess and desires of 'darker races' were embedded in the consciousness of many people. While the English gentleman shouldered the burden of civilising the 'natives', his wives, sisters and daughters were eternally under threat, in danger of being captured and conveyed to the harems and brothels of the 'mysterious East'.

77 Williams, Patricia J, *The Alchemy of Race and Rights*, Cambridge, MA, Harvard Univ. Press, 1991, 3.

78 Walzer, *On Toleration*, 60-66.

79 Kymlicka, Will, *Multicultural citizenship: a liberal theory of minority rights*, Oxford, OUP, 1995, 159. In the Australian context, indigenous women have been unable to access Aboriginal Legal Aid services to obtain Apprehended Violence Orders where the offending family member is also indigenous. Where they are forced to access non-indigenous legal aid services, or the limited number of gender specific indigenous services, the offender is able to access indigenous legal aid. This imbalance is the source of considerable resentment among indigenous women's groups, as is the suggestion that, by raising their voices against this injustice, they are being disloyal to their Aboriginality.

80 Walzer, *On Toleration*, 60-66.

81 Because culture is fluid, rather than fixed, Euro-centric patterns of sexism were frequently internalised by Native American and First Nations Men and reinforced by non-native law. In Canada, the *Indian Act* 1876 (as amended in 1951) by s 12(b)(1) built in patrilineal assumptions into its definition of 'Indian'. An Indian woman who married outside her tribe (together with her children) was stripped of her Indian status. The Canadian legislation was not amended until after the 1985 protest to the United Nations. See Jaimes, M Annette (with Theresa Halsey), 'American Indian Women: At the Center of Indigenous Resistance in Contemporary North America' in McClintock, Anne, Aamir Mufti & Ella Shohat, eds, *Dangerous Liaisons: Gender, Nation & Postcolonial Perspectives*, Minneapolis, University of Minnesota Press, 1997, 298, 313-316. Jaimes notes at 316 the battle Indian women were compelled to wage against their own men to reassert their traditional leadership and comments: 'Along the way, the Tobique Women's Political Action Group was forced to confront the broker class of their own male population, who had been placed in positions of "leadership" by the Canadian rather than their own governing system and who were thus threatened by the women's actions; the women physically occupied tribal office buildings and effectively evicted the men, beginning in September 1977'.

82 Jaimes, 311. The author comments concerning poverty and despair among Native Americans, 'On balance, the situation breeds frustration and rage of the most volatile sort, especially among native males, who have been at once heaped with a range of responsibilities utterly alien to their tradition – "head of the household," sole "breadwinner," and so forth – while being structurally denied any viable opportunity to act upon them. In perfect Fanonesque fashion, this has led to a perpetual spiral of internalized violence in which Indian men engage in brutal (and all too often lethal) bar fights with one another and/or turn their angry attentions on their wives and children. Battering has become endemic on some reservations, as well as in the Indian ghettos that exist in most US cities, with the result that at least a few Indian women have been forced to kill their spouses in self-defence'. The story is much the same in Australia. See Smallwood, Margaret, 'This Violence is Not Our Way: An Aboriginal Perspective

on Domestic Violence' in Thorpe, Ros and Jude Irwin, eds, *Women and Violence Working for Change*, Sydney, Hale & Ironmonger, 1996, 129. See further, Atkinson, Judy, 'Violence in Aboriginal Australia: Colonisation and Gender' (1996) 14 *The Aboriginal and Islander Health Worker* 5.

83   During the early nineties, battered indigenous women in Australia faced a catch 22 situation. All too often, when they sought help from indigenous legal services they were advised that help was unavailable as the service was representing the male partner in the magistrate's courts.

84   Cf Jaimes, 298. For a somewhat different perspective see Ng, Roxana, 'Sexism, racism & Canadian nationalism' in Gunew, Sneja & Anna Yeatman, eds, *Feminism and the Politics of Difference*, St Leonards, NSW, Allen & Unwin, 1993, 197. See further Huggins, Jackie, 'Pretty deadly tidda business' in Gunew & Yeatman, 61 and Yeatman, Anna, 'Voice and representation in the politics of difference' in Gunew & Yeatman, 228.

85   Generally see Delgado, 'Critical Legal studies and the Realities of Race', above. Echoing Delgado, Patricia Williams writes of her experiences in sub-letting an apartment and contrasts them with those of a white male colleague, noting that whereas he opted for informality and a verbal agreement she 'signed a detailed, lengthily negotiated, finely printed lease firmly establishing [her] as the ideal arm's-length transactor'. See Williams, above, 147. Martha Minow makes very similar points in Minow 'Interpreting Rights', above.

86   Dean, Jodi, *Solidarity of Strangers: Feminism after Identity Politics*, Berkeley, University of California Press, 1996, 93.

87   Dean, 93-94.

88   Dean, 103-104.

89   *State of Washington v Wanrow* 559 P 2d 548 (1977). For a discussion of some of these issues see Donovan, Dolores & Stephanie M Wildman, 'Is the Reasonable Man Obsolete? A Critical Perspective on Self-Defence and Provocation' 14 *Loyola of Los Angeles LR* 435 (1981) and Schneider, Elizabeth, 'Equal Rights to Trial for Women: Sex Bias in the Law of Self-Defence' 15 *Harv CR-CL LR* 623 (1980). Disturbingly, in *Malcolm Thomas Green v The Queen* (1997) 191 CLR 334 the High Court of Australia by a majority held that an unsolicited homosexual advance was capable of constituting provocation at law. For a sensitive discussion of these issues see Comstock, Gary, 'Dismantling the Homosexual Panic Defense' (1992) 2 *Law and Sexuality* 81; Dressler, Joshua, 'When "Heterosexual" Men Kill "Homosexual" Men: Reflections on Provocation Law, Sexual Advances, and the "Reasonable Man" Standard' (1995) 85 *Journal of Criminal Law and Criminology* 726; Mison, Robert B, 'Homophobia in Manslaughter: The Homosexual Advance as Insufficient Provocation' (1992) 80 *California Law Review* 133; Moran, Leslie J, *The Homosexuality of Law*, London, Routledge, 1996, 183-184. See further Yeo, Stanley, 'Sex, Ethnicity, Power of Self-Control and Provocation Revisited' (1996) 18 *Sydney Law Review* 304. In *R v Brown* [1993] 2 All ER 75 the defence of consent was disallowed where the defendants had engaged in consensual sado-masochistic practices.

90   *Khorasandjian v Bush* [1993] 3 WLR 476, Berns, Sandra S, 'The Hobart City Council Case: A Tort of Sexual Harassment for Tasmania?' (1994) 13 *UTLR* 112, *Norberg v Wyndrib* (1992) 92 DLR 4d 449. More generally see Bender, Leslie, 'An Overview of Feminist Torts Scholarship' (1993) 78 *Cornell LR* 575.

91   *Amadio*, above.

92   *Green v The Queen*, above.

93   *Green v The Queen*, above.

94   *Green v The Queen*, above.
95   The quotation below is taken from the second day of hearings in *Osland v The Queen*. See http://www.austlii.edu.au/.

> McHUGH J: It seems to me, to talk about the reasonable apprehension of an ordinary person with the subjective perceptions of a battered woman is almost a contradiction in terms.
>
> MS SCUTT: All right. That is one of the reasons why we put our argument as we did in relation to battered woman reality. I will just go to those points that my learned friend made, if I may. What we say is that the problem with calling it "battered woman syndrome" rather than "reality" is that there is an inward focus on the woman's mental state, and that is the starting and the ending point. There should be an outward focus on the violence, that is the reality of the external circumstances under which the woman is living, operating and so on.
>
> When you have looked at those external circumstances, you measure the subjectivity and the reasonableness by that, because if you think about it, if a man were genuinely in a situation where for 13 years he had been subjected to continuing violence, if the Court would – I am not asking them to do it now; I am asking you to do it later – to look through that litany of violence to which she said she was subjected and others said she was subjected, I ask the Court to think that if a man had genuinely been in that circumstance, would it have been reasonable for him to have killed?

96   Cornell, Drucilla, *The Imaginary Domain*, New York & London, Routledge, 1995, 3, 16.
97   Abella, 6. While she writes in the Canadian context, the process she describes is equally in play in Australia. The presence or absence of a constitutionally entrenched bill of rights is less important by far than the perception of groups and individuals that they possess certain rights and their willingness to defend them.

Chapter 3

Equal Opportunity: Rhetoric and Reality

The Australian Legal Framework: The More Things Change

As we saw in the first chapter, both the States and the Commonwealth have enacted legislation proscribing sex discrimination. While, in some states, sex discrimination legislation was enacted in the early 1970s[1] the Commonwealth legislation was not enacted until 1984.[2] This chapter will focus upon the Commonwealth legislation and upon the curious way in which the Australian regime is bifurcated and some of the consequences of that approach. Under sex discrimination law the legal regime has been described as 'privatised', depending entirely upon the willingness of individual claimants to approach HREOC, and thus depending upon whether those injured by discriminatory practices are prepared to confront their employers and challenge their behaviour and their practices. In addition, because remedies under the *Sex Discrimination Act* 1984 rely primarily upon the conciliation of complaints, there is relatively little case law, the vast majority of complaints being resolved at the conciliation stage. Only a few cases proceed to the tribunal level, and even fewer to the federal court. Although occasional high profile cases emerge[3] overall the educative role of the law has been blunted by the reliance upon conciliation and the need for an individual complainant. Additional complications arise because the Commonwealth and the States share responsibility and the protections actually available depend upon whether an individual complainant is able to invoke State or Commonwealth law.

Equal employment opportunity legislation is of slightly more recent origin, and emerged because of the limitations of legislation proscribing sex discrimination but lacking positive measures to effect structural change and eliminate discriminatory practices. The *Affirmative Action (Equal Employment Opportunity for Women) Act* 1986 (Cth) was intended to combat the structural factors, including the entrenchment of the 'family wage' in industrial awards until the late 1960s and a history of very low levels of female employment,[4] which made Australian workplaces among the most sex segregated in the OECD. The legislation was broadly based but modest in its ambitions. Despite its title, it did not mandate affirmative action as commonly understood, for example by incorporating a formal requirement for a quota as in the United States and Sweden.[5] Rather, it sought to initiate change through a set of formal structural arrangements intended to alter workplace cultures and thus break down the sex segregation in Australian workplaces. While the legislation prohibited both direct and indirect discrimination, its formal requirements were limited to compelling covered workplaces[6] to comply with eight steps and to provide a brief report for public scrutiny and a more detailed report for evaluation by the Affirmative Action Agency (now the Equal Opportunity in the Workplace Agency). Each covered workplace was required to formulate an EEO policy, appoint a senior person to take carriage of that policy, consult with trade unions and employees, particularly women, analyse its employment profile, set EEO objectives and monitor and evaluate its program. The locally specific focus of the program and the fact that it institutionalises self-regulation are both noteworthy. The shape of individual EEO programs is thus highly dependent upon the ethos of the particular enterprise and the understandings of senior individuals within it. The only available sanction involves the naming of non-compliant organisations in Parliament, a feature that both made it acceptable to the business community and severely limited its impact and its ability to break down the gendering of workplaces. Under the EEO framework:

> Employers can confine themselves to remove what they consider to be discriminatory from employment policy and practice, and not take positive action to redress past discriminatory practices, or to change the values, power structures and culture of the organisation.[7]

It is instructive to compare the Australian approach to that adopted by Sweden in the early 1970s. Like Australia, Sweden is a country with a relatively small population concentrated in a very few urban areas. Because of a history of industrial concentration in the major cities, employment opportunities in regional centres were very limited. To correct this, beginning in 1965 the Swedish government provided significant inducements to firms prepared to relocate to regional areas, in the hope of reducing unemployment and underemployment in those areas and creating a more diversified labour market. During the 1970s as part of its overall equal opportunity strategy, the government made location assistance conditional upon reserving 40 per cent of the total training positions in the relocated firm for each gender. Those firms electing to participate were entitled to receive a combination of depreciation loans and regular location loans to finance up to 70 per cent of the cost of buildings and plant.

> Depreciation loans or grants are initially given to enterprises as loans. If a firm receiving such aid complies with all of the requirements, including the sex quota, 30 percent of the loan is forgiven after the first year, 20 percent in the second year, and 10 percent each year thereafter. The regular loans are offered on more attractive terms than firms in these areas would otherwise have to pay.[8]

Where firms fail to meet their targets, sanctions are available. In such cases, the depreciation loan is typically converted to a location loan, a significant penalty for non-complying firms. There has been little opposition to the quota system, either from firms or from male workers. Barrett suggests that this is largely because the program provides gains for all parties. As she notes:

> An aspect of Swedish EEO policy that merits imitation is its links with other government programs that benefit firms and male workers ... If firms and male

workers stand to gain from these programs, they are more likely to accept gender quotas than they would under US-style affirmative action programs that are set up as zero-sum games. In the Swedish system everyone wins, while in the US system gains for women are at the expense of males and are perceived as costly to firms.[9]

The Australian EEO program provides neither incentives making participation desirable and offering benefits to all nor meaningful sanctions for failure to comply. Perhaps even more seriously, it stands alone, having structural links neither with the broader sweep of labour market policy nor with placement and training programs. While significant efforts have been made to encourage girls and young women to consider a broader range of career options, these lack formal links with EEO and with labour market policy. Essentially a bureaucratic and administrative exercise, it seeks to alter workplace cultures by requiring firms to develop an EEO policy and appointing a relatively senior person to implement it. It is, therefore, unsurprising that EEO was regarded as an inefficient imposition on established management practices and workplace cultures, particularly given a private enterprise culture that valued 'fit' above 'merit'.

During the decade and a half since enactment, evidence continues to mount that it is precisely the values, power structures and culture of organisations that must change if meaningful progress is to be made. Within every large organisation, there are numerous micro-organisations, each with its own sub-culture, its embedded power structures and associated values. These organisational sub-cultures are differentiated by perceived status, by responsiveness to unionisation, and by sub-cultural phenomena including the performance of particular kinds of gender roles.[10] In Australia, these organisational cultures and sub-cultures are the legacy of more than 60 years of government policy aimed at maintaining and reinforcing the 'family wage' and restricting the employment available to women, especially married women. This policy shaped employment practices, permeated the ethos and shaped the structures of the trade union movement, and almost thirty years after its abandonment, remains a potent cultural force. As Bryson notes:

> The historical evidence shows that women were actively excluded from the workforce and their independent economic activity within households was redefined as non-economic. During the nineteenth century domestic labour was classified in official statistics; at the beginning of the twentieth century, it was redefined as non-economic and expunged from the national accounts.[11]

The result has been a set of institutional structures, both within workplaces and within the organised trade union movement, that view the gender gap as a function of women's difference and disregard the ways in which existing organisational cultures and practices have acted to advantage men and continue to do so.[12]

The concordance between workplace cultures and trade union cultures has had a second effect, one that is equally important. Once the gender gap becomes linked to female deficits rather than occupational cultures, and is thereby absorbed into the rhetoric of disadvantage, the door is left open for other groups to put forward superficially similar claims. Thus, the continuing contraction in core unskilled, largely male, labouring and manufacturing jobs and the expansion in contingent semi-skilled and skilled service and hospitality industry positions, despite their lack of institutional history and structural embeddedness, are now being identified as a source of male 'disadvantage' warranting institutional intervention.[13] Removed from the context in which these changes have occurred and the associated organisational structures the tale of male disadvantage is plausible, even persuasive. Institutionally, however, it is implausible. The shift has not been from core male unskilled and semi-skilled labouring and manufacturing jobs to core female jobs enjoying the same relative security and benefits. Rather, the shift operates along two independent but related dimensions: from labouring and manufacturing jobs to service and knowledge industry based jobs and from core positions to contingent positions, although there are some indications that the latter trend is being reversed in the services sector.[14]

Australian research into contingent employment and the conditions with which it is associated[15] suggests that the disadvantageous conditions that characterise contingent work are largely a consequence of the fact that the work involved 'has traditionally been seen as women's work'.[16] Only in emerging fields, such as technology based work, are there signs that a relatively advantageous form of fixed term full time employment is emerging, and here, of course, access depends upon high levels of technical skills and training. The evidence to date suggests that this new and relatively advantaged form of employment is gendered male. ABS statistics suggest that 75 per cent of those working in computer maintenance services are male, as are 67 per cent of those working in computer consultancy services. Only in relatively low paid data processing and information storage and retrieval services do women predominate, 80 per cent of those working in this area being female, reproducing the distinction between the secretary and the manager.[17]

The rhetoric of male disadvantage conceals the fact that the profound contraction in core unskilled and semi-skilled employment that has pushed increasing numbers of men into contingent work[18] or unemployment is largely a product of external forces, including the dismantling of high levels of tariff protection.[19] Despite the efforts of some groups and individuals to use these developments to mobilise sympathy for the male 'victims' of equal opportunity laws, there is little evidence of any connection, causal or otherwise. Instead, despite the recurrent suggestion that women are 'flooding' the labour market, and 'edging out' men,[20] the evidence suggests that women are overall simply increasing their representation in fields with a history of significant levels of female employment and that male losses are concentrated in the contracting manufacturing sector.

EEO: Reality and Perceptions

Despite a regulatory approach that has been characterised as 'gentle', 'loose' and 'weak',[21] when EEO was introduced in parliament, opposition was widespread. Conservative politicians deemed it an attack on the family unit[22] while business interests viewed it as anti-competitive.[23] In contemporary variations, these polarised positions continue to marshal considerable support.[24] While some feminist scholars have, almost from the outset, expressed concerns that the legislation would be unable to meet the expectations it generated, in the eyes of its detractors it attained overwhelming potency. Among feminist scholars debate continues over whether, as Margaret Thornton argues, the *Act* is

> a classic piece of edentate, or toothless, legislation, in which the state has unsuccessfully sought to mediate the diametrically opposed interests of subordinated women workers and management.[25]

While not disputing Thornton's central argument, Valerie Braithwaite suggests that while the *Act* has failed to achieve cultural change, it has been surprisingly effective in setting up

> interlocking implementation chains at elite levels through the principle of redundancy: implementing the affirmative action legislation is not only being fair to women, but is good management practice.[26]

Despite this success it appears largely to have failed in implementing cultural change within the workplace and in mobilising and involving the energies of the majority of men and women who remain outside the cultural elites responsible for its implementation. In this way, Thornton's critical claim is, to some extent, borne out. Those who benefit most from EEO legislation are those who are already most like 'benchmark men' and, therefore, those least in need of assistance.[27]

Despite evidence that the impact of the *Act* was relatively modest, following the election of a Liberal government in 1996, an independent Committee was established to review it. Two issues were of particular concern. The Committee sought to determine whether, as frequently alleged by business interests, the *Act* restricted competition. It also sought to identify the net cost of compliance and to seek ways of reducing that cost.[28] As a consequence of that review, the Committee recommended that all reference to affirmative action be dropped from the title of the legislation. The *Affirmative Action (Equal Opportunity for Women) Act* 1986 is now known as the *Equal Opportunity for Women in the Workplace Act* 1999. According to the Assistant Director of the Affirmative Action Agency (now the Equal Opportunity for Women in the Workplace Agency), Tracey Carpenter, this change reaffirms the *Act's* commitment to fairness and merit and distances it from US style quotas.[29]

This apparently innocuous justification makes a number of highly contentious claims. Carpenter does not fully acknowledge that fairness and merit are not settled and defined concepts but contested terrain. She treats them as givens, as a set of qualities pertaining to particular relationships and individuals that can be applied unproblematically within a variety of settings. In reality, both fairness and merit are situationally determined cultural signifiers, sufficiently porous and open textured to be permanently open to challenge.[30] Fairness can be seen either as procedural or as substantive. If fairness is seen as merely procedural, as a matter of the right procedures and their consistent and 'neutral' application, it is profoundly conservative and favours the status quo. While it will pick up egregious departures from those procedures, it is unable to go beyond that and ask whether the procedures themselves produce particular kinds of outcomes and whether those outcomes are fair. Within this framework, merit becomes propertised, is understood as an identifiable set of measurable characteristics which are relevant to an equally identifiable skill set relevant to particular positions or to promotion from level to level. The merit principle thus requires an unproblematic matching of the traits possessed by a particular individual with the skill set required by a particular position. This understanding of merit conceals a set of further variables: the positions, experiences and understandings of those whose responsibility it is to make judgments of merit; and, more fundamentally, the cultural signifiers attached to particular positions and thus to what does or does not constitute merit in those positions.[31] These cultural signifiers demarcate the organisational culture, and the commitment of that culture to fairness and equity.

Inevitably, gender is among these cultural signifiers, as are the assumptions associated with the gendered characteristics of particular positions.[32] None of this is new; indeed, it is not even particularly surprising. As Alice Kessler-Harris notes:

> In the free market, theoretically demand and supply determine price. But in practice, wage theorists recognize a variety of ... "exterior factors" in determining the wage. These exterior factors are influences on the labor market that emerge from ... non-market factors ... In this widely accepted model, workers compare their wages to those of other workers; pride and dignity prevent them from settling for less than their peers are getting. Other economists talk about "job clusters": firefighters insist on parity with police; steelworkers strike to maintain equivalent wage nationwide ... [33]

Kessler Harris continues:

> Like the wage, the labor market is a regulating device, the product of a long history of social relationships heavily influenced by traditional conceptions of gender roles.[34]

While Kessler Harris speaks of the United States, the patterns she describes are deeply familiar. They are symptoms of features only too common in Australian workplaces: high levels of sex-segregation and wages patterns that both reflect this segregation and are historically dependent upon the now-abandoned family wage. In this context, Carpenter's affirmation of merit is a disturbing note, one that fails to contextualise 'merit' and to explore the ways in which merit is itself open to abuse.

Carpenter also identifies a number of other changes to the legislation that, according to her, will have the cumulative effect of making 'the legislation more business-friendly'.[35] While the coverage of the legislation will not change, reporting requirements are to become biennial rather than annual. The original eight-step program is to be abandoned in favour of a streamlined approach that will require organisations to analyse their EEO issues, identify priority EEO areas, develop an action plan, and establish the measures used and the outcomes sought.[36] Assessment of compliance will also be greatly simplified, becoming a simple analysis of whether or not the organisation complies, replacing the current five-point scale ranking the level of compliance. While these changes will reduce compliance costs, they will have little if any impact on the cultural norms which restrict female participation and which have, over more than a decade, remained largely impervious to change through both EEO and sex discrimination legislation.[37]

Eveline argues that one of the reasons that EEO has largely failed to deliver on its initial promise, particularly in terms of breaking down the extraordinarily high levels of sex segregation in business and industry, is because it has institutionalised talk of 'disadvantage'.[38] Where 'disadvantage' is institutionalised as a normative tool:

> 'The problem' is identified as 'women's disadvantage', or Aboriginal disadvantage' or 'disadvantaged groups'. In fact, the 'disadvantaged' are often 'commatised', as Mary O'Brien reminds us: where the lists of disadvantaged sweep across 'blacks (comma) unemployed (comma) gays (comma)' and so on. This form of argument 'otherises' the problem and normalises the standards by which those terms are measured – whites, men, employed and employers, heterosexuals and so on. In Australia more recently, we see the discourse of disadvantage turning to encompass groups who were previously the unnamed advantaged, with the news media trumpeting about 'boys' disadvantage' in schools, 'men's disadvantage' in university admissions, or 'men's disadvantage' in unemployment.[39]

As we saw in chapter 1, the father's rights movement is mobilising the rhetoric of disadvantage to protest the 'anti-male bias' (read 'male disadvantage') in parenting and child support arrangements and to demand 'equal opportunity' in the Family Court. The evidence suggests that their lobbying efforts and the claims of 'disadvantage' which have formed the centrepiece of their submissions have born fruit, both in terms of the 1995 amendments to the *Family Law Act* 1975[40] and the 1998 Men and Family Relationships Forum in Canberra.[41] Because of the ease with which it can be captured, the rhetoric of disadvantage enables groups who continue to occupy relatively privileged positions within the economic and social structures of a given society to mobilise the assistance intended for historically disadvantaged groups and individuals. Claims of disadvantage also serve another purpose, that of drawing attention away from the structural factors sustaining discriminatory practices and focusing it on individual isolated grievances. Discrimination is thus defined as a deviation from normal practices, rather than acknowledged as structurally embedded in existing workplaces.

In fact, the levels of sex segregation in Australian business and industry have remained essentially unchanged since the early 1980s, suggesting that both the *Affirmative Action (Equal Opportunity for Women) Act* 1986 and the *Sex Discrimination Act* 1984 have failed to deliver in this area. In 1984, OECD figures suggested that Australia had the most sex-segregated workforce in the OECD area.[42] The overall picture remains similar today.[43] Sex segregation is problematical for two reasons. First, the number of 'female' occupations is tiny in absolute terms compared to the number of 'male' occupations.[44] Second, female dominated occupations tend to be clustered at the lower levels of the occupational hierarchy and characterised by high levels of contingent employment, a fact that depresses wages and perpetuates the gender gap.[45] As Anker notes:

> Women all around the world tend to be working in a small set of occupations – and in addition these occupations tend to have *lower pay, lower status and less decision-making authority* than the types of occupations in which male workers tend to be located. Further more, the main occupations in which women work have characteristics which are *consistent with the types of stereotyped traits often attributed to women* ..., such as a supposedly caring nature; greater honesty; greater manual dexterity, especially with fingers; more experience and skill at typical household tasks; greater willingness to be subservient and take orders; less physical strength; less ability in maths and science.[46]

In Australia, while the overall level of sex segregation has not changed significantly, a more detailed analysis suggests that women are gradually moving out of highly feminised industries while men are 'consolidating within masculinised occupations'.[47] According to Pocock:

> In 1986, 73 per cent of women worked in disproportionately female occupations, and this fell to 69 per cent in 1995, while the expected proportions in each year are 29 per cent. Calculating the same ratios for disproportionately male occupations reveals that a growing proportion of men are found in male-dominated jobs; the actual ratio rose from 80.5 to 82.4 per cent, while the expected values fell. This suggests that beneath the steady overall sex-segregation ratio, what we are witnessing is increasing entry of women into 'men's' jobs, while men are not shifting ...[48]

The cultural implications of these figures are particularly interesting. They suggest that some women are becoming ready to widen their occupational choice and to compete in traditionally male domains while men are reluctant to abandon occupations that validate particular gender roles, even against a background of contracting opportunities in these occupations and in the face of increasing competition from women. The one exception, it would appear, is the retail sector, a traditionally female sector that has shown a marked increase in male employment over the last two years. The statistics do not, however, break down the sector into its constituent parts, some of which, such as appliance and motor vehicles sales have been traditionally male.[49] The critical questions are sub-sectoral, both in terms of the occupational classifications within the sector and the constituent parts within the industry. Pocock suggests that detailed analysis suggests that female entry into traditional male occupations

> has been strongest in the upper levels of the occupational hierarchy ... [and that] female domination is increasing in traditionally feminised occupations like teaching, nursing, numerical clerking, sales, filing sorting and copying, material recording and dispatching, and in receptionist and telephonist jobs.[50]

Pocock's analysis is borne out by the work of Peetz et al who suggest that in terms of gender equity:

> There are two clear occupational associations. Professionals tend to be associated with good equity performance while workforces dominated by sales and personal service workers and manual workers are associated with poor equity performance. In part, this divergence reflects the ability of workers in these areas to influence management. For example, the early movements in support of equal pay came from professionals: teachers. The apparent differential may also reflect the relative sophistication of employment relations in such workplaces. In terms of industries, only finance has considerably better than average equity performance, although communications, government administration, and health and community services also perform well. Conversely, construction, with its predominantly male workforce, performs poorly, as does manufacturing. This is likely to reflect the cultures of both management and employees in these industries.[51]

Thus analysis of recent statistics suggests that while the *Affirmative Action (Equal Opportunities for Women) Act* 1986 may have facilitated access to traditional male occupations for a minority of highly educated women progress overall has been relatively slow. It also suggests that education is a significant factor, both because of its impact upon workplace culture and because workplaces where high educational levels are commonplace are more likely to have developed sophisticated policy structures designed to enhance equity. The poor performance of the retail sector on the gender equity index is interesting and suggestive, given the unusual and apparently rapid movement of men into a female dominated sector over the last decade. One wonders if the movement of men into this sector is related to its poor performance on the gender equity index, perhaps because, despite a history of female concentration in the sector its overall ethos, including the lack of gender equity, is congenial to men, at least in some sub-sectors.[52]

In part, undoubtedly, these differences can be explained by the limited coverage of the legislation. Data in the 1995 *Australian Workplace and Industrial Relations Survey* (AWIRS 95) suggests that among uncovered workplaces 58 per cent of those workplaces having men-only jobs in 1990 still had men-only jobs in 1995. The picture was very different in covered workplaces. Among covered workplaces, only 10 per cent of those having men-only jobs in 1990 still had men-only jobs in 1995.[53] In this context, it is important to note that, 'seventy-three per cent of workplaces have fewer than 20 employees, and this is also where the vast majority of women are employed'.[54] While the sample size in AWIRS 95 was very small, it is clear that while some progress has been made further progress may well depend upon social and political willingness to extend the scope of equal opportunity legislation to cover workplaces with fewer than 100 employees.[55]

The former Director of the Equal Opportunity for Women in the Workplace Agency, Fiona Krautil, notes that while the evidence suggests that covered workplaces have made significant progress in recruiting women into management roles, uncovered workplaces have made no progress whatsoever. As a consequence, despite the progress made in covered workplaces, the proportion of women in management in Australian workplaces declined marginally between

1990 and 1998.[56] The glacial rate of change and its uneven distribution alerts us to a further dimension. Margaret Thornton argues that:

> EEO can ... be deployed to facilitate the retention of hegemonic masculinity... Its essential malleability, designed to permit workplaces to fashion practices to suit particular cultural norms, has not worked in the interests of women. Minimalist legislative prescripts have resulted in regimes of veritable self-regulation. Given the masculinist and managerialist orientation of corporate authority, we would be deluding ourselves if we were to think that EEO could function as a feminist instrument.[57]

While the Equal Opportunity in the Workplace Agency claims to have encouraged organisations to look at their policies and practices in a range of relevant areas, the simplified four-point program put forward suggests that employers will be able to evade the issue with relative ease. Particularly worrying from the perspective of any real potential for change is the overall direction taken by the Agency in recent years. While good EEO practices are fairly clearly good for business, if they are to bring about cultural change they are likely to be uncomfortable for both organisations and individuals while change is occurring. Given that the *Act* involved relatively modest structural changes,[58] and the fact that the evidence suggests that those changes have had a beneficial effect on productivity, thus producing significant gains for the enterprises involved, the new direction is disturbing.[59]

The Family Friendly Workplace: Myth or Reality?

The currently fashionable rhetoric of simplicity, merit and 'business-friendly' regulatory regimes has been accompanied by a new set of 'soft and fuzzy' buzzwords. The notion of a 'family friendly' workplace has become an icon of the nineties. It promises much, employee driven flexibility, access to workplace based childcare facilities, parental leave, permanent part-time work with access to penalty rates, the ability to move in and out of the workforce without loss of career path and promotion opportunities.[60] Heavily promoted by Liberal Party policy, it became a centrepiece of their 1998 election campaign. It is well to consider some of the business agendas underlying this rhetoric. Martina Nightengale warns of the perils of language:

> Take for instance the word 'flexibility' which is central to this discussion. The connotations have immediate and coercive appeal. As individuals, we are offered the choice of flexibility or rigidity. Given these stark alternatives, everyone would want to be flexible because to be otherwise implies its negative opposite. To unravel the industrial relations debates it is necessary to understand that terms such as 'flexibility' have quite different meanings, depending on who is speaking and whose interests are being represented. To the BCA, flexibility means the 'freedom' to do whatever employers consider necessary to increase profits and maximise the use of plant and equipment. In this context, award conditions such as

overtime, penalty rates and stipulation about the span of hours are 'restrictions' which must be removed.[61]

Anne Junior[62] notes that there are two forms of permanent part-time work, only one of which is family friendly in reality as opposed to rhetoric. The 'parental leave' model, familiar in public service workplaces, involves a temporary reduction in hours from full-time to part-time to accommodate specific worker needs. Workers retain the option to return to full-time work, retain access to the benefits and entitlements associated with permanent employment, and remain on the 'career track'.[63] The second model is very different. In this employer driven model on-going permanent part time jobs, primarily in the service sector, form a distinct segregated sector. These are typically entry-level positions without opportunities for advancement or recognisable career tracks employing mature and experienced women who have taken career breaks.[64]

A report recently released by the Work and Family Unit of the Department of Employment, Workplace Relations and Small Business downplays the importance of measures such as on-site child care centres, family rooms, paid parental leave, career breaks and purchased leave schemes. According to the Executive Summary:

> While paid maternity and paternity leave are obviously important conditions for employees, and are very beneficial for employers in terms of increasing retention rates, they are accessed at most only a few times during the working life of an employee. Similarly, on-site child care centres are a great facility, particularly if no other child care providers are available close to work and home, but they are only used by parents with children of a particular age.
>
> We found that there are other provisions that are arguably just as important to employees with family responsibilities, *and that cost the employer little to provide*. Provisions such as flexitime, control over start and finish times, influence over the pace of work, access to a phone at work to use for family reasons and access to regular part-time work, can assist in promoting a flexible workplace that directly benefits employees.[65] [Emphasis mine.]

The 'flexibilities' advocated are precisely those based on the assumption that women are 'contingent workers', that their primary focus is and ought to be their families, and therefore those that do least to facilitate equal sharing and break down conventional gender roles either at home or at work. Unsurprisingly, given that 'employees with family responsibilities' remains code for 'women', some current psychological literature suggests that they are also the practices that are least likely to promote male involvement in families. Silverstein and Auerbach suggest that:

> In social contexts where either the fathers or the mothers have few benefits to exchange, paternal involvement is low. When both fathers and mothers have benefits that contribute to family well-being, paternal involvement is relatively high. Thus, improving employment opportunities for women, as well as men, is crucial to increasing father involvement. These findings suggest that in our current cultural context, it is economics not marriage that matters.[66]

Chapter 1 introduced some of these issues and cited studies suggesting that the benefits of flexibility were largely illusory. Belinda Probert argues that many of the new enterprising bargaining agreements have eroded the distinction between casual and part-time status.[67] Despite the rhetoric of permanency, these new permanent part-time positions do not provide more predictable working hours but greatly increase the span of hours within which part-time employees may be required to work. While some of the benefits of permanent status are undoubted welcome, in Australia many casual workers have traditionally worked very regular hours for extended periods with the same employer.[68] As business interests increasingly appropriate the rhetoric of the family friendly workplace, we need to think about what a family friendly workplace might actually look like and what changes might be needed to make it a reality. I am profoundly pessimistic about its possibility, not least because the evidence suggests that in many workplaces working hours are gradually being extended beyond the 37.5-hour norm. As ordinary working hours expand, with 50 to 60 hours a week becoming conventional, family space shrinks.

Those fields that are making the greatest progress towards eliminating sex-segregated workplaces are also those in which working hours have spiralled out of control. The presence of family friendly policies, maternity and paternity leave, permanent part-time career track positions, family leave, workplace-based childcare counts for little against a backdrop of workplace expectations dictating a 60-hour week so that 'part-time work' often approaches 40 hours per week. Inevitably, those who fail to meet these expectations are perceived to be less than serious about their work, other than dedicated professionals. It is, perhaps, little wonder that in professions such as law, despite the rapid increase in the proportion of women among law school graduates, less than half of those entering practice remain in the profession after five years. In research on the Victorian Bar, Rosemary Hunter found:

> [T]he prevailing attitude around mothering and part-time work amongst members of the profession was shown to associate these with lack of commitment or even incompetence ... It was interesting to discover that barristers who had taken extended leave from the Bar for reasons other than parenting had not experienced any stigma and had far fewer difficulties re-establishing their practices when they returned to the Bar. By contrast, the research shows that competing family responsibilities, and attitudes at the Bar towards them, are possibly the largest contributing factors to women leaving the bar.[69]

Very often it seems that only feminised occupational enclaves: clerical and low level administrative work, sales and personal service, and teaching (especially primary teaching), have partly resisted the pressure towards spiralling hours. Critically, it is in some of these feminised ghettos (particularly those in workplaces too small to be covered by the *Act*) that 'flexible permanent part-time workers' appear to be supplanting both casual and full time employees and that the distinction between ordinary hours and out-of-hours work is collapsing. Research done by HREOC in 1996 emphasised the potentially discriminatory nature of these changes. The report suggested in Recommendation 1.2:

That the Sex Discrimination Commissioner review awards and federal agreements for their directly and indirectly discriminatory impact on women. Further, that systemic discrimination against part-time, casual workers and non-English speaking background women workers be investigated, in terms of their pro rata access to family-friendly working time arrangements, training, career progression and other work conditions and benefits. In particular, that the Commissioner investigate the indirectly discriminatory impact of rostering arrangements on women.[70]

Quite obviously, a workplace that does not provide paid maternity and paternity leave, family leave, and some flexibility in working hours does not qualify as family friendly. Equally obviously, once we assume that a family friendly workplace is important, not simply as a way of minimising attrition by talented female staff, but because it enables both men and women to be more productive within their workplaces, within their communities and within their homes, we come to question more broadly existing workplace structures. Perhaps workers as well as employers need to question whether the idea of 'normal working hours' has outlived its utility. Against the background of the factory labour practices of the industrial revolution, the eight-hour day was a magnificent achievement. As, in many professional workplaces, expectations once again creep towards ten or 12 hours daily, we need to ask whether we are working longer, rather than smarter.

We also need to question whether different working patterns may not be appropriate to different life stages, for both men and women. There is no real reason why an eight to ten hour day might not be appropriate for single workers without family responsibilities and why that could not be scaled back to a six hour day during the peak child-raising years, again, for both men and women.[71] The outcome need not be lessened productivity; indeed I suspect that individual productivity would be largely unchanged and possibly increased.[72] Staggered shortened working hours for men and women with family commitments would facilitate the combination of caring work and waged labour and would maximise the time available for family life. If a six hour day were the norm during this period, it would be possible for start times to be staggered, allowing one partner to start at 8:00am and leave at 2:00pm and the other to start at 10:00am and leave at 4:00pm. Similar arrangements should be feasible for shift workers. In this way, both parents could, if they wished, maintain their position on career pathways. The cost of childcare would be reduced because the hours would be minimised, and space would remain for family life and for the work of relationship building, something increasingly important given that relationships are no longer determined by traditional gender roles. Existing arrangements are, after all, institutional arrangements that are beneficial and efficient only to the extent that they serve the needs of all of the people concerned. If they do not, as the current employer led push for 'flexible permanent part-time work' demonstrates, they can be changed. We need to ensure that the calls for change are not one-sided and that changes are negotiated from a position of equality rather than inequality. In this respect, it is noteworthy that a report prepared for the HREOC specifically recommended (Recommendation 1.1):

> That the Sex Discrimination Commissioner continue to monitor the impact of flexible working time arrangements on women, particularly part-time and casual workers and NESB workers. Further that the Commissioner monitor the long-term impact on women's access to employment, pay equity and occupational and industry gender segmentation of changes to working time arrangements introduced in certified agreements.[73]

Earlier we noted the way in which the discourse of disadvantage directed attention away from structural issues and directed it towards particularistic claims advanced by interest groups. As Nightengale recognised, the rhetoric of flexibility serves similar purposes. While some flexible practices can contribute to a family friendly workplace, many other forms of flexibility, including those sought by employer groups as attributes of flexible permanent part-time positions, are distinctly family unfriendly. Structural factors, such as the overwhelming domination of women in part-time positions in certain feminised occupations, particularly in the sales and services sectors in workplaces too small to be covered by EEO legislation, disappear. All that remains are the claims advanced by employer's groups in these sectors: the need for a flexible and experienced workforce, the need to eliminate penalty rates which reduce competitiveness, and, in particular, the need to be able to increase hours of work during periods of high demand and maintain minimum hours during periods of low demand. Unsurprisingly, these accord well with the new EEO rhetoric of simplification and the need to make EEO policy 'business friendly'. On 2 August 1999, the front page of the Sydney Morning Herald carried the following story:

> A Sydney mother of three is fighting a NSW Industrial Relations Commission test case for the rights of working mothers to resist employer pressure to work inconvenient hours. Tele-sales operator Ms Kym Wood is refusing to accept an order from the Steggles chicken company at Marsden Park in Sydney's west, that she start work at 6:30 am, claiming that her employer's demands conflict with her responsibilities as a mother ...
>
> Steggles tele-sales employees received letters in June directing them to work different shift hours. Ms Wood said she was one of four told to start at 6:30 – two others were to start at 7 am and another two to start at 7:30 am.
>
> When management refused to allow her to swap with one of the 7:30 shift times, she called for help from her union, the Australian Services Union. She says two other women with children have since resigned, forced out because they could not work the earlier hours. Ms Wood is now starting at 7:30 but working an hour less each day.[74]

In the predominantly female services sector, for those women who from choice or necessity prefer full time employment, the increasing reliance on family-unfriendly hours has the effect of forcing women back to part-time status, potentially constituting indirect discrimination under the terms of the *Sex Discrimination Act 1984*.[75]

Sex Discrimination Law and the Uncovered Workplace

While much of what I have written thus far has been concerned specifically with EEO legislation, an educative kit[76] from the Human Rights and Equal Opportunities Commission provides a series of case studies of complaints subject to confidential conciliation as provided by the *Sex Discrimination Act* 1984.[77] The interaction between EEO legislation and anti-discrimination legislation is particularly instructive. What emerges over and over again is the interplay between casual and permanent part-time status and other forms of overreaching, often accompanied by sexual harassment and/or discrimination based on pregnancy. Something else emerges as well, a pattern of manipulating hours of work,[78] particularly but not exclusively, with part-time employees, as a form of 'discipline', whether for simply being female and moving into a position of responsibility in a male field,[79] for becoming pregnant,[80] for resisting sexual advances,[81] or for seeking time off to care for a sick child.[82] Some of the stories told are striking. We are told that 'Ms Hurley', a trainee supermarket manager, was transferred to 'light' duties and had her hours reduced from full time to 4 hours per week when she became pregnant, it being 'company policy' to transfer all pregnant employees to 'light duties'.[83] The change, of course, also moved her from a career track position to a position of significantly lower status and opportunities, and constituted direct discrimination on the basis of pregnancy. Similarly, 'Ms Callos', a casual employee in a doctor's surgery who had been working 10 hours a day on her rostered days on, had her hours reduced to 4 hours per day following taking agreed annual leave and the disclosure of her pregnancy. In the examples provided, the vast majority of the workplaces were clearly too small to be subject to EEO legislation.[84] The legislative preference for private conciliation means, in effect, that these forms of manipulation seldom make their way onto the public record, whether by way of judicial proceeding or otherwise. Hunter notes the difficulties this form of privatisation poses in practice:

> [T]here is also a danger that a privatised dispute resolution process will inhibit both the publicisation and the elaboration of sex discrimination legislation. Public hearings (and media reports of them) can be an important source of information about the legislation ... Publicity encourages potential complainants to invoke the legislation, and acts as a deterrent to employers. By contrast, a private dispute resolution process has no empowering or educative effect ... In the words of one commentator, alternative dispute resolution "poses the risk of invisibility" and important community interests and tenuous rights hard won "could fade from the public agenda". Indirect discrimination provisions in particular remain misunderstood and underutilised in Australia as a result of the lack of publicity given to this form of discrimination.[85]

The ease with which 'flexible hours' can become 'abusive practices' emphasises the double bind faced by casual and permanent part-time employees. Those who seek flexibility to meet childcare responsibilities may find themselves transferred from a position of considerable responsibility to one with significantly less responsibility and working hours that make it impossible for them to pick up their children from crèche and school.[86] While, in all of the examples cited above, the matters were resolved through confidential conciliation, they provide a striking counterpoint to claims of progress and illustrate the social costs of exempting businesses employing less than 100 workers from EEO requirements. Clearly, an educational opportunity has been missed. Many small to medium employers undoubtedly believe that, since they are not subject to EEO reporting requirements, equal opportunity principles have no application to their particular circumstances. The failure to adhere to and implement equal opportunity practices may, in turn, allow a climate in which discriminatory practices go unnoticed simply because they are part of the existing workplace culture and no real motivation for change exists. Because complaints are effectively privatised, and resolution through conciliation is usual, there is little incentive for such enterprises to rethink their practices. Changing practices imposes a direct, readily internalised cost on the enterprise and on the individuals involved in maintaining discriminatory practices. The potential for a sex discrimination complaint is relatively slight, since the legislation requires an already disadvantaged individual to lodge a formal complaint against her employer. While conciliation is argued to be optimal because it is quicker and less costly than litigation, a conciliated settlement seemingly, at least if the examples given in 'Harsh Realities' are representative, provides little more than a 'moral victory' for the complainant and imposes minimal costs on the enterprise. Studies on the behaviour of firms in other settings suggest that unless the likelihood of detection is high and the cost imposed significantly greater than the benefit to be gained from continuing with current practices, it will be rational for the enterprise to do nothing and to simply factor the cost of an occasional complaint into its business practices.[87] Despite the publicity given to a very few high profile cases, the social and business climate needed for change is lacking.[88]

The Segregated Workplace: EEO and its Failures

The Australian workforce remains one of the most sex-segregated in the OECD despite more than ten years of equal opportunity and sex discrimination laws.[89] We noted earlier some of the reasons for the persistence of sex-segregation and identified two variables as particularly significant. The first and most significant variable relates to the coverage of the EEO regime and complementary laws proscribing discrimination on the basis of gender. The various mechanisms put in place to induce cultural change and to break down entrenched patterns of segregation were introduced first in large public sector workplaces such as universities and phased in gradually in private sphere workplaces, eventually extending to all workplaces with 100 or more employees. Given that many Australians are employed by workplaces with fewer than 100 employees, and a majority of women are employed by workplaces with fewer than 20 employees, the coverage of the EEO regime lacks depth and leaves the great majority of Australian working environments untouched. Unsurprisingly, the study by Peetz et al[90] clearly showed that while workplaces covered by EEO had made some progress towards breaking down patterns of sex segregation, this progress did not extend to the uncovered workplaces in which most women are employed.

While the picture with respect to sex discrimination laws is somewhat better, their privatised nature, the fact that the onus is firmly on the complainant renders them relatively ineffective as an agent for cultural change. Margaret Thornton reminds us that even making a complaint can be onerous. A complainant must both recognise the fact of discrimination and be willing to persevere with a complaint in the face of corporate power. Because many women are socialised not to complain, taking this step can be exceptionally difficult.[91]

The implicit definition of sex discrimination as abnormal and exceptional, rather than structurally normal and embedded in workplace cultures and practices, a definition reinforced by the individualised nature of the complaints mechanism, has allowed 'business as usual' to prevail in most workplaces. The patchwork quilt of commonwealth and state coverage exacerbated these structural difficulties. State legislation was implemented at different times in different jurisdictions, South Australia being the earliest and Tasmania and Queensland the laggards. While Commonwealth legislation was enacted in 1984, the reach of this legislation was and is limited, leaving significant gaps in the coverage, in Tasmania forcing one complainant to bring a successful common law action in trespass.[92] Equally unsurprisingly, the incidence of sex discrimination complaints has not abated and shows few signs of doing so.

Several inferences can be drawn from these statistics. First, EEO requirements have a consciousness raising effect, alerting management to legal obligations both in terms of the formal EEO requirements and in terms of obligations under sex discrimination laws. Second, where EEO requirements have not been introduced, management may feel entitled to discount both the importance of equal opportunity and its obligations under sex discrimination laws or simply be unaware that it has such responsibilities.

A 1997 research paper by Clare Burton[93] suggested a further, and disturbing, impediment to change, this time in terms of access to senior positions. According to Burton:

> There are clear indications that within many Australian companies the merit principle is not widely understood and applied.
>
> The private sector does not share the history of the public services with respect to the supplanting of patronage systems with merit-based appointment processes. In the public sector this occurred well before and therefore independently of the contemporary concern with equal employment opportunity and anti-discrimination laws and principles.
>
> The private sector is inclined to view the merit principle as constituting a set of regulations which government imposes through the anti-discrimination and affirmative action laws.[94]

Burton's analysis highlights the role of 'informal cultural practices' in selection for management level positions, noting a long tradition in management literature 'of extolling the virtues of "fit" and "comfort" in the choice of senior management team members'.[95] While I earlier noted my scepticism concerning merit, and the ways in which merit can be co-opted, that scepticism exists within a set of understandings that suggested that, at the very least, formal procedures with tightly defined criteria and set pathways for review are more likely to attain equitable outcomes than informal procedures without carefully structured skills based criteria and few, if any, pathways for review.[96] Criteria based upon "comfort" and "fit" ensure continued homosocial reproduction, not least because most people tend to be more comfortable with people like themselves and with those with whom they share similar values and experiences.

A variety of seemingly innocuous selection criteria may also play a role in sustaining the sex-segregated character of workplaces, as may occupational health and safety regulations. Thus, selection criteria based on height, in the absence of a duties based requirement for a minimal height, is likely to disproportionately exclude women and members of certain racial groups. Similarly, legislative requirements restricting hours of work for women but not for men or limiting the maximum weight to be lifted by a women in certain industries will also have the effect of maintaining occupational segregation, particularly where these restrictions are limited to traditionally male occupations and are not present in traditionally female occupations, for example, nursing. There is some evidence that the current push for flexible hours may also be indirectly discriminatory in practice, where employer designed flexible practices disproportionately affect women, for example, by rendering them unable to meet family responsibilities.

Other factors are also at work. In the United States, where occupational counselling and testing form a significant part of student counselling services in universities and community colleges, considerable work has been done on the correlation between occupational segregation and the perceptions of students as to their capacity to fulfil the educational and performance requirements of various occupations. Betz and Hackett tested male and female university students on a group of 20 occupations that were strongly differentiated by gender. They found that male students were significantly more likely than female students to believe that they could complete the educational and performance requirements for traditional male careers, while the difference between the self-perception of male and female students as to their ability to fulfil the educational and performance requirements for traditionally female careers was somewhat less marked. This suggests that one of the reasons for the persistence of occupational segregation may be found in self-perceptions of career choosers as to their ability/inability to perform the required tasks. Among traditionally male occupations, the differentials were greatest for the following occupations: engineer, drafter, highway patrol officer, and mathematician, in that order. Among traditionally female occupations, the differentials were greatest for secretary, home economist, social worker and dental hygienist. Among female occupations, only that for secretary approached the order of magnitude of those for engineer and drafter respectively.[97] According to Betz and Hackett:

> Self-efficacy expectations, or beliefs in our capabilities to successfully perform a
> given behavior or class of behaviors, are postulated to influence behavioral
> choices, performance, and persistence.[98]

The persistence of sex segregation is of critical importance because of three associated features. First, the available evidence suggests that young women's aspirations are concentrated in a much more restricted area of the labour market than are young men's although with the growth of the services sector this may be changing.[99] Second, studies in the United States and elsewhere suggest that occupational sex segregation is responsible for approximately one third of the earnings gender gap.[100] The literature suggests that socialisation patterns and educational choices are significant as are self-perceptions of a possible negative response from peers and co-workers among those entering traditionally sex-segregated fields. Finally, the wages in female dominated fields are significantly lower than those available in male dominated fields at least in part because of the failure to implement comparable worth rigorously.

A recent ILO report suggests the reduction in the gender gap in Europe and the United States is largely a consequence of increasing penetration by women into formerly male dominated fields.[101] The report also notes that:

> The risk of occupational downgrading following a labour market break to have
> children is compounded if the training system relies on informal work experience
> instead of recognized transferable skills.[102]

This latter factor is said to explain why the gender gap has persisted more strongly in the UK and the USA where formal training schemes are not well established in comparison to the Scandinavian countries and Germany. In the Australian context, it highlights the potentially discriminatory impact of changes to working hours that militate against access by women to training and career progression and deprive them of the opportunity to develop recognised and transferable skills.[103] As the flexibility agenda gathers momentum, proposed amendments[104] to the *Workplace Relations Act* 1996 threatened to further downgrade existing protections. One of the proposed amendments deleted reference to skill based career paths from s 89A(2)(a) of the *Workplace Relations Act* 1996, further marginalizing those with interrupted career paths. While the Senate ultimately rejected the Bill, largely because the Australian Democrats joined forces with the Opposition, it emphasises the conflict between the efficiency agenda of the government and business representatives and equitable outcomes for women and other disadvantaged workers. In a political environment that is increasingly hostile to equity claims, these developments emphasise the fragility of the gains already made.

Concluding Thoughts

The earnings gender gap is a complex phenomenon, and equal opportunity law is only one part of a complex legal and social story. In Australia, the separation between equal opportunity law and practice and sex discrimination law and practice has, to a certain extent at least, sent mixed signals, perhaps suggesting to small business that neither equal opportunity nor sex discrimination are of real concern to them. Despite this, by world standards, the Australian gender gap is remarkably narrow, at least on the surface, almost certainly because of the centralised wage fixing system which prevailed until recently and which facilitated the push towards equality. It may well be that the gender gap has now narrowed to the extent where further progress is only possible if a concerted push is made to minimise sex segregation in the workplace, given ILO statistics suggesting it is responsible for up to one third of the gender gap.

Other disturbing features of the Australian scene are becoming more deeply entrenched. The gap between the top ten per cent and the bottom ten per cent of wage earners has widened significantly in the last decade. Because women have historically been clustered in the relatively poorly paid services sector and this has persisted into the present, it is unsurprising that the gender gap has once again widened.[105]

As a particular political and industrial philosophy increases its grip on the industrial relations agenda, other disturbing features are emerging. The mantras of the nineties – flexible practices, free trade, and globalisation – are beginning to bite and it is becoming clear that their impact is gendered in very particular ways. As the manufacturing sector continues to contract, following world wide trends, increasing numbers of skilled and semi-skilled men are either consigned to unemployment or forced back on relatively poorly paid forms of contingent employment in the retail and services sectors. They are clearly among the losers from the current economic agenda and it is not surprising that their anger has been displaced and directed towards equal opportunity and sex discrimination laws. Women are also among the losers, although the nature of their losses is often obscured by continuing increases in female employment, initially in contingent positions and more recently in full time positions. With the continued push for flexible practices and the historical reluctance to fully invoke the indirect discrimination provisions of the *SDA*, women are finding it harder to reconcile their family responsibilities with the demands for extended hours of work and the gradual erosion of the notion of 'ordinary working time'. Significantly, it is in areas of female workforce concentration, particularly in the services sector, in which these changes are currently having a significant impact. In some cases, women have been forced to move from full-time employment or to significantly cut back their hours because of the impact of changes to their rostered hours. Still more disturbingly, women in the casual workforce, a majority of whom worked remarkably stable hours, have often been significantly disadvantaged by a shift to permanent part-time positions. Despite the apparent advantage of pro-rata benefits including sick leave, holiday pay and superannuation, management imposed flexible hours have frequently proved incompatible with child care and after school pick up times and other family responsibilities.

A picture is beginning to emerge, one that is replicated in other jurisdictions, of the earnings gender gap as one element in a complex social fabric linking the various institutions affecting both the family and the market. At its centre stands the shadowy figure we met in the last chapter, the unencumbered citizen. The unencumbered citizen is both like and unlike the workers we have glimpsed in this chapter. The unencumbered citizen is well represented among the casualties of the contraction of the manufacturing sector. Here there is evidence suggesting that the unencumbered citizen of economic and political theory is becoming truly as well as theoretically unencumbered, both without employment and without lasting relationships and the possibility of forming them. Those who have been unmoored by the collapse of employment in the manufacturing sector are not the 'incorporated male family selves' of whom Patricia Mann[106] writes so tellingly. Increasingly they are without employment prospects and without social prospects, both economically and affectively disadvantaged.[107] As Mann notes:

> When men became economic individuals they also became incorporated family selves, with all the responsibilities and rewards of being the head of a patriarchal family. Contrarily, as women become economic individuals their economic independence promotes the breakup of incorporated family selves. People still live within family units, of course. But there is no more life-time incorporation under a male head of household. Families are now limited partnerships. The end of modernism is assured when the familial moorings of men, women, and children basic to modern liberal society cease to be either practically or normatively secured, and the social structures of kinship and of workplace as well cease to function in predictable ways.[108]

This does not, however, mean that the incorporated male family self is a vanishing species. He is not; but increasingly, the phenomenon is class based. As the gap between the top and bottom ten per cent of wage earners widens, unemployment statistics remind us that Australia is at risk of following the United States and the United Kingdom in the development of a permanent under-class. The incorporated male family self (aka unencumbered citizen) continues to occupy the majority of seats at boardroom tables, to dominate the upper echelons of legal practice and medical specialties, and to retain his hold over senior managerial positions. The profile among the barristers interviewed by Rosemary Hunter is not atypical. According to Hunter:

> In relation to relative family responsibilities, 19 of the male barristers and 15 of the female barristers interviewed had children. The majority of the fathers (14) had wives or partners who had taken, or were taking, the role of primary carer on a full-time basis. By contrast, none of the 15 mothers had a partner who had taken primary responsibility for the care of household and children.[109]

Here, the incorporated male family self remains normatively embedded, despite the inroads made by women into managerial and professional positions over the last three decades.[110] It is precisely this embeddedness and cultural and workplace practices which reflect it which block further change. A report published by the ILO indicates that among the priorities is

> the development of ways, which can include more flexible working hours, reduced hours of work and adequate child-and elder-care facilities, to enable both women and men to combine the building of a career and the raising of a family.[111]

The tension between family roles and market structures is a constant reminder of this embeddedness. In this chapter, we have explored the impact of equal opportunity programs and some of their significant failures. In the next chapter, we will turn from the ways in which equal opportunity and sex discrimination law have impacted upon the market to the evolution of the family over the last three decades and the role of family law in that evolution. We are interested both in the ways in which families have changed, at least in part in response to changes in family law, and in sites of resistance. Because this exploration will take place against the background of the changes brought about by equal opportunity and anti-discrimination law, evidence of tension and dissonance will be of particular significance.

Notes

1 See chapter 1.
2 *Sex Discrimination Act* 1984 (Cth).
3 The furore in August 2000 over a federal court decision that Victorian state laws excluding lesbians from IVF treatment violated the *SDA* is an example of one such high profile case, one very much one the margins compared to the 'normal' matters involving discrimination on the basis of pregnancy and sexual harassment. See *McBain v State of Victoria* (2000) 177 ALR 320. That matter is currently before the High Court, the Catholic Church arguing that the *SDA* proscribes discrimination between men and women, and not between different classes of women.
4 In 1966, 37% of Australian women were in the workforce. In 1998, 54% of Australian women were in the workforce. Comparable US statistics suggest that in 1965 about 39% of American women were in the workforce and by 1997 almost 59% were in the workforce. Australian changes mirror those in the US. The US statistics are from data provided by the US Census Bureau accessed online at http://www.census.gov/ on 12 November 1999. Australian statistics are sourced from the ACTU accessed on line at http://www.actu.asn.au/ on 12 November 1999.
5 Most US affirmative action programs do not, in fact, involve quotas. Rather they involve a variety of tactics intended to increase the diversity of the workforce. According to a report by the National Women's Law Centre to the Leadership Conference on Civil Rights: 'In employment, examples of affirmative action programs are recruitment and outreach efforts to include qualified women in the talent pool when hiring decisions are made; training programs to give all employees a fair chance at promotions; and in some cases the use of flexible goals and timetables (not quotas) as benchmarks by which to measure progress toward eliminating severe under-representation of qualified women in specific job categories'. Many of these measures

are commonplace in the affirmative action strategies of Australian employers, at least in the public sector. See http://www.civilrights.org/aa/women.html accessed on 12 November 1999. The Swedish approach is very different and required that in firms given certain forms of relocation assistance 40% of all new staff hired be of the underrepresented gender. See Brown, Charles & Shirley J Wilcher, 'Sex Based Employment Quotas in Sweden' in Brown, Clair & Joseph A Pechman, eds, *Gender in the Workplace*, Washington DC, The Brookings Institution, 1987, 271.

6   In the first phase, it applied to institutions of higher education and organisations employing more than 1000 people. Tertiary institutions were required to make their first report under the *Act* on 1 August 1987, while large organisations made their first mandatory annual report on 1 February 1988. In the second phase its operation was extended to organisations employing more than 500 people and their obligation to report commenced on 1 February 1989. In the third, and final, phase, it was extended to all workplaces employing more than 100 people and the reporting obligation for these organisations commenced on 1 February 1990.

7   Kramar, Robin, 'Equal employment opportunity: An essential and integral part of good human resource management' in O'Neill, Graham L & Robin Kramar, eds, *Australian Human Resources Management: Current Trends in Management Practice*, Melbourne, Pitman Publishing, 1995, 223, 233.

8   Brown & Wilcher, 274.

9   Barrett, Nancy S, 'Comments' in Brown, Clair & Joseph A Pechman, eds, *Gender in the Workplace*, Washington DC, The Brookings Institution, 1987, 299, 299.

10 Some insight into the processes involved may be gained from Baron, Ava, 'The Masculinization of Production: The Gendering of Work and Skill in US Newspaper Printing, 1850-1920' in Helly, Dorothy O & Susan M Reverby, eds, *Gendered Domains: Rethinking Public and Private in Women's History*, Ithaca, Cornell University Press, 1992, 277. Baron examines the impact of the introduction of the Linotype machine and the battles over whether operating the Linotype was to be gendered female or male. Her discussion is useful, both because it makes the process transparent and because it emphasises that different characteristics are selected according to whether the work is being defined as masculine or feminine. Baron makes the point that it is possible to characterise the same task as masculine or feminine; that is, gender is a function, not of the position and the aptitudes required, but of its cultural and political characterisation by workers, employers and trade unions.

11 Bryson, 180.

12 Pocock, 'Gender and Australian Industrial Relations Theory', 10-11. See also Casson, Louise, 'Jobs for Women Campaign' (1985) May *Refractory Girl* 30 on the campaign against AIS/BHP.

13 It is no accident that the UK Men's Movement has identified this particular trend as socially destructive and, simplistically, attributes it to the rise in female employment. Essentially, the UK Men's Movement suggests that this trend (prevalent in most OECD countries) is destructive of masculinity and of the male social role, attributing to it a rise in male criminality and violence. See http://www.ukmm.org.uk/ accessed 14 November 1999.

14 On Friday, 12 November, 1999 The *Australian* newspaper carried a front page story by George Megalogenis entitled 'Women Win the Jobs Race' detailing a rise in full time female employment and a decline in full time male employment and suggesting a causal connection. The story noted that a majority of the new opportunities were in the services industry. It is perhaps significant that these are areas in which the earnings gender gap appears to be increasing. Statistics are taken from ABS Cat. 6302.0 as

reported by the ACTU in 'Equal Pay: A Union Priority' at http://www.actu.asn.au/ accessed on 11 November 1999.

15 These include relatively poor pay, limited opportunities for control over how work is done, little control over the pace and design of the work, limited access to decision-making, to workplace management and to consultation. See Hall, Richard, Bill Harley & Gillian Whitehouse, 'Contingent Work and Gender in Australia: Evidence from the 1995 Australian Workplace Industrial Relations Survey' (1998) 9 *The Economic and Labour Relations Review* 55, 77.

16 Hall et al, 77. See generally Hunter, Rosemary, 'Part-time work & indirect discrimination' (1996) 21 *Alternative Law Journal* 220.

17 See ABS, 'Computing Services Industry, Australia: 1992-93', ABS Cat. 8669.0, March 1995.

18 Megalogenis, above, suggests that men now hold 66.6% of all full time jobs and 26.7% of part time positions, a marked change from the position two decades ago when men held 72.3% of full time positions and only 20.8% of part time positions.

19 Some of these forces were detailed in chapter 1.

20 Megalogenis, above, states 'The October figures reinforce the pattern of the past 20 years, which have seen women flood the labour market, edging out men'.

21 Braithwaite, Valerie, 'Designing the Process of Workplace Change through the Affirmative Action Act' in Gatens, Moira & Alison Mackinnon, eds, *Gender and Institutions: Welfare, Work and Citizenship*, Cambridge, CUP, 1998, 107, 107.

22 According to Catherine Harris, Director of the Affirmative Action Agency, Senator Crichton Browne described it as 'diabolical and draconian'. See Harris, Catherine, 'Women, men and work: time for a new dialogue', 11 August 1998, The Sydney Institute accessed on 5 July 1999 at http://www/eeo/gov.au/.

23 Harris, 2. See further, Thornton, *The Liberal Promise* and Thornton, Margaret, 'The Seductive Allure of EEO' in Grieve, Norma & Ailsa Burns, eds, *Australian Women: Contemporary Feminist Thought*, Melbourne, OUP, 1994, 215. The recent changes to the legislation and the diminution in reporting requirements are designed specifically to make EEO more 'business friendly' and to allay concerns that it covertly imposes a quota system and leads to appointment other than on merit.

24 Conservative politicians and social theorists continue to view EEO as an attack on the family. See Tapper, Alan, 'Family Policy and Family Problems in the Australian Welfare State' and Joseph, Gerard, 'Objectives for Family Policy' in Barcan, Alan R and Patrick O'Flaherty, eds, *Family, Education and Society: The Australian Perspective*, A PWPA Australia Publication, Canberra, Academy Press, 1995, at 67 & 83 respectively. Both argue that what is required is a return of women to domestic duties, and increasing support for the male breadwinner family, preferably by reducing support for sole parent families and encouraging married women to remain at home.

25 Thornton, 'The Seductive Allure of EEO', 220.

26 Braithwaite, 126.

27 Thornton, 'The Seductive Allure of EEO', 217. I have adopted Thornton's terminology.

28 Underlying these dual mandates is, of course, a profound shift in public culture, one in which equity is subordinated to efficiency.

29 Carpenter, Tracey, 'The Regulatory Review of Affirmative Action legislation, and what this means for organisations', 24 February 1999, Equal Employment Opportunity Network (EEON) Victoria accessed on 5 July 1999 at http://www/eeo.gov.au/.

30 These ideas are hardly new. Clare Burton expressed similar views in 1985. See Burton, Clare, 'Merit and gender: organisation and the "mobilisation of masculine bias"', paper presented at the conference 'Defining Merit', Macquarie University, 1985.

31 In some cases, employment or promotion requirements that inadvertently discriminate against a historically disadvantaged racial or gender group constitute indirect discrimination. According to Hunter & Shoben: 'In the context of employment discrimination, it refers to an employer's use of an unvalidated device, such as one for selection or promotion, that disproportionately excludes a protected group. Under current law, an employer's use of a device such as a physical agility test, an aptitude test, or an education requirement that more adversely affects a protected group is unlawful unless the requirement is demonstrably job related'. Hunter, Rosemary & Elaine Shoben 'Disparate Impact Discrimination: American Oddity or Internationally Accepted Concept?' 19 *Berkeley Journal of Employment and Labor Law* 108, 109.

32 For a fascinating discussion of the operation of these signifiers see Evaline, Joan, 'Heavy, Dirty and Limp Stories: Male Advantage at Work' in Gatens, Moira and Alison Mackinnon, *Gender and Institutions: Welfare, Work and Citizenship*, Cambridge, CUP, 1998, 90-106.

33 Kessler-Harris, Alice, 'The Just Price, the Free Market, and the Value of Women' in Helly, Dorothy O & Susan M Reverby, eds, *Gendered Domains: Rethinking Public and Private in Women's History*, Ithaca, Cornell University Press, 1992, 263, 268.

34 Kessler-Harris, 271.

35 Carpenter, 3.

36 This sounds remarkably like the description of affirmative action in the USA in n 5.

37 As this was being written a front-page story in the *Courier Mail* identified discrimination based on pregnancy as commonplace in Australia. Deeply entrenched workplace cultures, particularly in private enterprise, have failed to take on board the prohibition against discrimination based on pregnancy or potential pregnancy contained in anti-discrimination legislation. See McKenna, Michael & Michelle Hele, 'Women's hard labour, workforce still discriminates on pregnancy', The *Courier-Mail*, 14 July 1999.

38 Eveline, 90.

39 Eveline, 90-91. In this context, it is well to reflect on the distinction between civil rights and human rights discussed in chapter 2.

40 See Dewar & Parker, 79.

41 The Commonwealth Attorney General's Department hosted this conference on 9-11 June 1998.

42 Pocock, Barbara, 'Gender and the Labour Market' (1998) 40 *Journal of Industrial Relations* 580, 589-91. Swedish research suggests that 33% of women work in disproportionately female occupations while 40% of men work in disproportionately male occupations. See also Swedish Institute, Sept 1997, 'Equality Between Men and Women' at http://www.si.we/eng/esverige/equality.html accessed on 29 November 1999, 11 which suggests that one explanation for the apparently high levels of occupational segregation may be found in the partial transfer of carework from the home to the public sector and the disproportionate representation of women in that sector.

43 Anker, Richard, *Gender and Jobs: Sex segregation of occupations in the world*, Geneva, International Labor Office, 1998, 159 suggests that women's over representation in the clerical and sales sectors is significantly higher than the OECD average and that women's overrepresentation in the clerical sector is higher in absolute terms than that of any OECD country except Turkey. According to Anker, 210, 48.2% of the Australian labour force works in either female dominated or male dominated occupations.

44 Anker, *Gender and Jobs*, 222-223 suggests that out of 7300 occupations currently in the data set only 700 are female dominated, or slightly less than 10% while about 52% are male dominated.

45 Anker, *Gender and Jobs*, 186 suggests the Scandinavian countries are an exception in this regard, having established separate but reasonably equal labour markets for men and women.

46 Anker, *Gender and Jobs*, 293.

47 Pocock, 'Gender and the Labour Market', 591.

48 Pocock, 'Gender and the Labour Market', 591.

49 Megalogenis, above.

50 Pocock, 'Gender and the Labour Market', 593.

51 Peetz et al, 30.

52 Caution is warranted given that US data suggests that female domination of the retail sector has decreased significantly since 1983 (from 69.7% to 65.7%). All US data is sourced from http://www.census.gov/ accessed on 12 November 1999.

53 For discussion and analysis of this data see Peetz et al, 30.

54 Nightengale, Martina, 'Women and a flexible workforce' in Edwards, Anne and Susan Magarey, eds, *Women in a Restructuring Australia'*, St Leonards, NSW, Allen & Unwin, 1995, 121, 134.

55 Small workplaces are, unfortunately, exceptionally well represented in complaints under the *Sex Discrimination Act* 1984.

56 Krautil, Fiona, 'Action News Issue 40' December 1999, Equal Opportunity for Women in the Workplace Agency, accessed on line on 23 July 2000 at http://www.eeo.gov.au/.

57 Thornton, 'Embodying the Citizen', 222.

58 See the discussion in the first paragraph.

59 Peetz et al suggest that high levels of gender equity show a positive correlation with enhanced productivity at 15-18. Chart 2.1 Gender Equity and Productivity Change (16) is particularly interesting.

60 Caution is indicated here. Some of the forms of flexibility emphasised by Liberal Party policy have historically been available in occupations that are both poorly paid and sex-segregated. They have been bitterly resisted in professional and managerial areas. See Hunter 'Part-time work & indirect discrimination', 220. See further the discussion of the gendering of opportunities in the legal profession in Hunter, Rosemary, 'Gender and legal practice' (1999) 24 *Alternative Law Journal* 57.

61 Nightengale, 126. BCA stands for Business Council of Australia.

62 Junior, Anne, 'Permanent part-time work: new family-friendly standard or high intensity cheap skills?' (1998) 8 *Labour & Industry* 77.

63 Even here, caution is needed. These very important guarantees do apply to public service workplaces and to organisations such as universities. While they are theoretically available in other large workplaces, and in firms of professionals, very often their ostensible availability is associated with subtle cultural norms that discourage access. Thus in many law firms, for example, while maternity leave and part-time work are theoretically available, accessing them carries with it the danger of relegation to the 'mommy track'. Women who have accessed extended maternity leave have found upon their return that they have lost their place on the 'partner track' and, in some cases, that their partnership contract has not been renewed.

64 Junior, 80.

65 Department of Employment, Workplace Relations and Small Business, 'Executive Summary: Work and Family: State of Play 1998' accessed at http://www.dewrsb.gov.au/ on 19 July 1999.

66 Silverstein & Auerbach, 401.

67 Probert, 40.

68 Probert, 41. Probert cites a number of studies suggesting that working outside of ordinary hours, variable hours, and a decrease in the range of hours that attract penalty pay are common outcomes of enterprise bargaining.

69 Hunter, 'Gender and Legal Practice', 61.

70 HREOC, Stretching Flexibility: Enterprise Bargaining, Women Workers and Changes to Working Hours' accessed at http://www.hreoc.gov.au/ on 15 November 1999.

71 In Sweden, both parents are entitled to reduce their working hours while their children are young to six hours per day at reduced wages. See Bradley, David, *Family Law and Political Culture*, London, Sweet & Maxwell, 1996, 81-82. See also Swedish Institute, 'Equality Between Men and Women', 14.

72 'Putting in the hours', which often happens in organisations with a work culture which equates extremely long hours to productivity, is not necessarily the same as working efficiently and productively. There is evidence to suggest that productivity declines as fatigue sets in.

73 HREOC, 'Harsh Realities' accessed at http://www.hreoc.gov.au/ on 2 February 2000 with a forword by the Sex Discrimination Commissioner, Susan Halliday, provides a series of case studies of conciliated complaints under the *Sex Discrimination Act* 1984. See Recommendation 1.1.

74 Norington, Brad, 'Working Mother Tests Family Friendly Hours' The *Sydney Morning Herald*, 2 August 1999, 1.

75 HREOC, 'Stretching Flexibility', 1 emphasises that 'case studies showed actual and potential sex discrimination in changes to working time arrangements and in their implementation. Parties need to be aware of the potentially discriminatory impact of changes to working time arrangements, particularly the disparate impact on part-time workers'.

76 Generally see HREOC, 'Harsh Realities'.

77 See National Pregnancy and Work Inquiry, 'Pregnant and Productive: It's a right not a privilege to work while pregnant', accessed on 02 October 1999 at http://www.hreoc.gov.au/. The study found that 55% of the complaints were from workplaces employing fewer than 20 people and 84.6% came from private industry.

78 The most remarkable example was that of a supermarket butcher who rose to the position of manager but found that because her employer did not refill the positions she had previously held she found herself working excessive hours (starting at 5:00am daily) sometimes for thirteen or fourteen days in a row. 'Harsh Realities', 13.

79 HREOC, 'Harsh Realities', 13 & 16.

80 HREOC, 'Harsh Realities', 1-2, 4, 5 & 9. See further *Shelley Lee v Diana Clyne* No. H96/107 and *Delia Baker v. Wendy Lea Light & John William Light Trading as The Finishing Touch Beauty Therapy* No. H93/042, unreported HREOC decisions accessed at http://www.austlii.edu.au/au/cases/cth/hreoc/ on 11 September 1999.

81 HREOC, 'Harsh Realities', 6-7, 11 & 14.

82 HREOC, 'Harsh Realities', 6-7.

83 HREOC, 'Harsh Realities', 1-2.

84 HREOC, 'Harsh Realities'. Eighteen examples out of 27 were clearly small workplaces. In the others it is difficult to determine the actual size of the employer, but the employer could have been part of a large chain.

85 Hunter, Rosemary, 'Sex Discrimination and Alternative Dispute Resolution: British Proposals in the Light of International Experience' (1997) *Public Law* 298, 306.

86 HREOC, 'Harsh Realities', 7.

87 In the cases sketched in HREOC, 'Harsh Realities' the maximum compensation received was $20,000 and the compensation was generally under $10,000.

88 Hunter, 'Sex Discrimination and ADR', 299.

89 See n 48 and the associated text.

90 Peetz et al, 30.

91 Thornton, 219.

92 Berns, 'The Hobart City Council Case' discusses the facts and holding in this unreported case.

93 Burton, Clare, 'Women in Public and Private Sector Senior Management', a Research Paper for the Office of the Status of Women, Department of the Prime Minister and Cabinet, August 1997 accessed at http://www.dpmc.gov.au/osw/ on 30 June 1999.

94 Burton, 'Women in Management', 14-15.

95 Burton, 'Women in Management', 14. It is worth noting the connection of this sort of preference with the felt need of both Nealani and Matsuda to adopt a 'raceless persona', that is, to speak, dress and behave in such a way as to minimise differences and thus enhance comfort and fit.

96 This, of course, ties directly back to the discussion of the minority preference for rules and procedures rather than broad standards and informality discussed in chapter 2.

97 All statistical data is taken from Betz, Nancy F & Gail Hackett, 'Manual for the Occupational Self-Efficacy Scale' accessed at http://seamonkey.ed.asu.edu/ on 13 November 1999.

98 Betz & Hackett, above. The male occupations were accountant, drafter, engineer, highway patrol officer, mathematician, physician, probation officer, sales manager and school administrator. The female occupations were art teacher, dental hygenist, elementary school teacher, home economist, medical technician, physical therapist, secretary, social worker, travel agent and X-ray technician. Interestingly, differentials were minimal for lawyer, physician, probation officer, school administrator and sales manager among the male occupations, while among the female occupations they were minimal for art teacher, medical technician, travel agent and X-ray technician indicating that the gendering of these jobs is either not well entrenched or is beginning to break down.

99 According to ILO, 'World Employment Report 1998-99, Women and Training in the Global Economy' accessed at http://www.ilo.org/ on 14 November 99: '"Occupational segregation by sex is extensive in each and every country in the world" ... Half of the world's workers have occupations in which their own sex dominates by at least 80%. But male-dominated occupations – construction worker, policeman, technician, manager, architect, engineer – are seven times more common than female-dominated occupations – secretary, teacher, cashier, nurse, maid, etc. Female occupations, as a rule, tend to be "less valuable, offering lower pay, lower status and fewer advancement opportunities than male occupations"'.

100 Anker, Richard, 'Theories of occupational segregation by sex: An overview' (1997/3) 136 *International Labor Review* accessed at http://www.ilo.org/ on 14 November 1999.

101 See ILO, 'Women and Training in the Global Economy', above.

102 See ILO, 'Women and Training in the Global Economy', above.

103 Smith, Meg & Peter Ewer, *The Position of Women in the National Training Reform Agenda and Enterprise Bargaining*, WREIP, Department of Employment and Training, Canberra, 1995.

104 See *Workplace Relations Legislation Amendment (More Jobs, Better Pay) Bill* 1999.

105 See Chapter 1.

106 Mann, 131-141.

107 Generally see Faludi. Susan Faludi interviewed many of these 'unmoored' men for
    Stiffed. See also Silverstein & Auerbach, who suggest that social conditions such as
    poor education and lack of employment are responsible for lack of father involvement
    in 'underclass families'. Because they have little in the way of resources to contribute,
    their bargaining power is minimal, and they are unlikely to remain involved.
108 Mann, 21-22.
109 Hunter, 'Gender and Legal Practice', 59.
110 See ILO, 'Breaking through the glass ceiling: Women in management', *World of Work*
    No. 23 February 1988, accessed on 18 November 1999 at http://www.ilo.org/. The
    report notes the impact and gendered nature of family responsibilities, suggesting that it
    is almost impossible for a woman with family responsibilities to compete with an
    incorporated male family self! It notes further that: 'At lower management levels
    women are typically placed in non-strategic sectors, and in personnel and
    administrative positions, rather than in professional and line management jobs leading
    to the top. Often these initial disadvantages are compounded by women being cut off
    from networks, formal and informal, so essential for advancement within enterprises. It
    is notable that in large companies and organizations where women have achieved high-
    level managerial positions, these are usually restricted to those areas considered less
    vital and strategic to the organization such as human resources and administration'.
111 ILO, 'Breaking through the Glass Ceiling', above.

Chapter 4

The Fragile Family

Families Then and Now

During the three decades since 1970, if the workplace has seen radical change, so too has the family. Families are smaller, apparently increasingly fragile[1] and, more than ever, contested terrain. 'The family' has become a site of public contestation, as debates flood the mass media. Sole parents, same sex couples, working mothers, declining fertility and marriage rates coupled with high divorce rates form part of a discourse of moral panic swirling around the 'future of the family', and, by extension, the future of society.[2] Like the debates on female employment that we encountered in the last chapter, with their core texts of women 'flooding' the workforce and 'edging men out' in the 'jobs race', at the heart of these debates is a discourse of blame. Variously blaming 'feminists', lesbians, gay men, working mothers, and women who seek fulfilment in marriage, the theme is one of crisis, specifically a crisis of masculinity as traditional male roles in the workforce, in the family and in the community are eroded by social change. While these debates occur in the public sphere, they are anchored in the politics of the private. Here, there are no unencumbered citizens, no rights bearing individuals; indeed the underlying fear is that these fully encumbered individuals will seek to exercise the formally equal rights of the political and thus destroy the fragile fabric of the social. More and more, these debates reveal profound fissures in the façade of equal citizenship, as gender lines criss-cross those of ethnicity and aboriginality, class and sexuality. Here, even more than in the often politically charged arena of race, often it seems that law fears to tread, perhaps because if it does so it risks contamination by a resurgent social. As Nancy Levit, writing in the US context notes:

> Maybe gender differences are so sacred and pervasive, so structural to the family, to economics and politics – even more than racial differences – that it is more threatening to the Court even to consider pronouncements about separation of the sexes. This may parallel the reasoning why certain basic necessities of life, such as food, shelter, and peace, are not guaranteed by or even mentioned in the Constitution – and not because we think they are unimportant. On the contrary, perhaps they are too important. In both instances – the Supreme Court leaving untouched the issue of gender separatism and the Constitution not providing for basic needs – there are unexpressed assumptions about what it is appropriate for a government to do.[3]

In this chapter, I will look at some of the statistical information behind these debates, at its uses and misuses, and at family law and the Family Court and the ways in which both have become flashpoints embodying these fears. I will also look at the interaction of legal and judicial understandings of equality and at contemporary understandings of the best interests of the child and explore the ways in which those understandings remain gendered and the impact of this for men and women and for their children.[4]

We live in an era in which, increasingly, statistical information has become, not simply a matter of monitoring and tracking demographic change, but an ideologically charged tool, an essential weapon in debates about gender and gender roles. Perhaps we are finally witnessing the fulfilment of the process begun by *Lord Hardwicke's Act* 1753 (UK) which implemented the registration of marriages as a process through which the population could be tracked and monitored, safeguarded against pollutants. If, at the time of *Lord Hardwicke's Act*, the threat was of the dilution and subversion of property, today it is of the dilution and subversion of gender and of gender roles.

Often, although this is seldom acknowledged in mass media reporting, the demographic changes cited are merely local instances of global phenomena and those phenomena are intimately connected to broader forces of social change: increasing levels of education, economic well being and urbanisation. What often appears transparently clear from the statistical data is itself open to interpretation, although when we try to explain the underlying social phenomena we move rapidly from the relative simplicity of the statistical accounts to the emotionally and ideologically charged arena of politics. In the next section we will examine social trends in three areas that have become flashpoints and which circle 'the family' as an ideological construct: fertility rates, marriage rates, and divorce rates. The picture these will give us provides a telling counterpoint to the trends towards the 'family unfriendly workplace' and to the glacial pace of decline in sex segregation in the workplace that we explored in the last chapter.

A Recipe for Moral Panic

Fertility Rates

One critical flashpoint in current skirmishes is found in the politics of motherhood. While many of the most telling debates focus on a media-fuelled divide between mothers in the waged labour force and those who prefer to be full time mothers, the subtext of these debates is linked with concern at falling fertility rates and the alleged 'selfishness' and 'individualism' of those who postpone or decline motherhood.[5] Clearly, fertility rates are falling, in many jurisdictions below population replacement level. The evidence suggests that this process has been underway for more than a century.[6] In fact, fertility rates are declining throughout the industrialised world and are beginning to decline in developing countries as the forces of modernity transform children from economic assets to economic liabilities. According to the World Resources Institute 'the total fertility rate in developed countries is 1.6 children per woman; however, it is still 3.1 children per woman in developing countries'.[7]

The data also suggest that, to an increasing extent, women in developed countries are waiting until they are older to begin their families, often bearing their first child in their late twenties. This pattern is not limited to liberal democratic states such as Australia and the United States, but is present throughout the developed world. The most precipitous drops in fertility in the developed world have not been countries such as Australia, Canada and the United States, but in countries such as Italy, Japan, Portugal and Spain where social supports enabling women to maintain workforce participation while raising families are negligible. Divorce rates in these countries are also relatively low (although rising) suggesting that the critical links are to increased educational opportunities and an enhanced standard of living rather than to changes in EEO law and in family law. Female workforce participation in many of these countries is negligible, with only 36 per cent of Italian women and 34 per cent of Spanish women in the workforce. In the Scandinavian countries, while fertility rates are slightly below replacement, the decline since 1970 has been minimal in most countries, and the same is true of some other developed social welfare states.[8]

The picture in countries such as Australia, the UK and the USA is very different. In Australia, in 1971 the fertility rate was 2.87; in the United States it was about 2.4, down from a high of 3.7 in the late 1950s; and in Canada it was 2.12. By 1998, the Australian fertility rate had fallen to 1.76, while that in the US had fallen to about 1.9 and that in Canada had dropped to 1.57 in 1987 before levelling out at about 1.7. The picture in the UK was remarkably similar, with a fertility rate of 1.7, although the evidence suggests it is continuing to drop. By world standards for industrialised countries these figures are not unusual, although countries such as Italy, Greece, Germany, Spain and Malaysia have fertility rates in the order of 1.3 and Japan and other Western European countries have fertility rates in the order of 1.6.[9] The overall figures mask considerable internal variability, both by socio-economic status and by racial and ethnic origin and this is as true of Australia as it is of the United States and Canada.[10] The trends in Australia, the United States and Canada are remarkably similar, and this too is hardly surprising. Overall, fertility rates are inversely correlated to both education and socio-economic status, women with higher levels of education having fewer children than those with lower levels of education although Australian evidence suggests that this may now be changing and that working class women are postponing childbearing more frequently than their better-educated sisters.[11] According to the World Resources Institute:

> Demographic experts believe that the shift from high to low birth rates, and from low to high life expectancy is brought about by 'social modernization'. This complex of changes involves improved health care and access to family planning; higher educational attainment, especially among women; economic growth and rising per capita income levels; and urbanization and growing employment opportunities.[12]

The concern over declining fertility rates now, as in the past, signals a further and deeper concern. It is not simply that fertility rates have declined below population replacement level, but that the decline was initially most rapid and most significant among well-educated middle class women who are, it is suggested, fleeing from responsible motherhood within the confines of male-headed families.[13] While the myth of well-educated women fleeing motherhood has captured the popular imagination, current Australian trends suggest that less well-educated women are also pursuing careers, travelling or saving towards home ownership and are delaying marriage and childbearing until their goals have been realised. Research suggests that the relevant social indicators of a below replacement fertility rate are:

> Longer full-time education of women, more cohabitation or living alone and increasing female labor-force participation are often identified as relevant social trends leading to later motherhood, more children born out of wedlock, a rising voluntary childlessness and further declining family sizes.[14]

Given the (unwarranted) persistence of the belief that women deliberately become pregnant in order to access social welfare benefits,[15] one clear sub-text is that the 'wrong women' are bearing the children and that this is itself a symptom of social decay and the unravelling of the national fabric.[16] The decline in fertility rates has been accompanied by a steady increase in the median age at which women bear their first child, which, in both Canada and Australia has now risen to the late twenties, suggesting that many women delay childbearing until their education is completed and they have established themselves in careers.[17] It is clear that, across the developed world, women now have access to the educational and social opportunities necessary for meaningful choice, and that a significant number are choosing to seize educational opportunities and career opportunities and to defer marriage and childbearing, sometimes indefinitely.

Against this background, it is interesting and suggestive that the only nation in which there has been a sustained resurgence in the fertility rate to close to replacement levels after a sharp decline is Sweden, where it occurred against the background of generous universal paid maternity and paternity leave and excellent support structures including high quality subsidised child care.[18] The Swedish picture is also noteworthy because women who are well educated and have secure and well-paid employment are more likely to have children than are those yet to complete their education or who are unemployed or poorly paid, a pattern strikingly different from that in Australia and the United States.[19] Sweden also has a very low percentage of teenaged mothers, a consequence of strategically planned intervention to provide high levels of sex education, ready access to contraceptive information for teenagers and access to abortion in the event of contraceptive failure.[20] The Swedish experience suggests that given a meaningful choice, women prefer to bear children when their economic and social position ensures that they and their children will enjoy a reasonably comfortable and secure life.[21]

The percentage of children born to unmarried women has also increased significantly during this period. In Australia, 24 per cent of all births were to unmarried women in 1993, a rise of 16.6 per cent since 1971, and the rate is continuing to rise, reaching 27.4 per cent in 1996.[22] The rate of increase in other countries is similar. In Canada, for example, 27 per cent of all births in 1996 were to unmarried women, an increase of 17 per cent over figures for the early seventies, while in the United States comparable figures are 31 per cent and 20 per cent. In Sweden, in 1993, 50 per cent of all births were to unmarried women, an increase of 32 per cent. The Swedish picture apparently differs from that in other jurisdictions in that the majority of these births were to unmarried parents living in stable de facto relationships and it has been suggested that this may be a return to traditional patterns of family formation rather than a new development.[23] Equally significant, de facto relationships in Sweden are a common prelude to marriage across the social spectrum. In Australia, the available evidence suggests that they are more common among lower socio-economic groups and among previously divorced people, a pattern that also has historic roots.

Seventy-nine per cent of Swedish children live with both biological parents, the proportion in single parent or step-parent households being significantly lower than in the US (68 per cent) and Australia (74 per cent).[24] The statistics for jurisdictions other than Sweden do not identify the proportion of children born to women in stable, non-marital relationships, whether heterosexual or homosexual. The Swedish data are particularly interesting against the background of widespread mass media attention in Australia and the United States to the unstable nature of de facto relationships and the unsatisfactory nature of their outcomes for children.[25] If Swedish outcomes are, as a preliminary examination of the data suggests, somewhat different, that difference may be correlated to the economic status of the households and the social supports available for child rearing rather than to any intrinsic advantage as between formal marriage and other forms of permanent or semi-permanent relationships. In both the United States and Australia, casual and de facto relationships appear to be more common among the economically marginal, again a different picture from that in Sweden.

Marriage and Divorce Rates

During the same period, marriage rates have fallen substantially and it is clear that, on average, the age at first marriage is increasing and that the marriage rate is falling in absolute terms. In the US the crude marriage rate fell from about 11 in 1970 to 8 in 1998, although it is still high in world terms, while in Australia it has fallen from 8 to 5.8 during the same period. These rates are still relatively high compared to France and Germany where the crude marriage rate is just below 5, and significantly higher than that in Scandinavian countries.[26] These changes are, in part, accounted for by an increasing tendency for couples to live in de facto relationships prior to or instead of legal marriage and by significant changes in social attitudes. Marriage is now only one of a number of social choices, as it was in the past.[27] In many countries, including Australia, many of the social (and legal) consequences of marriage now attach to de facto relationships[28] and the stigma attached to children born outside of legal marriage has largely been eliminated, although single mothers continue to be pathologised by some elements of the popular press.

During the same period, divorce rates have risen significantly. ABS statistics suggest that:

> About 43% of all marriages are likely to end in divorce; 8% within five years of marriage, 19% within ten years, 32% within twenty years and 39% within thirty years.[29]

While these figures are lower than comparable figures for the United States, they are high in absolute terms and close to those for Canada and the United Kingdom.[30] Yet these figures are merely a representation in statistical terms of the legal, social and economic changes of the last three decades. Other statistics are much more difficult to obtain from reliable sources although they are frequently aired by various interest groups. It is difficult, for example, to obtain accurate longitudinal information as to which spouse initiated dissolution, and even more difficult to determine whether the spouse actually initiating dissolution also made the decision that the marriage was at an end. Dissolution may be sought for any one of a number of reasons, ranging from a decision that continued marriage no longer meets the needs of the individual to desertion by a partner. According to a survey conducted by the Australian Institute of Family Studies:

> Nearly two-thirds (64 per cent) of women compared with one-fifth (21 per cent) of men indicated that it was mostly themselves who had made the decision to separate. Conversely, more than half (53 per cent) of men compared with 20 per cent of women said that the decision had been mostly made by their former partner. According to 26 per cent of men and 16 per cent of women, the decision was jointly made.[31]

The same study indicated that 83 per cent of women and 67 per cent of men had no regrets concerning separation. What this study does not provide, of course, is longitudinal information capable of suggesting whether it has become, as is sometimes intimated, increasingly common for women to initiate separation and/or dissolution.[32] Where some longitudinal data is available, as in the UK and Australia, the picture is variable. In the UK, the numbers of men and women seeking divorce in 1961 were roughly comparable, with women filing about 57 per cent of all petitions. By 1971, the percentage of women filing for dissolution had increased to 60 per cent and by 1986 to about 72 per cent, a significant increase.[33] More recently, the percentage in the UK appears to have stabilised and is holding steady.[34] The available Australian statistics suggest that in 1988 women filed 51 per cent of petitions, men filed 37 per cent, and 11 per cent were joint. Ten years later the proportion filed by women had decreased to 50 per cent, those filed by men had declined to 31 per cent and 19 per cent of petitions were joint.[35] Unfortunately, data prior to 1988 is not readily available and thus it is difficult to determine the magnitude of any trend. It is significant, however, that in 1988 divorces where children were involved, women filed 55.3 per cent of petitions, men filed 35.9 per cent and 8.8 per cent were joint. By 1998, the proportion of men filing had decreased to 29.2 per cent, the proportion of women filing had increased to 58.6 per cent and the proportion of joint filings had increased to 12.2 per cent. Where no children are involved, applications are much more likely to be joint (27.7 per cent) and the discrepancy between the percentages for each party is significantly less, in the order of 5.5 per cent.

It is difficult to know what to make of these differences, however it seems clear that women are significantly more likely to file where children are involved. A number of explanations are possible. Filing affords an opportunity to establish interim parenting arrangements, and may be desirable for that purpose. Equally, and plausibly, particularly for less affluent families, separation and divorce may entail relatively little disruption for some women, particularly if they retain possession of the family home. The resources available to them through Parenting Payments may not be substantially less than those actually available prior to separation and will be under their direct control, an important consideration in some cases, particularly where the relationship has been violent.

Accurate data for Canada has proved difficult to access, as Statistics Canada does not hold such data,[36] however research into custody awards suggests that men filed about 40 per cent of petitions in 1982 and women filed about 60 per cent of petitions.[37] Meaningful comparison with Sweden is even more difficult. In Sweden, divorce is a legal entitlement rather than a consequence of the breakdown of a potentially lifelong union,[38] a factor that might be thought to have considerable impact upon willingness to file for divorce. Likewise, given that Sweden has allowed joint filing since the 1970s and in a childless marriage divorce is immediate where uncontested, comparisons are somewhat complicated. While statistics circulating on some men's group web sites suggest that some 75 per cent of divorces in Sweden are initiated by women, given the prevalence of joint filing and the absence of any source for the statistics cited this figure must be treated with caution.[39]

Fragmenting Families

The enactment of the *Family Law Act* 1975 brought no-fault divorce to Australia and established the Family Law Court as a specialist tribunal. While reducing the grounds for divorce to the single category of irretrievable breakdown, it also sought to uphold marriage as a fundamental social institution and to entrench protection for those women whose primary social role had been that of wife and mother. Thus, the legislation provided that the Court should have regard to 'the need to preserve and protect the institution of marriage as the union of a man and a woman to the exclusion of all others voluntarily entered into for life'. Perhaps more significantly, as originally enacted, s 75(l) emphasised the 'need to protect the position of a woman who wishes only to continue her role as a wife and mother'.[40] Section 75(l) has since been amended and now emphasises 'the need to protect a party who wishes to continue that party's role as parent'. These provisions reflected the continued importance of socially conservative elements within parliament and served as a clear signal that broader change in social roles and relationships formed no part of the legislative intent. Here, there were no unencumbered citizens and the structure adopted for the social welfare safety net meant that, in effect, the state replaced the husband, leaving conventional gender roles otherwise intact.[41] The more recent formulation, however, is capable of a far broader reading, and can be interpreted to reinforce the principle of continuing parental responsibility and to apply equally to residential and non-residential parents.

Enactment of the *FLA* was followed by an immediate upsurge in dissolution rates, in large part attributable to those who had already determined that their marriage was at an end and were waiting for the abolition of fault-based grounds. While the rise in dissolution rates has been gradual following the initial 'spike', it is not clear whether this is, as widely assumed, attributable to no-fault divorce or whether it simply represents the continuation of a gradual upwards trend already established during the 1960s and early 1970s.[42] While a causal connection is widely assumed, the available statistical data suggests that this is not necessarily the case and that the trend line was already established before the enactment of the *FLA*.

When the *FLA* was enacted no legislative standard for property distribution was established. Although the possibility of imposing a broad deferred community property regime had been considered, Parliament did not take up this option. Instead the *FLA* called for the exercise of substantial judicial discretion and relied upon an analysis of needs and contributions,[43] the intent being that a clean break[44] was desirable and that, where possible, the ongoing needs of the custodial parent should be met through the distribution of property. The quantum of child support payable was also a matter for judicial discretion, and the eligibility of the custodial parent for a sole parent's benefit was routinely taken into account in calculating the amount, the aim being to maximise the resources available to the custodial parent while leaving the non-custodial parent sufficient resources to form a new family. While the legislative framework was formally gender neutral,[45] early first instance decisions reflected a clear maternal preference.[46] Although these decisions were overruled, and a maternal preference forcefully disapproved, in retrospect it seems likely that the first instance tribunals inferred a maternal preference both from prevailing social mores and from the explicit language of s 75(1) *FLA* affirming the legislative intention to protect a woman who wanted only to continue her role as 'wife and mother'.[47] The social welfare safety net provided resources at subsistence level to sole parents and their children. In this respect, Australian social and family policy remained firmly committed to traditional social roles, at least so far as parenting and the gendered division of labour were concerned, although these social roles were increasingly seen as independent of marriage as a social institution.

Although the changes to family law followed very closely upon the decisions of the Industrial Relations Commission entrenching equal pay for equal work, there is little evidence of broad political commitment to gender equality at the time of its enactment. Instead, the assumption was that traditional roles would continue for the great majority but that those who, from choice or necessity, engaged in waged labour were entitled to formal equality. When the *FLA* was enacted, national EEO legislation was almost a decade away, although South Australia had pioneered by enacting sex discrimination legislation in the early 1970s.[48] The legislative intention was to facilitate the termination of failed marriages with a minimum of rancour, while, so far as possible, ensuring that those committed to conventional gender roles were protected through maintenance and property settlements. The structure of these provisions[49] and of the social welfare regime[50] has undoubtedly played a significant role in the present social settlement in Australia and in the participation rates of sole parents in the labour market.[51]

Sole Parents: Myth and Reality

Until very recently, conventional gender roles have remained entrenched in Australian society. Female participation in waged labour has risen slowly but steadily although levels remain below those common in Europe and the US. Discriminatory practices continue to play a significant role in many workplaces. In part because of the way in which social welfare supports are structured and the cost of child care, it remains preferable for many sole parents, other than those with professional or trade qualifications, to work part-time rather than full time for an extended period as this maintains eligibility for the Parenting Payment (formerly sole parent's benefit) and for valuable ancillary benefits, including health care benefits. In many cases, even should a sole parent desire to return to work on a full-time basis, the additional cost of child care and work-related expenses and the loss of medical and other benefits associated with the parenting payment would make any real financial advantage minimal.[52]

Social attitudes complicate the picture further. Community disapproval of mothers in full-time employment, particularly when their children are relatively young, remains relatively widespread, at least if mass media accounts are to be believed. Paradoxically, many people also believe that sole parents (often referred to as 'single mothers') elect this 'lifestyle' because of the availability of social welfare benefits, the implication being that this is a career choice designed to facilitate 'sponging' off the state.[53] This rhetoric imagines the single mother as a teenager for whom motherhood is preferable to 'a real job' and is prominent on talkback radio and in letters to the editor in the popular press.[54]

The availability of a social welfare safety net is clearly a factor in separation decisions, and some sole parents feel that the parenting payment allows them greater control over resources than was the case while they were married, particularly where their partner was the sole wage earner. Writing in the US context, Nancy Dowd cites research suggesting that:

> For some women, single parenthood "can represent not only a different but a preferable kind of poverty". In one study, over half of the women had been battered by their partners; becoming a single parent removed violence as part of the price of access to resources. As single parents, women gain control of household resources. In contrast to the marital arrangement, where husbands

commonly control access to resources while wives commonly manage those they are given, single mothers have both control and management. They avoid marital fights over money and are able to make different choices in allocating scarce resources.[55]

A dichotomy is beginning to emerge between the perception of single fathers and single mothers, media accounts suggesting that a single father who gives up work or works part time to care for his children is praiseworthy, whilst a single mother in the same position is seen as 'lazy', possibly 'immoral' and as sponging off the state. This dichotomy is predictable: for a single father, active parenting is supererogatory, beyond role expectations. In this way, the choice to engage in full time parenting can be seen (at least in the short term) as a praiseworthy sacrifice of his career in the interests of his children. For a single mother, on the other hand, parenting is core: deficiencies incur opprobrium; dedication is presumed and hardly praiseworthy. Unlike a single father, she is presumed to have no career (other than reproduction) to sacrifice. She is simply a 'drain' on the resources generated by hardworking taxpayers. Sheila Shaver notes that the changes to social security provision in the late 1980s 'removed provision in social security for sole parents to maintain a distinctive female life-cycle pattern shaped by wifehood and motherhood'.[56]

Against this background, it is significant that ABS statistics indicate that in 1998 46.5 per cent of male lone parents were employed whilst about 44 per cent of female lone parents were employed, the majority on a part-time basis.[57] By contrast, the numbers of male sole parents in part-time employment was only marginally higher than the number employed full-time.[58] In this way, conventional marital roles continue to be reproduced following separation and divorce, mothers, sisters and girlfriends of lone fathers often assuming responsibility for household work and parenting, whereas female sole parents maintain their pre-divorce roles. Nancy Dowd argues that:

> Placed in the social context of work and family, the single-parent family develops within the marital family, harbingering the common parenting patterns at divorce. In that sense, every parent is a single parent, generally following a gendered parenting role. Mothers' parenting is characterized by all or the vast majority of unwaged household work and caretaking, combined with wage work constrained by the real or imagined responsibilities of caretaking. Fathers' parenting, on the other hand, is characterized by economic caretaking as the primary, although no longer sole, wage worker, combined with minimal caretaking and household work. After divorce, most children will live solely or primarily with their mothers, and be cared for nearly exclusively by them. Fathers do little or no caretaking after divorce, and many abandon even minimal caretaking within several years of divorce. Furthermore, many fathers, until recent strengthening of child support laws, gave up economic parenting as well at divorce or shortly thereafter.
>
> In a dual-parent family we can believe that the ideology of choice lies behind gendered patterns and outcomes. In the single-parent family, that façade is not present. The consequences of 'choices' made in dual-parent families distributing work and family responsibilities, most often along predictable gender lines, are

economic devastation and emotional abandonment if the patriarchal tie is broken.[59]

Against the background of a shift in government policy that dictated reliance upon private provision for children wherever possible and argued for the return of 'responsibility' and 'choice' to the private sphere, the late 1980s saw renewed legislative attention to the economic consequences of marital breakdown. A number of factors were critical in focusing the debate. First, it had become clear that escalating numbers of sole parents and their children were living in poverty. Following Prime Minister Hawke's 1987 promise that by 1990 no Australian child would live in poverty and increasing concern at the escalating cost of social provision for sole parents and their children, government policy swung decisively to emphasise individual responsibility rather than state provision. In response to widespread failure by non-residential parents to comply with maintenance orders and the judicial practice of setting child support payments to maximise the income of the custodial parent where that parent was in receipt of a sole parent's pension, child support legislation was enacted. In the case of custodial parents in receipt of the sole parent's pension, participation in the new arrangements was compulsory. The new regime was intended to transfer financial responsibility for children from the public sphere (through transfer payments) to the private (through state collection of child support). This legislation marked a significant turning point in terms of financial arrangements for children, one that has also been adopted in a significant number of US jurisdictions and in the UK.

In 1988 the *Child Support (Registration and Collection) Act* 1988 was enacted to commence the transfer of responsibility for the assessment and collection of child support payments from the Family Court to the Child Support Agency, a bureaucratic agency operating under the aegis of the Australian Taxation Office. The new arrangements became fully operational through the *Child Support Act* 1989. Assessment is according to an income-based formula tied to average weekly earnings and payable through the Child Support Agency.[60] Against the background of widespread avoidance of judicially ordered child support obligations, the *CSA* provides by s 3 that parents have a duty to maintain their children which is primary and which is not affected (s 3(2)(ii)) by 'any entitlement of the child or another person to an income tested pension, allowance or benefit'. As has been the case in most other jurisdictions implementing bureaucratic procedures for the assessment and collection of child support payments,[61] the *CSA* has generated considerable anger among non-residential parents and been the subject of numerous attacks by fathers' rights groups.[62]

Under the current arrangements, where the residence parent is not in receipt of more than the basic rate of the Family Tax Benefit, the residence parent (the payee) can opt to move to private arrangements, where both the amount and the manner of payment are privately arranged. Where the payee is in receipt of more than the basic rate of the Family Tax Benefit or receives the Parenting Payment, the options are more limited. While private collection remains an option, the amount of the payments will be determined by the formula, and the Family Assistance Office must be notified. If difficulties arise, a return to CSA collection is an option. The difficulty with all of these options is that any default, including by a self-employed payor where payments are made to the CSA direct, is, in the short term borne by the payee.

This contrasts profoundly with the approach in Sweden. There, remittance to the payee by the equivalent agency does not depend upon collection from the payer. Rather, the agency remits the agreed or ordered amount to the payee irrespective of whether the full payment has been received from the payer, and recovers the funds where necessary from the defaulting payer. This has the advantage from the payee's perspective of maintaining income and ensuring that the children are not disadvantaged. It also has the psychological advantage of allowing the agency to operate as a 'buffer' between the parents, reducing the potential for an acrimonious exchange over late or missed payments.

Despite the child support provisions and the potential benefit to residence parents some difficulties remain. Unlike the arrangements in Sweden where the child maintenance payment comes directly from the government and the non-residential parent has a legal obligation to reimburse the government[63] only the funds actually remitted to the CSA are available to the residence parent. The Swedish priority is to ensure that adequate funds are available to meet the child's needs and to ensure that these are available on a predictable basis.

The current Australian arrangements are more ambivalent. While, as part of an attempt to encourage fathers to maintain contact with their children, the child support payments are reduced where the father has the child for ten or more nights per year, and shared care is also recognised in the arrangements for Family Tax Benefit payments, the Parenting Payment (single) cannot be shared by two low income or unemployed parents, even if caring responsibilities are equally divided between them. Not only is this a disincentive to shared care by unemployed or very low income parents, but also, and more significantly, it reinstates the breadwinner homemaker bargain by assuming that one parent will assume responsibility for market labour while the other is responsible for parenting. Given the gendered distribution of residence arrangements, in practice this means that while fathers are rewarded for caring about their children through the reduction in child support payments and the ability to share Family Tax Benefit payments, they are not encouraged to care for their children. Instead, they are subject to the normal 'activity tests' associated with receipt of the Newstart allowance.

When the child support legislation was initially enacted, the liability was structured to recognise the residence parent's 'non-financial' contribution in caring for the child. Thus, even where both parents were engaged in waged labour, the financial liability of the residence parent was lower than that of the contact parent. During the years since the enactment of the child support legislation, the exemption applicable to the carer's earnings has been significantly reduced.[64] In the most recent changes the liable parent's exemption was raised 10 per cent and liability extended to those with total incomes under the exempt level, including persons in receipt of unemployment benefits and other transfer payments, who are now required to pay $260 pa or five dollars per week.[65] Julie Tolmie and Miranda Kaye note that:

This difference in financial liability, with the resident parent contributing less by way of financial support, is in fact an attempt by the legislature to recognise the non-financial contribution made by that parent in terms of their daily labour of caring for the children. The effect of measuring equity solely in terms of the financial contributions made towards the support of the children is to render this actual work of caring, generally performed by women, unvalued and invisible.[66]

In another significant change, the Jobs, Education and Training (JET) program was introduced in 1989 to assist sole parents in entering or re-entering the labour force. It specifically targets those in receipt of income support payments for more than one year and whose youngest child is over the age of six years, those whose youngest child is approaching the age of 16 years, and teenage parents irrespective of the age of their child. Its introduction emphasised changing public perceptions of motherhood. 'Motherhood' was no longer seen as an exclusive role and distinctive female lifestyle, but as a temporary and transitional phase, a career interruption rather than a career in itself. Coupled with the simultaneous amendments to the *Social Security Act* 1947 reducing the age at which the youngest child ceased to be eligible from 18 (25 if in full time education) to 16, these changes effectively ended an era in which female sole parenthood was seen as a distinctive and valuable lifestyle entitled to public support.[67] When they are read in conjunction with the child support legislation a clear shift towards individual responsibility and provision and an emerging model of 'mother as worker' can be discerned, although the policy signals are mixed, as the availability of the basic parenting payment to partnered women with low personal incomes but employed partners emphasises. A number of significant practical barriers remain. Many female sole parents, particularly those in their thirties or forties, lack the education and skills for employment providing other than a marginal income.[68] Even those with prior employment history are likely to have worked in 'female dominated' areas of employment typically characterised by poor rates of pay, casual employment and lack of career paths and training programs.[69] These collective 'deficits' and the marginal rates of pay available for such work means that even those sole parents who obtain full time employment tend to cycle on and off benefits as, for example, they withdraw temporarily to care for a sick child or parent.[70] According to a paper prepared by Carmen Zanetti,[71]

> the educational disadvantage of sole parent pensioners has turned out to be greater than originally anticipated. One of the hallmark outcomes of JET is that it is delivering skills formation to a generation of women who missed out on education.[72]

Zanetti also notes that the average age of sole parent pensioners has increased from about 28.3 in 1975 to 33 in 1994, and that very few sole parents are teenagers.[73] Reflecting increased emphasis upon education for girls and women, teenage sole parents are significantly better educated than those in older age groups, although they are believed to be at risk of long-term dependency.[74]

In line with the increasing emphasis upon private provision, the Minister for Family and Community Services recently flagged the possibility of further reforms to eligibility for the parenting payment. Noting that increasing numbers of Australian lone parents are reliant upon income support payments[75] the Minister has foreshadowed a major policy shift aimed at encouraging sole parents to re-enter the workforce. One publicly mooted reform involves reducing the ceiling age for the youngest dependent child from 16 to 12,[76] reflecting the fact that 67 per cent of mothers with children between ten and 14 are in paid work, roughly half of them full-time.[77]

Within this context, the 1995 reforms to the *FLA* are both critical in their symbolism and potentially revolutionary.[78] Kathleen Funder suggests that the reforms had their genesis in

> widely expressed concerns that custody and access provisions of the Family Law Act 1975 encouraged a mind set among parents which disposed them to see themselves as 'winners' or 'losers'. [According to Funder] [n]otions of parental ownership and exclusive control of children appeared to underpin many intractable disputes over children and the reforms attempted to remove concepts which suggest parental rights and powers.[79]

Against this background, and, in particular, agitation from an increasingly vocal and influential fathers' rights movement, custody and access were replaced with a conception of joint parental responsibility. The parent with primary responsibility for day-to-day care, formerly the custodial parent, is now styled the residence parent; the other parent, the 'contact' parent. More radically, in the Australian context, the objects stated in s 60B2 apply to all parents, whether married, separated, living in a de facto relationship, or unmarried, implementing a policy of encouraging continued contact between fathers and their children, even where the parents have never lived together.[80] According to s 60B2:

(a) children have the right to know and be cared for by both their parents, regardless of whether their parents are married, separated, have never married or have never lived together; and

(b) children have the right of contact, on a regular basis, with both their parents and with other people significant to their care, welfare and development; and

(c) parents share duties and responsibilities concerning the care, welfare and development of their children; and

(d) parents should agree about the future parenting of their children.[81]

The recent emphasis upon the importance of shared parenting following divorce, in practice an emphasis upon the importance of the father to child development, in practice introduces a further form of dependence and can lay the groundwork for ongoing conflict. While the legislation explicitly provides that the child has a 'right' to contact with both parents, in practice that 'right' imposes an obligation on the residence parent to facilitate contact but does not impose a corresponding obligation on the contact parent to utilise it. Contact parents, typically fathers, depend upon residence parents to facilitate contact and to perform a majority of the parenting duties. Residence parents typically depend upon contact parents to provide agreed financial support and to comply with contact arrangements, such as picking up and returning the children at the scheduled times. In practice, this can be very difficult for sole parents. As Stoltz notes, while:

> It can be an advantage for single mothers who suffer from severe time constraints to have someone with whom to share the responsibility of the children, but this can also mean a new form of dependence. It can be extremely difficult for the single mother when a father who was uninterested in the family suddenly wants, and also gets, all the attention from the children. Women who divorce need manifold economic and social resources in order to survive a divorce successfully. If this stress on the role of the father is not also combined with a policy directed towards the social and economic situation of single mothers, the final result will be unsatisfactory for women.[82]

A survey conducted by the Australian Institute of Family Studies for the Attorney-General's Department immediately prior to the implementation of the recent reforms, sought to measure the respondents' acceptance of the concept of parental responsibilities under the four family conditions specified in the proposed legislation. The areas explored included physical and emotional care, contact, and financial support. Support for shared care where parents are separated or divorced commanded about 50 per cent support across the survey population, contact commanded about 60 per cent support, and shared financial support 70 per cent agreement. Somewhat predictably, where parents were married, support for shared care and contact was significantly higher, about 80 per cent in each case. Surprisingly, however, support for shared support was only marginally lower, about 67 per cent, perhaps indicating widespread support for the increasing workforce participation of women. Perhaps most interestingly, a tiny minority (one per cent) rejected shared care where parents were separated, and a similar minority rejected shared support where parents were married.[83] While this survey suggested broad support for the overall thrust of the reforms, Funder notes that:

> Sharing responsibility however can mean taking responsibility for almost none to almost all of the parenting of a child. Self attribution of a greater proportion of a socially desirable behaviour is an almost universal bias.[84]

How little these social attitudes accord with the reality of parenting following divorce is highlighted by the statistics concerning the living arrangements of children following divorce. According to ABS statistics:

> After separation, children of all ages were more likely to live with their mother than their father. ABS Family Characteristics Survey (1997) data showed that 96% of 0-4 years olds, 89% of 5-11 years olds and 82% of 12-17 years olds whose parents had separated were living with their mother.[85]

When the statistical information is read against the backdrop of 'standard' contact arrangements following divorce[86] and the economic information cited earlier in this chapter[87] it is clear that neither shared caring responsibility nor shared financial support are anywhere near a reality, a fact that fuels the ire of fathers' rights groups.[88] This, too, should not be surprising. As Nancy Dowd suggested, 'single parenting is the most common pattern *within marriage* as well as after divorce'.[89] Upon dissolution, the patterns which prevailed during marriage are replicated, both because parenting patterns are entrenched and reinforced by community attitudes and because social support systems in employment actively discourage equal parenting by men and women. Against this background, the concerns of the fathers' rights movement are easy to read simply as a protest against the imposition of child support payments and their assertion of willingness to engage in 'equal parenting' as an attempt to privilege 'caring about' as the moral equivalent of 'caring for'.[90] Dowd notes further and I think tellingly that:

> The failure of family law with respect to fathers is not that it has failed to increase fathers' rights, but rather that it does not require that fathers fulfill their nurturing responsibilities or impose consequences for the failure to do so. Any version of custody short of joint physical custody presumes less than equal paternal involvement. If the right to custody exists without a corresponding duty or responsibility, when that right is juxtaposed against a gendered pattern of marital household and child care responsibility, it may operate as a weapon to deny support, rather than a protection of fathers' relationships with their children ... Custody arrangements that permit fathers to abandon nurturing responsibilities without economic or other compensation for the lack of caretaking allow fathers to be "take it or leave it" parents.[91]

Custody arrangements that permit fathers to delegate nurturing responsibilities to a new partner, or to female kin, have the same effect, granting social permission for withdrawal from engagement in and responsibility for carework. In contested parenting disputes lawyers acting for fathers often frame their arguments for paternal residence against evidence of the suitability of the father's kin or new partners as 'substitute caregivers' than on the basis of the father's actual pre-separation role in parenting or capacity for care giving. Against the background of economic arrangements that still condemn those actively engaged in carework to the 'mommy track' this delegation is hardly remarkable. As we saw in the last chapter, family friendly policies remain illusory for the majority of workers, the pressure continues to work longer rather than smarter, and there is no evidence that what Dowd terms 'a child-centered caregiving model for fathers' is a reality in Australia any more than it is in the USA. Even as family law tiptoes towards a model of equal parenting, market structures and residual community attitudes ensure that such a model remains unattainable.[92] Richard Collier emphasises that in the UK

> what emerges from [custody] cases, and family law generally, is not just the class-based version of familial masculinity so evident in recent debates surrounding the Child Support Act 1991. It is also a valorization of the masculinity/work relation, albeit with some flexibility around working hours. It is this which negates the value of men's involvement in childcare at the same time as it promotes the ideal of breadwinner masculinity ... Whether a man works or not is not so much a moral choice as something which is presumed. As a father his natural primary duty

is *to employment and not to childcare.* This means that the man who actually gives up employment to care for children is not seen as acting on any 'natural' nurturing instinct but is, rather, acting against this natural breadwinner masculinity.[93]

What emerges is a tangle of entrenched community attitudes and behaviour patterns, continued resistance to the kind of alternation of workplace practices and patterns that would make equal parental responsibility within marriage feasible, and a set of social indicators that generate widespread alarm but produce nostalgia and the desire to recapture an imagined past rather than create a positive future.

Against this background, and despite widespread criticism of the Family Court,[94] the evidence suggests that despite some inconsistencies at first instance, it maintains a relatively even-handed approach to changes in gender roles.[95] Unlike UK courts, the Full Court today appears relatively even-handed in respect of parenting arrangements, there being no recent evidence of disapproval of a father who elects to act as a full time parent, at least where the children are under school age. Likewise, there is little evidence of disapproval of a mother in full time employment, even where the father appears able and willing to provide full time care.[96] This contrasts sharply with the continued reliance upon stereotypical gender roles in the UK (which excludes men from full time parenting) and with the 1980s Canadian pattern (which favours an employed father able to provide a mother surrogate over an employed mother reliant upon day care).[97]

In Sweden as well the late 1990s brought profound changes to the administration of family law. While joint legal custody had long been the preferred model in Sweden where the parents had been legally married, in 1998 it became possible for the first time for the court to order joint legal custody (and in some cases joint physical custody) over the objection of one of the parents. These changes apply irrespective of whether the children were born to a legally married couple, to a cohabiting couple or to an unmarried couple who had not cohabited.[98] For legally married couples joint custody is automatic. For others, it is necessary for the couple to register an agreement providing for joint custody and about 90 per cent of cohabiting couples and about 45 per cent of couples who have not cohabited register such an agreement.

In Sweden, as in Australia, an overriding aim of the legislation is to keep parenting issues out of court proceedings, thus producing a preference for out of court mediation where disputes arise. While the legislation provides that joint custody should not be ordered against the will of a parent where the other parent is an unsuitable custodian, where the parent has assaulted the other parent or the child, or where conflict is deeply entrenched and the parents are unable to cooperate, in practice joint legal custody has become normative. Even in cases where there has been significant violence, contact will typically be ordered. As in Australia, the introduction of joint legal custody has provided contentious, and the absence of any legal definition of the rights and obligations of joint legal custodians has exacerbated the problems associated with the new legislation.

There is little statistical information on the outcomes of litigation under the new provisions. Under the previous law, in which there was a strong preference for joint custody, although it was not compelled against the will of either parent, there was joint custody in about 40 per cent of cases where the parents either no longer lived together or had never cohabited.[99] In the minority of cases where custody was litigated to appellate stage, where the parents had been married joint custody was the outcome in 35 per cent of cases, the mother received sole custody in 46 per cent, and the father received sole custody in 19 per cent. Where the parents had never been married, joint custody was the outcome in 41 per cent, the mother received sole custody in 37 per cent and the father received sole custody in 22 per cent.[100]

Together with the legal emphasis upon the child's need for stability and contact, has come an increasing willingness to take the child's wishes into account, even where there is evidence that the child has been pressured to favour one parent. In this way, considering the child's wishes is part of a wider legislative aim of compelling the parents to cooperate, it being hoped that parents would recognise that conflict was not in the best interests of the child and would, therefore, cooperate. Schiratzki suggests that:

> The development over the last decades can be described figuratively in terms of the legal system's abdication. Until 1977, when joint custody was made possible for unmarried couples, it was up to the courts, in each divorce case involving children, to settle the parents' dispute and award one of them sole custody. With time, the court's task as regards custody disputes has become to ensure that joint custody is not manifestly incompatible with the child's best interests. From being cases settled by the court, custody cases have become the subject of the parents' own conflict-solving abilities.[101]

Many of these features are replicated in other jurisdictions, including Australia. The transition from judicially mandated to 'mutually agreed' parenting arrangements, in Australia as in Sweden, has come about, at least in part, through the interest of governments not only in minimising conflict but also, and more importantly, in minimising the costs involved in the administration of family law. Mediation, both in Australia and Sweden, is seen as a cost effective alternative to litigious settlement and as less likely to promote continued conflict. While it has been accompanied by what amounts to a discourse of empowerment, specifically one of empowering the parents to make arrangements that meet their needs and those of their children, in Australia at least the rhetoric of empowerment is accompanied by the threat of denial of legal aid if a parent is unwilling to participate in mediation. Where a parent is unable to establish that they have participated in good faith in mediation, the likelihood of a grant of legal aid for judicial proceedings is substantially diminished. In Sweden, Schiratzki suggests that:

> A striking feature regarding custody issues are thus the efforts made to keep disputes on custody away from the courts ... The new law aims at relieving the pressure on the courts and creating better conditions for voluntary agreements. This is done by highlighting the possibilities of solving custody-related conflicts through co-operation talks (Ch. 6, s. 18 of the Code on Parenthood) as well as the courts' ability to issue a joint custody order against the wishes of a parent (Ch. 6,

s. 5 CP), are also seen as important tools for creating better conditions for voluntary agreements. The ambition to keep custody issues out of a court is based on the premises that mediation is cheaper than court proceedings, and out of court mediation is considered to give better results than dispute settlement before the court. In contrast to court proceedings, mediation is believed not to increase the hostility between the parents.[102]

As in Australia, parents bargain in the shadow of the law, and, as in Australia, a reduction in the availability of legal aid becomes another form of coercion, directing the financially weaker parent away from the courts and into mediation. Schiratzki's observation concerning the involvement of children is exceedingly interesting. In Australia, as in Sweden, the wishes of the children are an important consideration and will be taken into account by the Court in making a decision and where the children are of a suitable age they will be encouraged to express their views, both in the course of family counselling and, where one is appointed, to their separate representative. Whether, in practice, this means that the children are indirectly co-opted into the dispute resolution process by being encouraged to take sides, or whether this is simply an outgrowth of entrenched conflict between the parents and unconscious or conscious manipulation to encourage them to do so is not clear. It is clear, however, that as governments seek ways of minimising the costs of administering the courts and associated agencies efforts (including coercive efforts) to redirect the parties into various forms of alternative dispute resolution become increasingly important. What is not clear, in Australia or in Sweden, is whether these efforts, which fall most heavily on the 5-10 per cent of couples where the dispute is deeply entrenched, do, in fact, produce positive outcomes for the children and for their parents or whether the children are simply further exposed to risk.

Concluding Thoughts

This chapter began by looking at a series of demographic indicators that have, over the last few years, been used to legitimate a discourse of moral panic. Against the background of relatively high divorce rates, political and social attempts to stigmatise sole female parents and to valorise fatherhood, and a political agenda clearly aimed at reducing the overall level of state provision and returning 'responsibility' (including economic responsibility) to the individual, a steady and discernable shift has taken place in two bodies of law impacting upon the family. These changes must be understood within the context of other changes, such as those to EEO law and policy. Here it is essential to begin to tie some of the threads together and to offer a way to understand these legal changes as part of a wider story.

First, as feminist commentators have noted, there has been a decisive shift in social welfare law. When the *FLA* was introduced in 1974, it was introduced against the background of a social welfare safety net that enabled mothers to continue following a distinctive female life cycle shaped by wifehood and motherhood.[103] The explicit provisions of the *FLA* guaranteeing protection for a woman who wanted only to continue her role as wife and mother reinforced the safety net. The child support decisions of the Family Court reflected the overall parameters of this social settlement, pegging the quantum of child support to the 'free zone', the level of overall income that did not affect pension entitlements, both minimising the financial burden on the non-custodial parent and maximising the total income available to the custodial parent.

That social settlement, one in which the social behaviours associated with mothering and carework were supported by a male breadwinner within marriage and supported outside marriage by the state indirectly shaped the aspirations of girls and young women. For those who were not obviously academically talented and whose family traditions did not consciously value education (at least beyond year 10 or leaving certificate level) a pattern was established for girls in which a school leaver would work in a shop or factory until marriage and then embark on what was to be a lifetime pattern of carework, with, perhaps, casual part-time employment or assistance in a family business as the children grew older. Given that fewer than 40 per cent of Australian women were in waged labour, there was little cultural or economic incentive to develop marketable skills. Even for girls who aspired to teacher's college or perhaps nursing, the social expectation was of marriage followed by childbearing and rearing, with, at most, a qualification to fall back on should the unthinkable happen. The overall result, one that is hardly surprising, is precisely the pattern noted by Zanetti, a significant educational deficit among female sole parents that is exacerbated by the overrepresentation of non English speaking background (NESB) women among them.[104]

In retrospect, it is easy to see how the forces of social change overtook the elements in that social settlement. Even before its shaping, the decisions of the Arbitration Commission recognising equal pay for equal work set a series of changes in motion which have, over time, made it increasingly unlikely that working class families could live reasonably comfortably on one income. Second, to an extent not fully recognised at the time the *FLA* was enacted, the safety net provisions made it possible for women to escape not only violent and abusive marriages, but also relationships which had become unsatisfying for other reasons without the dislocation which attends the loss of familiar roles. That the overall impact of these changes has been less significant in Australia than elsewhere may be attributed, at least in part, to the persistence of a social welfare safety net that simultaneously reinforced dependence within relationships and supported a distinctive female life cycle shaped around motherhood and wifehood should relationship breakdown occur. The combination of a welfare structure oscillating uneasily between a 'male breadwinner' pattern and a 'citizen mother' pattern reinforced female dependence on two levels: within marriage as wife and mother, and outside marriage as state dependent.

Against this background, an overtly re-distributive family law system provided, on two quite distinct levels, an incentive for dissolution for those who found relationships difficult. For women from low-income families, a group in which NESB women were and are over-represented, the safety net provided an independent and reliable income under their personal control. For those from households with significant property available for distribution, the explicit requirement that non-market contributions be valued equally to market contributions could yield a settlement permitting a reasonably comfortable life and a degree of independence otherwise unavailable. Together, these legal structures have provided an environment in which market participation by female sole parents has remained relatively low. While women represent an increasing proportion of the total workforce in Australia,[105] female sole parents apparently lag behind in workforce participation.[106] In the next chapter, we will look at the structure of the social welfare safety net in Australia, particularly as it applies to sole parents, and at its impact on the choices women have made in the past and are making in the present.

Notes

1   To some extent, this increasing fragility is illusory. In the pre-modern era, families were often fractured by death; step-parents were common, as were informal unions, particularly among the working class. See Berns, Sandra, 'Women in English Legal History: Subject (almost), Object (irrevocably), Person (not quite)' (1993) 12 *Univ. Tas LR* 26.

2   In August 2000, the declared intention of the Howard government to amend the *Sex Discrimination Act* 1984 to permit discrimination based upon marital status in some contexts is symptomatic of these debates. While the threat is in a seemingly peripheral area, whether single women and lesbian couples should be able to access IVF, and was prompted by a recent Federal Court decision declaring that Victoria's regulatory scheme regarding access to IVF services violated the *SDA*, it is symptomatic of the wider debate.

3   Levit, 88.

4   Boyd, Susan, 'Child Custody, Ideologies, and Employment' (1989) 3 *Canadian Journal of Women and the Law* 111 discusses the conflict between the ideology of motherhood and the ideology of equality in Canadian disputes over parenting and argues that the combined effect of these ideologies is to elevate the value of paternal parenting (even where there is little evidence of performance as opposed to rhetoric) and to simultaneously propel women into paid employment and insist that full time employment is incompatible with primary parenting.

5   In Australia this debate has been fuelled by the political decision to treat the structural supports needed by working mother as issues associated with family policy rather than industrial relations policy, thus explicitly pitting the interests of mothers in the waged labour force against those of full time carers.

6   In Australia, concern over falling fertility rates, often cast against the threat of the 'yellow peril', were significant during the Federation era and led to the introduction of a maternity benefit following the turn of the century.

7   Data held by the World Resources Institute accessed at http://www.wri.org/ on 27 November 1999.

8   In Sweden, remarkably, fertility rates rose to above replacement levels in the 1980s, apparently as a consequence of generous paid maternity leave provisions and excellent social support systems, particularly in the area of child care.

9   Fertility rates appear to be higher in those countries that make more generous provision for maternity and paternity leave and provide more adequate support structures for

combining workforce participation and child rearing. In Japan, fertility rates are continuing to fall rapidly and there is increasing concern by the Japanese government.

10   Australian statistics are taken from ABS Cat. No. 3301.0 accessed on 18 November 1999 at http://www.abs.gov.au. American statistics are taken from Social Security Area Population Projections accessed on 19 November 2000 at http://www.ssa.gov/. Canadian data are taken from Statistics Canada, 'Fertility Projections for Canada, Provinces and Territories 1993-2016' Catalogue No. 91F0015MPE, 9 downloaded from http://www.statcan.ca/ on 23 November 1999. World comparators are available from United Nations, 'World Fertility Patterns' available at http://www.undp.org/popin/ accessed on 24 November 1999.

11   ABS Cat. No. 3301.0, 'Births Australia' accessed at http://www.abs.gov.au/ on 24 November 1999. The statistical profile for Canada and the United States is similar. In 'The Big Baby Bust', The *Australian*, 22 November 1999 new ABS statistics were cited suggesting that fertility among working class women was beginning to decline. See also Retschlag, Christine, 'School's out on low birth rate' The *Courier Mail*, 14 December 1999. According to Retschlag, 'Among the 25-29 age group the percentage of childless women rose by 7.2 percent for those with a degree, 12.4 percent with those with a post-school qualification and 10.1 percent for no post-school qualification'. See also 'Delay brings the best of both worlds', The *Courier Mail*, 14 December 1999 on the joys of late motherhood among professional women.

12   Infoplease Almanac, World Statistics, 'Births to Unmarried Women, by country, 1970-1993' accessed at http://www.infoplease.com/ on 28 November 1999.

13   In the United States, ethnic groups with fertility rates at or above replacement levels include Afro-Americans, Native Americans, Hispanics and Asians and Islanders. Birth rates among Afro-Americans, Native Americans and Asians and Islanders are currently below 2.5 and continuing to fall. See Ameristat, Population Reference Bureau and Social Science Data Analysis Network, 'Race and Ethnicity' on http://www.ameristat.org/ accessed on 27 November 1999. In Australia, the fertility rates of indigenous people and of Lebanese migrants remain well above replacement rates. See n 10 for sources.

14   United Nations Expert Group Meeting on Below Replacement Fertility, 'Future Expectations for Below-Replacement Fertility' accessed at http://www.undp.org/ on 27 November 1999. The same document indicated that the most fertile years for Australian women were 25-29, with one-third of all children being born to women in that age bracket.

15   This is a clear sub-text of the debates in Australia, Canada and the United States, and the available information suggests that similar beliefs are current in the United Kingdom. There is some evidence suggesting that, in the United States, single parenthood among African-Americans is 'the most advantageous family form for obtaining economic resources. The structure of public and private economic options provides support for the view'. Dowd, Nancy E, 'Stigmatizing Single Parents' (1995) 18 *Harvard Women's Law Journal* 19, 46. This is a consequence of government policies over an extended period. To the extent that a 'safety net' exists in the USA, it is available to female-headed families and it is unavailable if a man joins the household.

16   An allied belief is that most sole parents are teenagers. In Australia and Canada, the available statistical information suggests otherwise. In Canada, 57% of sole parents became so as a result of divorce or separation; in Australia the comparable figure would appear to be about 71.6%. See further the references in n 24 below and the associated text.

17   In Canada, for example, 'during the 8-year period between 1987 and 1994, the annual age specific fertility rates for maternal age group 20-29 declined from 97.0 to 92.1, a 5.1% decrease. For women aged 30-34, the corresponding rate increased from 77.1 in 1987 to 87.3 in 1994. Among women aged 35-44, the rate increased by 28.8% from 16.0 in 1987 to 20.6 in 1994'. Data sourced from the British Columbia Vital Statistics Agency (1996) accessed at http://www.hlth.gov.bc.ca/vs/stats/ on 27 November 1999.

18   After falling to a low of 1.6 in the 1970s, the birth rate rose rapidly in the 1980s, reaching 2.1 in 1990 before again dropping to 1.5 in 1998, largely as a consequence of a worsening economy. See Swedish Institute, (1999) 'The Swedish Population' accessed at http://www.si.se/eng/ on 28 November 1999. See further Swedish Institute, (1998) 'The Financial Circumstances of Swedish Households' accessed at http://www.si.se/eng/ on 5 December 1999.

19   Andersson, Gunnar, 'The impact of labor-force participation on childbearing behavior: pro-cyclical fertility in Sweden during the 1980s and the 1990s', Stockholm University Demography Unit, 28 July 1999, Table 1, 13. The evidence cited in n 11 suggests that the trend in Australia is moving in that direction. See further Furst, 39 who suggests that 'Swedish women had more children when their labour market participation was high. The connection between gainful employment and fertility suggests that it is your position in the labour market, i.e. your chances of being able to provide for yourself and your family, that decides when and if you bring children into the world'.

20   United Nations statistics suggest that the rate of teenage births in Sweden and Australia is below 25 per 1000 births. In the United States and Canada the rate is about double that figure. See UN 'World Fertility Patterns' accessed at http://www.undp.org/popin/ on 2 November 1999.

21   While in the past marriage was typically the key, given rising divorce rates and changing expectations, there is some evidence that women, like men, now wish to ensure that they are established in their careers before commencing their families.

22   ABS, Australia Now – A Statistical Profile 5.18 'Selected Summary Measures of Fertility and Mortality' accessed at http://www.abs.gov.au/ on 28 November 1999.

23   Bradley, 96. Glendon notes that spousals, that is, a promise to marry followed by intercourse gave rise to many of the incidents of marriage until early in this century, and suggests that cohabitation today is a resurgence of this practice. She also notes that under Swedish law those who opt for a civil ceremony may omit the exchange of vows for life. See Glendon, Mary Ann, *The Transformation of Family Law: State, Law and Family in the United States and Western Europe*, Chicago, Univ. of Chicago Press, 1989, 74-75.

24   'Births to Unmarried Women, by country, 1970-1993', above. See also Swedish Institute, 'Financial Circumstances' Swedish Population', above. According to this source, only 14% of children live in single parent households and 7% in step or blended families. In Australia 74% of children live with their natural parents, 8% in step or blended families and 18% in single parent households. Australian statistics are from ABS, 'Family Characteristics' 4442.0, April 1997. Comparable statistics for the USA suggest that about 68% of American children live with their natural parents while about 25% live in single parent households and 7% in blended families. Data obtained from Childstats 'America's Children 1999' accessed at http://Childstats.gov/ac1999/ on 29 November 1999. In Canada, data obtained from the Vanier Institute suggests that 78.7% live with their biological parents in two parent families. See Schlesinger, Ben, 'Strengths in Families: Accentuating the Positive' accessed at http://www.vifamily.ca/ on 2 December 1999.

25   Silverstein & Auerbach, above, suggest that this is an oversimplification and grossly
      misrepresents the true picture. ABS statistics suggest that those in de facto relationships
      in Australia tend to be less well educated and more likely to be impoverished than
      married couples, suggesting that factors such as poverty may be critical and also
      suggesting the persistence of traditional informal mechanisms among working class
      couples. The critical difference for Sweden seems to be the relatively even class
      distribution of unformalised relationships.
26   Infoplease Almanac, World Statistics, 'Crude Marriage Rates for Selected Countries',
      accessed at http://www.infoplease.com/ on 28 November 1999. In Sweden, for
      example, the crude marriage rate is 4.7 although it is unclear what the implications of
      this may be, given the open acceptance of informal unions. See Swedish Statistics and
      Information Page accessed at http://home1.swipnet.se/ on 4 December 1999.
27   For a discussion of traditional patterns of family formation in England prior to *Lord
      Hardwicke's Act* 1753, see Berns, 'Regulation of the Family', above.
28   In Australia, arrangements for children of de facto relationships now mirror those of
      legal marriage. Likewise, the social welfare system attaches the same consequences to
      de facto relationships as to marriage although this has not been extended to same sex
      relationships. See the discussion of the Australian and UK rules regarding social
      security benefits for unmarried cohabitants in Harris, Neville, 'Unmarried Cohabiting
      Couples and Social Security in Great Britain' (1996) 18 *Journal of Social Welfare and
      Family Law* 123. In Australia during the late 1980s intensified surveillance of sole
      parent pensioners became commonplace and was directed at determining whether they
      were cohabiting with a person of the opposite sex and therefore ineligible for the sole
      parents' pension. See Baldock, Cora Vellekoop, 'The Family and the Australian
      Welfare State' (1994) 29 *Australian Journal of Social Issues* 104, 112.
29   ABS, 'Australia Now: A Statistical Profile', accessed on 19 November 1999 at
      http://www.abs.gov.au/. Crude rates have risen from about 1 per 1000 in 1970 to about
      3 per 1000 at present.
30   The US divorce rate rose from about 2.5 in the mid-1960s to a high of 5.3 in the early
      1980s before falling to about 4.7. Current statistics suggest that about 50% of first
      marriages will end in divorce and about 60% of second marriages. Percentage statistics
      were accessed on 19 November 1999 from http://www.co.midland.mi.us/foc/stat.ht.
      Crude divorce rate statistics were downloaded from US Census Bureau 'Statistical
      Abstract of the United States' on 18 November 1999 at http://www.census.gov/.
      Currently, the Swedish divorce rate is 2.2 although given the number of informal
      unions some caution is need in interpretation. See Sweden Statistics and Information
      Page accessed at http://home1.swipnet.se/ on 4 December 1999. In Australia, the
      divorce rate is about 2.5 while in the UK it is close to 2.9.
31   Australian Institute of Family Studies, 'Media Release', at http://www.aifs.org.au/
      accessed on 22 November 1999.
32   The specific accusation is that no fault divorce and the availability of the parenting
      payment encourage women to jettison relationships that they find personally
      unsatisfying and that this undermines 'the stability of the family'.
33   UK statistics were accessed from http://www.statistics.gov.uk/ on 18 November 1999.
34   Haskey, John (Office for National Statistics), May (1996) *Family Law* 301. In 1994
      women filed 71% of petitions. Where there are children under 16, women file 78% of
      applications, however the percentage drops to 65% where there are no children under
      16. The UK figures are interesting because, unlike Australia, the UK has not fully
      moved to no-fault divorce. Joint filing is unavailable in the UK.

35 ABS, 'Marriages and Divorces' Cat. 3310.0, 1998, 49-50. Clearly, the trend is towards joint petitions and away from sole petitions filed by the husband. There is no evidence of a similar trend away from petitions filed by the wife.

36 Email communication from the research officer for Statistics Canada, 2 December 1999.

37 Mossman, Mary Jane & Morag MacLean, 'Family Law and Social Welfare: Toward a New Equality' (1986) 5 *Canadian Journal of Family Law* 79, 84.

38 Bradley, 72. Where there are no children and both parties desire divorce, it will be granted immediately. Where there are children, or the petition is opposed, there is a six-month reconsideration period after which the petition will be granted immediately if sought. There is no requirement for separation during the reconsideration period. The procedure is non-adversarial and it is not necessary that property issues and matters concerning children be resolved in advance. Since 1983, joint legal custody has been automatic upon divorce unless opposed. Parents are expected to resolve matters concerning residence and access without the intervention of the court.

39 See Hoffman, Bjorn, 'Fatherhood Education: A Way to a Richer Life' accessed at http://www.rb.se/man/engelsk/hoffmFN.htm on 19 December 1999. While Gunilla Furst does not provide statistical details she suggests that 'it is often the woman who takes the initiative in seeking a divorce and the grounds most often cited are dissatisfaction with the division of labor between the two partners'. Furst, 43.

40 See *Family Law Act* 1975 s 43(a).

41 The Supporting Mother's Benefit was introduced in 1973 and was extended to supporting fathers in 1997, becoming the Sole Parent Pension. See *Social Security Act* 1991 (replacing *Social Security Act* 1975) Part 2.10 Parenting Payment. It should be noted that s 500R provides that a parenting payment is not available to both members of a couple (thus effectively denying shared care) and that s 500E provides that a child can be a parenting payment child of only one person at a time.

42 See ABS *Marriages and Divorces Australia* ABS 3310, Table 5.4 accessed at http://www.abs.gov.au/ on 24 July 2000.

43 This regime itself was schizophrenic, at once directing the court to value non-market contributions equally with market contributions while prescribing a clean break, suggesting that once the resources provided by distribution of property had been exhausted it would be necessary for a former wife to provide for her needs and those of any children in her care either through market labour or through a residual social welfare net. See *Family Law Act* 1975 s 79(4)(c). The legislation was amended in 1998 to include superannuation in the property available for allocation. See *Family Law Act* 1975 s 79(7). Widespread discontent continues, both because it is not uncommon for a former wife with care of the children to be awarded a significantly greater share than a former husband and because where a family is of modest means, the amount available for distribution is likely to be negligible.

44 *Family Law Act* s 81.

45 Subject to the anomalous provisions noted earlier.

46 See *Epperson v Dampney* (1976) FLC 90-061, 75-302. Cf *Raby v Raby* (1976) FLC 90-104; *Hobbs v Ludlow* (1976) FLC 90-119; *Gronow v Gronow* (1979) 144 CLR 513.

47 The absurdity of this formulation escaped the notice of Parliament.

48 *Sex Discrimination Act* 1975 (SA) was repealed and replaced by *Equal Opportunity Act* 1985 (SA).

49 Both s 43 and s 79(l) were amendments to the original legislation as proposed by the then Commonwealth Attorney-General, Lionel Murphy and represented an attempt to mollify the more conservative elements in the community.

50   The Australian social welfare regime may be described as mixed, although like the UK
     and the USA social insurance provision for families where the primary breadwinner is
     unemployed presumes dependence and thus approximates a 'male breadwinner' model.
     The persistence of a widow's benefit also presumes a male breadwinner. It differs in
     that the parenting payment and its predecessor, the lone parent's pension, explicitly
     acknowledges the value of carework. There is, however, a lingering shadow of the male
     breadwinner model in that should a sole parent cohabit with a person of the opposite
     sex, that person will be (subject to certain criteria) presumed to be contributing to the
     support of the sole parent. Australia has never quite made up its mind whether to pursue
     a strongly male breadwinner centred policy or one affirming the 'citizen mother'. The
     Family Law Act 1975, as originally enacted, clearly reflected some 'citizen mother'
     assumptions. Despite the ambivalence of government policy, popular understandings
     clearly reflect the tenacity of the 'male breadwinner' model.
51   Current statistics suggest that only 37% of female sole parents are engaged in waged
     labour. See ABS 'Labour Force Status and Other Characteristics of Families', No.
     6224.0.40.001, Tables 13 & 25.
52   See the discussion of the poverty trap in Barclay, Susan, 'Where There's no Will
     There's no Way' (1990) 35 *Refractory Girl* 33 and Shaver, Sheila, 'Poverty, Gender
     and Sole Parenthood' in Fincher, Ruth & John Nieuwenhuysen, eds, *Australian
     Poverty: Then and Now*, Melbourne, Melbourne Univ Press, 1998, 276 especially 288-
     289.
53   Both the rhetoric and the terminology reflect US influence. Generally, on the US scene
     see Dowd, 'Stigmatizing Single Parents'. For a discussion of UK attitudes see Lewis,
     Jane, 'The Problem of Lone-Mother Families in Twentieth-Century Britain' (1998)
     20(3) *Journal of Social Welfare and Family Law* 251. Lewis notes at 253 that 'strong
     male breadwinner' countries are prone to moral panic regarding sole motherhood.
54   'Myth of the Single Mother Revealed', The *Sunday Telegraph*, 12 December 1999.
     'While it is often still expected that single mothers will be teenage girls on welfare,
     recent ABS statistics reveal this not the case. Less than 3 per cent of single mums are
     teenagers, with almost 70 per cent aged 30 and over'.
55   Dowd, 'Stigmatizing Single Parents', 58.
56   Shaver, 287.
57   The ABS defines an employed person as anyone working for one hour or more in the
     week prior to the survey. Interestingly, the proportion of female lone parents in full
     time employment is relatively close to the proportion of mothers in couple families with
     full time employment (22.5% and 26.5% respectively). This position is otherwise with
     respect to lone fathers, with only 57.9% of lone fathers in full time employment as
     against 84.1% of those in couple families. The unemployment figures for male and
     female sole parents indicate that unemployment is far greater than among their married
     counterparts, over 14% of female sole parents being unemployed. ABS *Labour Force
     Status and Other Characteristics of Families*, No. 6224.0.40.001, Tables 13 & 25.
58   Statistics are from 'Australia Now: A Statistical Profile, Labour: Characteristics of the
     Labour Force', Table 6.6 accessed at http://www.abs.gov.au/ on 12 December 1999.
     The significance of these figures is difficult to determine. It would appear from
     parenting cases in the Family Court that a significantly higher proportion of men than
     of women are able to rely upon the service of female kin for childcare. The
     'employability' of sole parents and their earning capacity is also relevant, given the
     persistent gender gap, particularly apparent in part time employment.
59   Dowd, 'Stigmatizing Single Parents', 59.

60 *Child Support (Registration & Collection) Act* 1988 s 43 provides for collection by deduction from salary or wages for wage earners. The 'disregarded income' amount for the liable parent is $9,947 and the support owing is based on income over that amount. Where the carer is employed, s 46 provides that the carer's disregarded income amount is equivalent to the 'all employees' average weekly earnings figure for the relevant period, currently approximately $30,347. The differential between the liable parent's disregarded income and that of the carer has fuelled the anger of the father's rights movement.

61 Sweden appears to be an exception, possibly because the obligation falls on both parents equally and a majority of Swedish sole parents are in the waged labour force. Only 35% of female sole parents and 15% of male sole parents are in receipt of means tested social assistance. In Australia, 58% of sole parents (more than 92% female) are in receipt of means tested social assistance according to Saunders, Peter, 'Poverty and Deprivation in Australia', Year Book Australia, 1996, ABS Cat. 1301.0.

62 See Mattias, Malcolm, 'Towards a Class Action' at http://www.familyequity.asn.au/ accessed 25 December 1999. According to Mattias: 'Many men live in cheap accommodation, are compelled to leave pad employment, forced into bankruptcy, lose contact with their children, lose any prospect of a comfortable retirement and a growing number ultimately commit suicide. Many innocent men do not survive this draconian system'.

63 See the discussion of the Swedish maintenance system in Bejstam, Lars, 'Social Benefits and Families with Children' in Wahlgren, Peter, ed, *Legal Issues of the Late 1990s*, Scandinavian Studies in Law Volume 38, Stockholm, Stockholm University Law Faculty, 1998, 217, 227-238.

64 Originally, the exemption was set at male average weekly earnings (about $39,000). It has since been reduced to all employees' average weekly earnings (about $30,000).

65 *Child Support Act* 1989 s 66.

66 Kaye & Tolmie, 'Discoursing Dads', above, 167.

67 The predecessor to the sole parent's pension, the supporting mother's benefit, was introduced into the *Social Security Act* 1949 in 1973 and extended to lone fathers via the supporting parent's benefit in 1977. A common pattern was for a divorced mother to receive the supporting parent's benefit until her youngest child was 18 (25 if still in full time education) and then to receive a Widow's Pension (B) until she was old enough to receive the Old Age Pension.

68 When women now in their mid-forties were teenagers, the family wage was still in place as were restrictive rules requiring married women to resign from public service positions. Their expectations would have been limited to wifehood and motherhood and career preparation and training would have been relatively uncommon. Women now in their mid-thirties were teenagers when EEO legislation was introduced, with, in many cases, their career paths already determined.

69 Taylor, Janet, 'Issues of Paid Employment for Mothers of Young Children' (1996) 17 *Women and Work* 12, 13 suggests that 'mothers who were not in paid employment were also significantly more likely than the employed mothers to be in NESB families (46 per cent), to have larger numbers of children (23 per cent had four or five children) and to have limited education (59 per cent have secondary schooling as their highest level of education and another 19 per cent have no more than primary schooling)'.

70 Paid leave to fulfil caring responsibilities is available primarily in the public sector and is a recent development.

71 Sole Parent Program Branch, Family Programs and Services Division, Department of Social Security.

72 Zanetti, Carmen, 'Sole Parents: Trends and Issues', December 1994 *Social Security Journal* 92, 99.

73 Zanetti, 94-95. Zanetti suggests that only about 3% of sole parents are teenagers and that the teenaged birth rate is the lowest since 1921.

74 Only 31% of female sole parents have any form of post-school qualification, and 57% did not complete the highest level of school. Male sole parents are comparatively better educated in that 46% hold post-school qualifications and only 42% did not complete the highest level at school. ABS, *Transition from education to work, May 1995, Table 17, 'Persons aged 15-64: Relationship in household and educational attainment'*. Married parents are significantly better educated, and this holds true for both men and women, although the difference between male and female educational levels remains relatively constant.

75 Newman, Jocelyn, 'The Challenge of Welfare Dependency in the 21st Century', 20 accessed at http://www.facs.gov.au/ on 13 December 1999 provides statistics suggesting that in 1989 240,000 sole parents were on income support payments, while in 1999 382,000 receive such payments. On current trends, the Minister suggests that by 2006 more than 475,000 will receive such payments. It should be noted, however, that Zanetti suggests that the growth rate of sole parent families calculated as a proportion of all families with children has begun to steady. In 1974 sole parent families represented 9.2% of all families with children, in 1985, 14.4% and in 1993 17%. See Zanetti, 94.

76 When the Supporting Mother's Benefit was originally introduced, where a child was in full time education the benefit was available where the youngest child was under 25.

77 In Australia, 49.4% of women and 66.8% of men are in paid work. In Sweden 67% of women and 70% of men are in paid work. In the UK, 63% of women and 76% of men are in paid work. Australian figures are for 1998 and are from ABS Wage and Salary Earners in Australia, Cat. 6248.0. The UK and Swedish figures are 1998 EUROSTAT figures cited in Furst, 30. While many Swedish women with young children work part-time, about 40% work fulltime and a further 22-23% work between 20 and 34 hours per week. In the UK, the New Deal for Lone Parents program specifically targets single parents with children five years and over. It seeks to place them in supported employment and facilitate return to the workforce. It provides assistance with childcare, job seeking skills and training opportunities as appropriate. Details may be found at http://www.newdeal.gov.uk/.

78 There is little evidence that this potential has been achieved, perhaps because the government's commitment is not to equal parenting, but cosmetic changes aimed at quashing resentment over the child support scheme and at reinstating 'symbolic fatherhood' by eliminating the alleged proprietary connotations of terms such as custody and access.

79 Funder, Kathleen, 'Australian Family Law Reform Act 1995' (1998) 12 *International Journal of Law, Policy and the Family* 47, 49.

80 Potential child support liability for a child born of a casual relationship is one of the new 'horror stories' fuelling the anger of fathers' rights groups. The Mens' Rights Agency includes on its web site the reprint of an article from The *Australian* citing a 'rodeo rider' who has fled to Canada to avoid child support liability for a child born of a casual liaison. See McGregor, Richard, 'Fathers force PM to review child support', The *Australian*, 17 April 1998 accessed on http://www.mensrights.com.au/ on 25 December 1999.

81 With the exception of the introduction of the notion of parental responsibility and the replacement of custody and access with residence and contact, this is remarkably close

to the current Swedish settlement, although differing in that it is embedded in an adversarial framework. In practice, Swedish parents are expected to arrange physical custody and visitation amicably, with the assistance of the child welfare service where necessary. Inquiries into the fitness of one or both of the parents for continued parenting are highly unusual. They are also expected to share in the economic support of their children, both during marriage and following divorce. See Nozari, Fariborz, 'The 1987 Swedish Family Law Reform' (1989) 17 *International Journal of Legal Information* 219, 223; Glendon, above, 226. Glendon notes the primary responsibility for the financial support of children remains with their parents, both during marriage and following divorce and this applies equally to the mother and father.

82 Stoltz, 441-2.

83 Funder, 56. Equally predictably, support for shared care and contact was significantly lower where parents have never been married, while support for shared financial support more nearly approached the level for the other groups.

84 Funder, 60. In this context, it is noteworthy that Bertoia & Drakich, above, cite at 602 one fathers' rights group member for whom 1% of the child care responsibility could be defined as 'shared parenting'. Joint custody did not mean an equal division of child care, but the 'right to exercise the level of parenting that went on prior to the divorce'.

85 ABS, 'Australia Now: A Statistical Profile – Population, Marriage and Divorce in Australia – 1998' accessed at http://www.abs.gov.au/ on 13 December 1999. These figures make an interesting comparison with Sweden where about 80% of single parent households are female headed according to Furst, 38. Joint legal custody is the norm in Sweden (and equates to joint parental responsibility in Australia) and applies to more than 80% of divorced and separated families. Where this is the case, the legal system has no involvement in parenting arrangements or the payment of child support. Where joint custody is not possible, the legal system is involved only to the extent requested by the parents. In Australia, 88% of children live primarily with their mother following separation or divorce, 78% of them in lone parent families. About 12% of children live primarily with their father, 6% of them in lone parent families.

86 The decided cases suggest that the 'standard' contact arrangement involves alternate weekends, one overnight stay in the 'off week' for older children and shared school holidays.

87 See n 58 and the associated text.

88 See, for example, Mathias, Matthew, 'Towards a New and Equitable Beginning for Members of Broken Families' accessed at http://www.familyequity.asn.au/issues.html on 13 December 1999.

89 Dowd, 'Stigmatizing Single Parents', 67. Emphasis mine.

90 Mattias, above, identifies the preference given the 'primary carer' as evidence of gender bias and argues: 'That is, where two parents are essentially "equal" in their parenting capacities, future decisions should favour the father, in order to re-dress the previous bias towards the mother. This is no more than women asked of men in women's quest for "equal opportunity" in the workplace'.

91 Dowd, 'Stigmatizing Single Parents', 67.

92 Sometimes, because of the uneven pace of legal change, and inattention to the interaction of different bodies of law, those couples that are able to co-parent effectively following divorce are effectively penalised if they need or wish to rely upon benefits such as the parenting allowance. See Otlowski, Margaret, 'Shared (Week About) Parenting Arrangements Leads to Neither Parent Qualifying for Sole Parent Pension: Legislative Changes Effective 1 July 1999 May Produce a Different Outcome' (1999) 5 *Current Family Law* 93 for an interesting discussion of *Lowe v Sectretary,*

Department of Social Security (1998) 24 Fam LR 120. Drummond J held that neither parent was eligible for the parenting allowance as it was calculated by reference to a fortnightly rate, and neither parent was eligible during an entire fortnight. Also of note is the reference to *Secretary, Department of Social Security v Field* (1989) 25 FCR 425 which held that a child must be in the care of one parent for a continuous 14 day period before dependency arose under *Social Security Act* 1991 s 5(2). Drummond J dismissed this reasoning and gave the statutory phrase its natural meaning, holding that the child was 'in the care of each parent' to the exclusion of the other during each alternate week.

93 Collier, Richard, '"Waiting Till Father Gets Home": The Reconstruction of Fatherhood in Family Law' (1995) 4 *Social & Legal Studies* 5, 19-20.

94 The Family Court is routinely castigated as a 'patriarchal institution' by elements within the women's movement and accused of gender bias by fathers' rights groups. Chief Justice Alastair Nicholson has been the target of sustained attacks by fathers' rights groups.

95 In *In the Marriage of JJ and DC Sheridan* (1994) 18 FLR 415, the Full Court overturned a first instance decision based in part on the view of the trial judge that it was inappropriate for the father to rely upon parenting payments in order to serve as a full time parent. According to the Full Court: 'To the extent that the trial judge may have assumed that it is inappropriate for a father who is capable of obtaining full-time paid employment to engage instead in full-time child-care or that a father in full-time paid employment presents a better role-model to his children than one engaged in their full-time care we would disagree. Each case must be decided on its merits and it is inappropriate to impose a stereotypical norm of proper parental roles'. See also *McMillan and Jackson* (1995) FLR 183, 192-193, where the Full Court strongly disapproved of remarks by the trial judge and stated that 'a judge must leave outside the court any pre-conceived notions which he or she may entertain, as a private individual, about the roles which males and females ought to adopt in society'. The situation may have been otherwise during the 1980s. Hasche suggests that during the 1980s the Family Court frequently applied a double standard, working mothers being regarded somewhat unfavourably while working fathers were accepted as the norm. Hasche, Annette, 'Sex Discrimination in Child Custody Determinations' (1989) 3 *Australian Journal of Family Law* 218.

96 See Pannell and Pannell (1996) FLC 92-660, 82,828.

97 Boyd, 111. In a remarkable parallel to the fathers' rights movement self-characterisation as 'disposable parents' Boyd suggests mothers are seen as fungible. According to Hasche, the Australian pattern during the 1980s was remarkably similar. Both are in sharp contrast to the tendency in some US jurisdictions to explicitly recognise the 'capacity and disposition of the parties involved to provide the child with food, clothing, medical care ... and other material needs'. See Mich Comp Laws Ann § 722.23© (Supp. 1981-82). For a general discussion see Polikoff, Nancy D, 'Why are Mothers Losing: A Brief Analysis of Criteria Used in Child Custody Determinations' (1992) 14 *Women's Rights Law Reporter* 175.

98 See Schiratzki, Johanna, 'Custody of Children in Sweden: Recent Developments' in Wahlgren, Peter, ed, *Legal Issues of the Late 1990s*, Scandinavian Studies in Law Volume 38, Stockholm, Stockholm University Law Faculty, 1998, 255.

99 Schiratzki, 256.

100 Schiratzki, 258.

101 Schiratzki, 259.

102 Schiratzki, 256-7.

103 At the time it was introduced it was possible for a separated or divorced mother to receive the mother's allowance until her youngest child turned 25 (if in full time education) and then receive a Class B Widow's Pension.

104 Today's 40-year-old sole parent was born in 1960 and was likely to be thinking about leaving school when the *FLA* was enacted. Even those born a decade later were born 14 years prior to the enactment of EEO legislation. Programs encouraging girls and women to prepare for careers other than motherhood were in their infancy when they were in their mid-teens. Today, many of these women are mature age students in TAFE colleges and universities and are preparing for the opportunities their lack of formal training has denied them.

105 UN statistics suggest that women represented 43% of the workforce in 1995. Comparable figures for other industrialised countries are as follows: Canada, 45%; UK, 43%; USA, 45%; Japan, 41%; and Sweden, 48%. Among the European countries with the lowest female participation are: Greece, 37%; Italy, 38%; Ireland, 33%; and Spain, 36%. 'See Economic Activity by Sex, 1995' accessed at http://www.un.org/ on 9 September 2000.

106 During the same year 14.6% of female sole parents were unemployed, and 50.4% of female sole parents with dependent children were labour force participants; that is, either in employment or available to start work within four weeks. These figures suggest that a majority of female lone parents are either in the labour force or unemployed and seeking work.

Chapter 5

Structuring Dependence: Family, State and Self

Introduction

In the last chapter we looked at the debates swirling around the 'future of the family', and at some of the current flashpoints. As we did so, it became clear that many of these 'debates' were internally contradictory, media attention focusing on the one hand on 'women flooding the workforce' and 'stealing men's jobs' and on the other on 'spiralling' numbers of female sole parents and the fear of long term welfare dependence.[1] This chapter will explore the structure of the social welfare safety net and the ways in which that structure has embodied and continues to embody assumptions about family ordering and appropriate roles for men and women.

Unlike previous chapters, which have largely focused on the present, this chapter will, initially at least, have a historical focus. Because of the revolutionary impact of the industrial relations and family law reforms of the late sixties and early seventies, we will begin in the late sixties. The children of the late sixties and early seventies are now men and women in their late thirties and early forties and many of them are sole parents. The choices made then, about industrial relations, about family law, and about the social welfare safety net, shaped the environment in which they grew up and studied and made choices – choices with a profound impact upon the people they are today and the possibilities that are now open to them. They grew up with the knowledge that divorce was a realistic possibility, although, perhaps inevitably, it was often seen as something that happened to other people and not something to consider ex ante. A vocational understanding of wifehood and motherhood shaped women's education while the requirements of the breadwinner role shaped that of men. While academically talented women may have profited from the educational reforms of the eighties, for many women aspirations did not extend beyond working in a shop or factory until marriage and children intervened. While their male counterparts studied vocational subjects and were apprenticed to trades and crafts, their vocational training was bound by the ubiquitous and often compulsory classes in sewing and cooking, in preparation for future domestic roles.

The uneasy tension between the liberalised divorce regime embodied in the *FLA*, even with its 'lip service' to those who wanted only to continue their roles as wives and mothers, and social norms that presumed that motherhood was a lifelong and exclusive career received little sustained attention.[2] Even less attention was paid to the inter-relationship between fault based divorce rules and the breadwinner homemaker bargain. The legislation and case law elucidating fault defined the public terms of the sexual contract and the lengthy waiting periods and evidentiary requirements ensured that its terms were difficult to evade for a majority of Australians.

At this time and for at least a decade afterwards, Australian family policy unequivocally affirmed the male breadwinner family and the focus of the welfare state was upon supporting this role. While the state stepped in as a replacement breadwinner where the breadwinner was unable or unwilling to fill his ordained role, family policy was directed towards supporting relationships of dependence. It is important to recognise that these relationships of dependence cut both ways. As Stoltz notes, writing in the context of Danish law:

> The concept of dependency is a difficult one. According to Fraser and Gordon (1994) it includes assumptions about human nature, gender roles, the causes of poverty, the sources of entitlement, and what counts as work and as a contribution of society. It also alludes to a state of independence, which is seen as positive and often connected to employment and economic independence. An alternative interpretation of dependency is emphasised when discussing the fact that the vast majority of mothers rely on another person's income, either in the form of some type of child support or the income of a husband who, statistically, earns three times what the woman earns. Fathers are also dependent in the sense that they rely on the unpaid labour of women to raise children and care for the home (this is also true of divorced or separated fathers).[3]

Unmentioned by Stoltz, but, as we saw in the last chapter, emphasised by Dowd, is another form of dependence, the dependence of fathers on the women with whom they cohabit to mediate their relationship with their children or step-children.

These same understandings shaped the education system. The pervasive failure of the educational system to deliver marketable skills and vocational options for non-academic girls and to encourage the aspirations of the more talented was a natural consequence of these expectations.[4]

Despite the far reaching nature of the changes initiated by the Equal Pay cases of the late 1960s and early 1970s, at a policy level these were not seen as incompatible with the male breadwinner orientation of the overall policy framework although in retrospect they clearly were. When the principle of equal pay for equal work replaced that of a family wage, a central support underlying the normative assumption of motherhood as an exclusive career was undermined. In a wages system increasingly focusing upon job attributes rather than upon employee 'status',[5] the justification for maintaining the minimum wage at a level sufficient to support a family was undermined.[6] The stage had been set. As Deborah Mitchell notes:

> [T]he falling real wages of men and their rising unemployment throughout the 1980s was accompanied by a growing perception that the male breadwinner unit was no longer capable of delivering the standard of living that Australian families expect ... This further reinforced the pressure on government to provide social

services and other supports that allow women to enter the labour market. Where this was not possible, there was increased demand from the unions and the electorate for transfer policies to supplement wages of low-income (typically one-earner) families.[7]

The emerging social settlement was internally contradictory. Formal equality prevailed in the waged labour market, although given the levels of occupational segregation it was largely illusory and many areas of employment openly or tacitly excluded married women. The underlying model of the worker had not changed. Although the family wage had been legally abolished, this was not accompanied by any recognition that workers might have family responsibilities and could not rely upon the services of (unwaged) others for domestic support. Entitlements available elsewhere, for example, maternity leave,[8] were only beginning to appear, and were and are largely unpaid. Both society and welfare state presumed a male breadwinner,[9] and in case of divorce or separation, the state as surrogate breadwinner.[10] By the beginning of the 1980s three features dominated the Australian landscape. They were: the erosion of the living wage and emergence of the dual breadwinner family, the rapid growth in the number of sole parent households reliant upon Commonwealth benefits, and a waged labour market and social welfare regime which remained structured around the breadwinner homemaker bargain. The relationship between them and the obvious tensions provide a backdrop against which legal and policy changes continue to unfold.

Given the emerging mantra of international competitiveness and economic rationalism a new labour market was taking shape, one with an increasing division between the haves and the have nots and in which economic rationalism was increasing assuming hegemony over social understandings. As Mitchell notes:

> In other countries the supports provided to working women are generally regarded as part of labour market policy. In Australia, however, the legacy of the male breadwinner construction of social policy has pushed changes in these areas into the orbit of family policy ... [M]easures designed to reflect the changing role of women have been grafted onto older policy structures that supported the male breadwinner-dependent spouse role model, creating potential conflict between working women and those at home.[11]

Institutionally, the specific needs of employed women are thus positioned as competing with the needs of those who work within the home. For this reason, the resources needed to create the conditions necessary for women to have a meaningful as opposed to formal choice to participate in waged labour are seen as depriving those who work within the home of an equal share. The labour market changes needed to provide men and women with the support required for participation in both waged labour and in family life collapse into preferential treatment for a special interest group. They are seen as equal opportunity issues and thus peripheral to both labour market policy and family policy, ultimately submerged in the rhetoric rather than the reality of choice. Market institutions are reified as naturally rather than socially constructed and the product of competitive forces. The legal and policy interventions that shaped its parameters, the interest group battles that entrenched particular assumptions and structures vanish, only to be replaced by a 'natural' and efficient institution at risk from exogenous change.

Of Breadwinners and Homemakers: Constructing Legitimate Dependence

Unlike other social democracies Australia was a relatively tardy entrant into the provision of broadly based social welfare benefits at the Commonwealth level. While a maternity allowance was introduced in 1912[12] as a response to declining birth rates, child endowment was not introduced until 1941, and was available only for second and subsequent children.[13] From Federation, the Commonwealth had constitutional authority to provide pensions for the aged and those unable to work because of disability or illness.[14] Despite an apparent lack of constitutional authority, the Commonwealth introduced widows' pensions in 1942-43 and unemployment benefits in 1944.[15] The widows' pensions, so called, provided benefits not only to widows, but also to deserted and divorced wives and to women whose de facto husbands had died and who were unable to support themselves. Single mothers were excluded, as were women deserted by de facto partners and those whose de facto husbands were imprisoned.[16] The Class A widows' pension was available to widows who had the custody, care and control of one or more children aged 16 or under[17] while the Class B widows' pension provided support for those women, aged 45 or more, who were no longer eligible for a Class A pension because their youngest child was over 16. Childless widows over 50 were also eligible; the presumption being that it was unreasonable to expect them to enter the labour market. In this way, the hegemony of the nuclear family headed by a male breadwinner was affirmed. Howe and Swain suggest that:

> The Widows Pension ... was part of a clearly defined social security strategy, which had as its first priority a full employment policy in the post-war period for male breadwinners. The welfare system supplemented the family wage and provided a security net for those outside the workforce – unemployed men, invalids and women deprived of a male breadwinner.[18]

For those ineligible for the widows' pension, private charity or state support were the only options. The Commonwealth welfare structure was a patchwork quilt of separate statutes, primarily because of the uncertain constitutional position, and most of the safety net was provided by the states and by private charitable organisations.

In 1946, a constitutional amendment gave the Commonwealth power to legislate across the entire sweep of welfare provision.[19] Shortly thereafter, the Commonwealth consolidated its various social welfare programs into one primary statute, the *Social Services Act* 1947. Structurally, little had changed. The widows' pension continued to provide benefits to deserted wives,[20] divorcees, provided they had not remarried, and women whose husbands were in mental institutions or imprisoned for more than six months. Benefits were also available to women whose de facto husbands had died, but only if they had been living with them for three years or more in a 'marriage-like' relationship. There were, however, significant gaps. The widows' pension was not available to deserted wives until six months had passed, an extended waiting period being deemed necessary to establish that the desertion was 'unjustified', highlighting the synergies between the social welfare system and notions of marital fault. 'Deserting wives' were not eligible. Neither were deserted de facto wives and those with husbands in prison. While they might apply for charity or for state benefits, the tone of moral disapproval was clear and the benefits were variable and confusingly structured, often necessitating multiple applications.[21] Section 62(1) required a woman seeking a pension to establish that she was of 'good character'.[22] If she was not 'deserving of a pension' or had disposed of assets to render herself eligible, she would be denied a pension. The widows' pension was intended to replace the support of a male breadwinner where that support had been lost through no fault of the woman's. In this way, eligibility was firmly linked to status and character.

While the pension was relatively generous[23] and a widows' training scheme was introduced in 1968 to encourage younger widows to enter or re-enter the workforce,[24] for divorced and separated women the pressure to seek maintenance from a former spouse was substantial, posing problems where the relationship had been abusive. Unmarried mothers were eligible for unemployment benefits, and, in practice, the requirement that they seek employment was not enforced. They were also entitled to a 'special benefit' from 6 weeks prior to the birth of the child until 6 weeks after birth, officially excusing them from seeking employment during this period. After its expiry, they were no longer entitled to the special benefit. For those who chose not to place their babies for adoption the only options were to apply for the unemployment benefit and actively seek employment or to seek assistance from the state in which they lived or from private charities.

Two 'quasi-universal' benefits available to mothers and their children continued to escape any means test. Mothers, married or unmarried, were entitled (and had been since 1912) to a maternity allowance paid on the birth of a child. Here, the exclusions were racial rather than financial or moralistic. When the maternity benefit was introduced, indigenous women, Asian women and natives of the Pacific islands other than New Zealand were excluded, reflecting the 'White Australia' policy of the era. As a consequence of international and Commonwealth pressure, the reference to Asians was deleted in 1926 and replaced by a provision excluding 'aliens'. The exclusion of indigenous and islander women remained in place until 1947, when the consolidated act provided that the maternity allowance could be granted to indigenous women at the discretion of the Secretary. The maternity allowance was abandoned in 1978.

Child endowment[25] was also available 'universally' and was not means tested. Initially it was quite generous, being set at close to 30 per cent of the minimum wage however its relative value declined over the years. In 1987 the Family Allowance Supplement replaced child endowment. It was subject to an income test, thus removing the remaining universal benefit payable to women.[26] An assets test followed in the early 1990s, reflecting changing social attitudes and the increasing desire to focus on those most in need. A program that began as recognition of the value of carework became a form of income support for low-income families, although payment continued to be directly to the mother. The shift in emphasis was significant, both because of the change from entitlement to benefit and because, in practice, the combination of an assets test and an income test acts as a disincentive to part-time employment for many women, reducing the likelihood that they will remain even marginally attached to the workforce.

Prior to the Equal Wage Cases of the late 1960s, the structure of the social welfare system, like that of the taxation system and the industrial relations system was based upon institutionalised dependence, although there were interesting partial exceptions, such as the maternity allowance and child endowment.[27] 'Legitimate dependence' received relatively generous support, both through the social welfare system and the taxation system; 'illegitimate' dependence was managed intrusively. The distinction between a 'benefit' and a 'pension' was critical. The former was a form of charity, a gesture of largess on the part of the community and typically, although not invariably, carried an obligation to seek employment. The latter, in the eyes both of the community and the recipient was seen as an entitlement. Pensioners were not expected to seek employment. The policy framework supported the male breadwinner family and full male employment, both by providing for their dependants in the event of serious accident or premature death and by guaranteeing income support following retirement.

In 1973, the introduction of the Supporting Mother's Benefit[28] marked a major policy change. While it was styled a benefit rather than a pension, there was no obligation to seek employment. In many respects, it was a halfway house between a benefit and a pension. While the terminology made it clear that it was not to be seen as an entitlement, but as minimum level of support for those in an unfortunate position, the absence of any obligation to seek employment sent different signals. In ordinary parlance, it and its successor, the sole parent's benefit, were typically referred to as pensions. The stated intention was to provide support to unmarried mothers who chose to keep their babies rather than place them for adoption. It

> [was] available to any single parent who has sole support of a child or children. It [was] usually sought only by those single parents for whom a Widow's Pension [was] not an option, that is by those who [were] not widows, divorcees or deserted wives... However, as a great deal of personal background may have to be aired to prove the fact of desertion, some women actually [chose] to apply for [Supporting Mother's Benefits] rather than the Widows' Pension.[29]

The Supporting Mother's Benefit cast a wide net, being available to all women with the sole support of one or more children under 16. Those who were entitled to the Widow's Pension could apply either for the Supporting Mothers' Benefit or the Widows' Pension. While the six-month waiting period remained in place,[30] the Supporting Mother's Benefit represented a significant weakening of the 'deserving poor' theme that had traditionally pervaded the benefit structure. The presumption of dependence remained and eligibility ended if the woman repartnered, thus reinforcing the normative position that state support was a replacement for the absent male breadwinner rather than an independent form of support for carework.[31] Cohabitation carried with it a presumption of social fatherhood, and a cohabiting male was deemed a replacement breadwinner.[32] No support was available to male sole parents. They were expected to apply for unemployment benefits and to actively seek employment, reinforcing the normative status of the breadwinner role and reflecting prevailing social mores.

When the *FLA* was introduced two years later, the Supporting Mothers' Benefit and s 75 of the *FLA* collectively provided female sole parents with the legal framework needed to pursue a 'distinctive female life cycle characterised by wifehood and motherhood' following separation or divorce. While the Supporting Mothers' Benefit, as originally conceived, was primarily intended to provide support for young single mothers, in the period between its introduction in the 70s and its absorption into the Parenting Allowance in the mid-90s, both the age profile of recipients and their status changed significantly. By June 1997, teenaged unmarried mothers represented only about three per cent of beneficiaries, reflecting enhanced access to birth control and abortion and increasing educational opportunities.[33] The most numerous group is aged between 30 and 39, closely followed by those aged 20 and 29. Most of these women became sole parents following the end of a marital or de facto relationship.[34] They typically have relatively poor educational levels and limited vocational skills in comparison to partnered parents, both male and female.[35] Many of them completed their education before the emphasis in the late 80s and early 90s on education and career preparation for young women. The presence of NESB women further depresses educational levels.[36] The combination of minimal education and non-English speaking background distinguishes female sole parents from wives in couple families, and may be a partial explanation of the somewhat lower employment levels among this group than among their married counterparts.

In 1977, the Supporting Mother's Benefit was replaced by the Supporting Parent's Benefit, extending eligibility to lone fathers, in belated recognition of the formal equality of the *FLA* and confronting the reality of rising unemployment levels and an accelerating divorce rate.[37] In parliamentary debate, Dr Klugman, speaking for the ALP opposition, noted that:

> Inasmuch as many lone fathers at the present time may be working because they have no alternative, this benefit will make it possible for them to give up work, in some cases at least, and to look after their children.[38]

The extension of the Supporting Mothers' Benefit to fathers, like the extension of the 'sickness benefit' to married women temporarily incapacitated for work, reflected increasing political sensitivity to obvious formal inequalities and to the increasing workforce participation of women. At the same time, however, an early sign of change in the policy environment emerged. Whereas the eligibility rules for the 'sickness benefit' had not previously been means tested on the wife's income as well as the husband's, the new benefit was fully means tested. Irrespective of whether the applicant was a man or a woman, a partners' income would henceforth be taken into account in determining eligibility.

As with the unemployment benefit, another normative assumption, equal sharing within the family unit, underpins the benefit structure. Even where the benefit rate included support for a partner and one or more children, the entire benefit was payable to the unemployed person and only one member of a couple was officially recognised as unemployed,[39] a factor which was critical in accessing training and other programs facilitating workforce entry.[40] Despite an Australian tradition of specific benefits payable to the mother, recognising that sharing within the family was not necessarily egalitarian; the pull of the normative nuclear family remained strong, as did the presumption of dependence.

The residual split between the Supporting Parents' Benefit and the Class A Widow's Pension was eliminated when the two programs were amalgamated into the Sole Parents' Pension in 1989, effectively ratifying what had long been the popular perception. As concern mounted about increasing long-term welfare dependency, particularly among sole parents, and recognition emerged that a substantial proportion of sole parents lived in poverty, this period also marked the introduction of the Child Support Scheme, intended to ensure that absent genetic and legal fathers provided support for their children. Parallel amendments to the *FLA* removed judicial discretion as to the quantum of child support payable, thus ending the judicial practice of considering the availability of the Supporting Parents' Benefit in determining the child support payable. These programs, while significant, were hardly revolutionary. Similar changes were occurring in many US jurisdictions[41] as well as in Great Britain and Canada as concern continued to mount over increasing levels of welfare dependence among sole parents and over the failure of many contact fathers to pay court-ordered child support.

Of potentially greater significance was the launch of the Jobs, Education and Training (JET) program to assist sole parents to re-enter the waged labour force. Significantly, given the pull of the normative nuclear family, Jan Gardiner suggests that:

> In line with the dominant discourse of maternal responsibility, ie: maternal primary care as normative throughout the child's formative years, the state's broad goal was entry into part-time employment.[42]

A little later she notes tellingly that:

> The state constructs parenting as the mother's primary (your most important) job and then decides it would be good for her to earn some extra income through paid employment. The mother is thereby positioned as wanting to remain primarily dependent on her surrogate provider, the state, and can regard her earnings from part time work as 'pin money', in much the same way she would, in earlier times, have regarded a personal allowance from a middle class husband – as distinct from allotted housekeeping money.[43]

If one measures the success of a program through a reduction in rates of welfare dependence, the evidence suggests that the impact of JET is modest.[44] Workforce participation rates[45] for both male and female sole parents remain below those in couple families, although whether this is a function of status or of educational level and vocational qualifications is not clear. Carberry et al cite statistics suggesting that in 1996 57.9 per cent of male sole parents and 22.5 per cent of female sole parents were employed full time, 9.5 per cent and 21.5 per cent respectively were employed part time, and 21.6 per cent of male sole parents and 47.4 per cent of female sole parents were not in the labour force. In couple families with dependent children the percentage of women employed full time was marginally higher at 26.5 per cent and the part time employment rate significantly higher at 34.3 per cent.[46] More recent Australian data suggests that the total participation rate for husbands is 75.8 per cent and for male lone parents 61.2 per cent, while the total participation rate for wives is 55.5 per cent and for female lone parents 50.2 per cent. While not broken down into full time and part-time participation, these figures suggest that participation rates for female sole parents are approaching those of partnered women, while the gap remains substantial between husbands and male sole parents. Where one compares the participation rates of those with dependents the divergences are much more marked. For husbands with dependents, the total participation rate is 92.8 per cent while that for male lone parents is 72.6 per cent. The differences in unemployment rates are equally striking. For husbands, the unemployment rate is four per cent, while for male lone parents the unemployment rate is 10.6 per cent. For wives with dependents, the total participation rate is 62.9 per cent, while that for female lone parents is 55.7 per cent.[47] As with men, the difference in unemployment rates is significant, the unemployment rate for wives being 4.2 per cent, and for female sole parents 14.6 per cent, although this may not be entirely accurate. Given the rate of hidden unemployment among women it may well be that a significant number of wives fall into the category of discouraged job seekers and do not appear as unemployed in the relevant statistics. These figures suggest that the gap between the participation rates of husbands with dependents and male sole parents is substantially greater than the gap between female sole parents and wives with dependents. The rate at which female sole parents participate in the waged labour force remains similar to the participation rates of mothers as a whole. The participation rate of male sole parents, while higher in absolute terms, is gradually becoming less similar to that of fathers as a whole.

These statistics suggest that many female sole parents with qualifications that enable them to earn a reasonable living do maintain labour force participation. Many of them may have been employed prior to the breakdown of their relationships. Those whose attachment to the labour force is more marginal, or who have chosen part-time employment in order to spend more time with their children may be less likely to continue in their employment following relationship breakdown. In many cases, this may be because the financial rewards are insufficient to make part-time employment worthwhile after work expenses such as transportation and clothing and the cost of childcare are taken into account. For those in casual work and other marginal forms of employment, these expenses and the lack of family friendly practices in workplaces represent a substantial barrier. Undeniably, it is significant that:

Part time employment for both wives and lone parents peaks with those whose youngest child is aged 5-9, at 39.6% for wives and 28.6% for lone parents. However, the rate of part time employment for wives is more than double that for lone parents for those with a youngest child aged 0-4 and between one and a quarter and one and a half times the rate for other age groups.[48]

Carberry et al suggest that both male and female sole parents perpetuate the gender roles that characterised past relationships.[49] They note that while the labour force participation of the husband in couple families appears not to be affected by parenthood, the participation of male sole parents is affected, although to a lesser extent than that of their female counterparts.[50] They conclude that the reduced labour force participation by both male and female sole parents with older children is more likely to be a consequence of the impact of lack of recent full time experience and a history of intermittent work patterns than of parenting responsibilities. In a market environment in which employability and career progression increasingly depend upon employment history and evidence of commitment, those with interrupted employment histories are unlikely to be competitive, particularly where they are relatively poorly skilled.

Here, of course, another facet of the breadwinner homemaker bargain is critical. While women have long been part of a secondary labour market emphasising casual and part-time employment with limited career tracks,[51] men have characteristically been positioned in the full time waged labour market. The expectations of these two market segments are very different. In the full time waged labour market, given continuing levels of sex segregation, a broken employment record continues to signal unreliability and a lack of commitment and career goals. Even in Sweden, with a 30-year history of commitment to equal participation in parenting and employment, men outside the public sector have been relatively slow to take the parental leave available and have often cited as their reason the fear of damage to their career prospects.[52] This fear is justified. In Australia, where such a commitment is almost non-existent, it is likely that men who absent themselves from the workforce to participate in carework for an extended period would find it very difficult to secure full-time employment when they sought to return.[53] Ageism further complicates the picture and makes it more difficult for both men and women to pursue changing career paths at different stages in their life cycle. Female sole parents who seek to re-enter the full time workforce as their children become older or their benefits run out encounter the same problem.

Despite the general egalitarian consensus in Sweden, recent evidence suggests that parenthood damages the career prospects of women working in the private sector and that sole parents are particularly disadvantaged.[54] As the economic downturn of the 90s took hold, employer demands for increased management driven flexibility led to the resurgence of the unencumbered worker as the ideal employee. As a consequence, women, in particular, female sole parents, were increasingly perceived as liabilities while men consolidated their position as responsible, desirable employees. These problems are exacerbated because the somewhat inflexible nature of the leave arrangements makes it impossible for parents to time-share periods of leave. More flexible arrangements might, for example, permit mothers to remain at home full-time for the first two or three months and share the remaining leave with their partners on a fractional basis with each partner working half-time and utilising leave entitlements for the remaining half-time. This kind of flexibility would overcome the perceived problem with the current arrangements, in which the mother typically takes the first four to six months after birth as parental leave with the father claiming the 'daddy month' and the mother returning to work. If the mother wishes to take further leave, claiming the 'daddy month' means that the mother will have two discontinuous career breaks, leading to negative career effects.[55] The Swedish evidence emphasises the critical point, that an interrupted career path, at least for women, is equated to a less desirable employee. While some of these effects were also apparent for men, an unexpected consequence appeared in the case of those men who took significant amounts of parental leave (20 per cent or more of the available leave). Hass notes:

> When the men who had taken at least 20% of the couple's leave were examined separately, even greater decreases in fathers' work commitment, preference for full time work, and income earning were found. Of the nine couples interviewed, in every case but one the father had changed significantly his orientation to employment; four worked part time; three took advantage of considerable job flexibility as teacher, administrator, or professor to leave work earlier and bring work home to do, and one worked a compressed work week of four days so he could be home for child care on Fridays.[56]

The significance of the Swedish study should not be underestimated. While, undeniably, these men were predisposed towards participating actively in parenting, given that they utilised leave entitlements at a rate more than double the Swedish norm, their commitment to the value of active parenting increased as a consequence of their experience, suggesting that positive incentives can and do produce lasting social effects.

Changes in the 90s: Parenting as Life Cycle Stage

In the mid-90s, following a review of the payment and benefit structures providing income support to Australians unable to support themselves, the structure and nomenclature of the benefit regimes were simplified and reorganised. Benefits became 'allowances', a majority of which were activity tested, although some categories were exempt from an activity test. The Job Start and New Start Allowances replaced the Unemployment Benefit, which had been payable at either a single or married rate. More significantly for present purposes, the married rate was abolished. In couple households with no children under 16, a 'partner allowance' was available only if the partner was 40 or older and had no recent workforce experience. It was not subject to an activity test. A partner under the age of 40 was simply another unemployed adult eligible for either the Job Start or New Start Allowance and subject to the same activity tests.

For low-income families with children, the Parenting Allowance partially filled the lacuna left by the termination of Child Endowment. It was not subject to an activity test and was available to a member of a couple who had primary care of one or more children under 16 and had low personal income. The Parenting Allowance was split into two programs. The Basic Parenting Allowance was payable free of an assets test and income tested only on the income of the primary carer. It was also non-taxable. The Additional Parenting Allowance replaced the combined married couple rate previously paid to an unemployed 'primary breadwinner', and provided full income support for unemployed and low income people with low income partners.

These changes marked a decisive break with the past. First, they made it clear that Australia no longer fit seamlessly within the strong male breadwinner category. Increasingly, at least in the social welfare area, a weak male breadwinner regime was beginning to emerge. Parental responsibility, not marital status, earned exemption from the activity test, the only exception being for partners who were over 40 in 1995 and who had no record of recent workforce activity.[57] Both spouses were to be treated as potential wage earners, and both were eligible for retraining and programs and job search allowances. Given the cut-off point of the Parenting Allowance, the phasing out of the Widow's Pension B, and the introduction of the JET program some years earlier, it was clear that the mood was changing. All families were potentially dual-breadwinner families, and the space for non-activity tested programs based on status was shrinking rapidly.[58]

Something else became clear as well, perhaps because increased attention was being paid to the demographic profile of individuals in receipt of benefits. Additional Parenting Allowance recipients were distinctively different from the broad group of partnered parents and from sole parents on several key demographic indicators. They were much less likely than sole parents to be employed, a significant difference given that the employment rates for female sole parents remain somewhat below those of married women with children. They were likely to have more children than sole parents; indeed, their fertility rate appeared to be slightly higher than that for women as a whole. In educational attainment, however, they were more like sole parents than like women in the overall married couple population, although they tended to be marginally better educated than sole parents. As a group, they were poorly educated, were largely content with traditional gender roles, and had larger families than the contemporary norm. Carberry et al suggest that:

> The facts tend to suggest that both sole parent pensioners and Additional PgA recipients are drawn from people with similar backgrounds, the main thing setting them apart being the presence or absence of a partner. Additional PgA recipients are almost certainly different from the broad sweep of partnered parents. This is not surprising, since many of them are partnered with people who are unemployed or employed in low paying jobs.[59]

During the late 90s further changes to the benefits regime saw the sole parents' pension merge with the Parenting Allowance, forming the Parenting Payment

(PP).[60] Despite the amalgamation of the programs, pension conditions for sole parents, including rates, the structure of the income test and concessions were retained. In another significant change, access to the JET program was extended to married parents, reinforcing the trend begun with the elimination of the 'married rate' of the unemployment benefit. While JET is not compulsory, its extension to married parents marks the first time that the partners of unemployed and low-income men have been encouraged to seek employment outside the home as their children grow older. Couples have been disaggregated into individuals, and are treated as such. Current trends suggest that some element of compulsion will be introduced, perhaps when the age limit is reduced from 16 to 12 in line with current government thinking. The current government rhetoric of 'mutual obligation' and the enthusiasm for work for the dole schemes clearly signals a gradual reduction in entitlements and a conditional approach to allowances.

Fiddling at the Edges: Old Reforms for a New Millennium

In the latest 'reforms', the distinction between family support payments through the social welfare system and rebates through the taxation system has all but vanished; reminding us that both taxation and welfare are parallel mechanisms for resource allocation. The new legislative framework, the *A New Tax System (Family Assistance) Act* 1999, has been harmonised with the *Social Security Act* 1991. The Family Tax Benefit Part A replaces the previous family allowance, the previous Family Tax Payment Part A and Family Tax Assistance Part A. Those eligible can claim their entitlements either through the social welfare system as a fortnightly or lump sum payment through Centrelink (the social welfare agency) or through the taxation system as an end of year lump sum payment or a reduction in their or their partner's withholding. Perhaps the most interesting aspect of the change in institutional arrangements is the alternative mechanism for claiming. The symbolic significance is substantial; the provisions are positioned as taxation relief measures and not welfare benefits, tacitly acknowledging the increasing stigmatisation of those in receipt of public assistance and reinforcing the desirability of paid work. Unremarkably, some of those claiming either a reduced withholding through the taxation system or a fortnightly payment through Centrelink have found the new arrangements a double-edged sword. In those families where fortnightly income is not predictable, either because of overtime or because of the variable income of a part-time wage earner, a significant number have been required to repay substantial sums with their tax returns because of increases in their income during the year.[61]

The overlap between social welfare payments and taxation rebates is clearer still in the case of the Family Tax Benefit Part B which replaces the basic parenting payment, the guardian allowance, the Family Tax Payment Part B, the dependent spouse rebate (with children) and the sole parent rebate. Like its immediate predecessor, the Family Tax Benefit Part B is designed to bolster the disposable income of families with one main wage earner, in that way compensating for the erosion of the family wage and sustaining the partial viability of the breadwinner homemaker bargain. While the benefit extends to sole parents, because it would be unacceptable for the Commonwealth to discriminate on the basis of marital status, its symbolic significance lies in the support it provides for the iconic family and thus for the incorporated male family self. As we saw in the last section, those partnered women who previously received the Additional Parenting Payment differed sharply from the majority of partnered women, holding largely to traditional gender roles, having limited education and lacking marketable skills and having larger families than the contemporary average. The Family Tax Benefit Part B targets families just above this threshold, in many cases families in which the alternative would undoubtedly be part or full time employment for a partner who may wish to retain a traditional role. It seems likely that the poorest of these families will be among those who cycle on and off unemployment benefits and thus will have a similar demographic profile to women who previously received the Additional Parenting Payment. The current Commonwealth government, in the lead up to the 2001 federal election has signalled further symbolic changes, most notably a 'baby bonus' of up to $2500 over a five year period for women bearing their first child who elect to remain at home or return to work only on a very limited basis. Like the Family Tax Benefit Part B, these provisions, cosmetically disguised as taxation rebates rather than social welfare payments represent a significant extension of a sustained attempt to replace the family wage with a social wage and thus to strengthen the breadwinner homemaker bargain, leaving the government as a 'replacement breadwinner' in the case of sole parents.

Women, Work and Families: Choices and Options

In the long term, given the desire on both sides of politics to reduce welfare dependence, particularly among the growing group of sole parents, it is not clear that the combination of taxation relief and assistance with labour market re-entry will have the desired effect. Research overseas suggests the critical factor in labour market re-entry appears to be the strength of labour market attachment prior to the birth of the first child and the supports available to sustain that attachment following childbirth. The kind of labour market attachment necessary is also linked to post-secondary educational qualifications and the development of a career track prior to parenthood.

European research comparing two cohorts of women found:

> That for those born in 1946, the time by which half the mothers had entered employment after their first child was 5.5 years, compared with 2.2 years for those born in 1958: the median gap was reduced twofold. In the 1958 cohort, mothers who returned to work earliest after their first child were those who were highly educated, those who were cohabiting, and those who delayed childbearing. Those who spent most time out of employment were those who had started, and mostly finished, childbearing earlier, who were living without a partner, and who had no educational qualifications.[62]

Many of the same trends are apparent in Australia.[63] In light of the conclusions reached by Dex and Joshi on examination of the UK data, a profile of mothers likely to have 'continuous' employment histories emerges.

> They have more education and more accumulated labour market experience from having delayed childbearing. Being in paid work continuously (including maternity leave) over the birth of the first child increased subsequent participation rates of mothers after controlling for other influences. For a standard mother with one young child under three, the total effect of taking maternity leave was to increase the probability of employment by around 25 percentage points. Further analysis revealed that maintaining employment continuity was more dependent on education, wages and the ability to take maternity-leave breaks than on age at the birth of the first child. These studies implied a polarisation in the women's labour force: a divergence between highly educated mothers with high wages and those with the least education and low wages.[64]

The research cited above suggests the importance of educational policy, and of an emphasis on both academic and vocational education for girls and young women. It also suggests, perhaps even more fundamentally, that those women who have established themselves in the labour market, at least where paid parenting leave is available for a reasonable period before and after childbirth, are more likely to sustain labour market participation than poorly educated women in marginal employment. Should their relationships subsequently fail, they will be in a relatively advantaged position. Given the Australian statistics cited earlier concerning the comparative educational disadvantage of sole parents, the findings from this research are clearly applicable to Australia. It would appear that women with limited education and weak labour market skills are both over represented among sole parents and more likely to experience prolonged periods on benefits. Because, broadly speaking, members of couples tend to come from similar backgrounds; it seems likely that many sole parents would have lived in financially marginal circumstances prior to relationship breakdown. Undoubtedly, this reduces the incentive to become or remain economically active since the perceived costs of economic activity may outweigh the gains.

Another factor, of greater significance when the majority of today's sole parents were young but still very significant, is the relatively low level of workforce participation by women of all ages in Australia. In 1996, approximately 47.4 per cent of women between 15 and 19 were economically active. The rate rose to about 69 per cent for those between 20 and 24, before declining to 62.9 per cent for those between 25 and 34. While it rose again to 67.5 per cent for those between 35 and 44 it declined quite rapidly thereafter, with only 40 per cent of those between 55 and 59 economically active and only 18.4 per cent of those between 60 and 65 economically active. By contrast in Sweden, only about 40 per cent of those in the lowest age bracket are economically active. By age 20 the Swedish participation rate rises to 90 per cent before peaking at about 98 per cent for those aged between 25 and 29. The decline thereafter is extremely gradual, with more than 80 per cent remaining economically active until age 59. For the oldest group, the decline was quite rapid, falling to about 40 per cent for those aged 65.[65]

Comparable statistics for the US and Canada suggest that 45 per cent of women between 15 and 19 are economically active. Thereafter the rate rises to about 72 per cent of 20-24 year olds and 78 per cent of 25-34 year olds and remains more or less steady until beginning to decline quite sharply for 55-59 year olds (60 per cent) and falling to about 40 per cent for those 60-64. Viewed against international comparators, several features are striking. First, the economically active proportion of the youngest group is very high in comparison to Sweden and somewhat higher than in the US and Canada. This suggests that Australian school retention rates may still be somewhat lower than those in the chosen comparators.[66] Second, the economically active proportion of 20-24 year olds in Australia is significantly lower than in Sweden and also lower than in the US and Canada.

The pattern of economic activity these figures reveal suggests that many young Australian women do not develop any real attachment to the workforce before beginning their families. This failure has a number of significant consequences. First, given current divorce rates, a significant proportion of female[67] sole parents are likely to be without substantial workforce experience and attachment in the future. Second, Australian workforce practices continue to discourage labour market attachment among young women. Paid maternity leave remains uncommon;[68] women are not covered by a national maternity leave insurance scheme as in Sweden (and the UK); and it is still relatively uncommon for permanent career track positions to be available on a fractional basis or time-share basis. While there are some signs of changing practices, they are largely confined to the public sector and to large enterprises.[69] Even where paid maternity leave is available, return on a part time basis is often deemed inappropriate, particularly for those in supervisory positions, although recent Equal Opportunity Tribunal decisions challenge this.[70]

Australian social policy seems schizophrenic. During the 1990s, means tested benefits for parents responsible for the care of children have become increasingly similar for partnered and sole parents. At the same time, efforts are being made to encourage sole parents to enter or re-enter waged labour; at least after their children reach school age. Only very recently has any similar pressure been extended to partnered parents receiving the parenting payment. In August 1999, the Commonwealth government announced a pilot project requiring five groups of Parenting Payment recipients to attend job-counselling seminars. Targeted groups include sole parents on benefits for more than five years, recently separated persons and those who have recently left paid employment, persons without earned income whose children are aged 12-16, and couples where neither partner has been in work for an extended period.[71] Maureen Baker argues, in the context of partnered parents, that:

> [P]olicies that pay mothers to stay at home and care for their children for extended periods of time (more than several years) serve to reinforce patriarchal relations. After several years at home, a woman's role as care provider and homemaker tends to be confirmed within her family. At the same time, her job skills, employment experience, and earning capacity are eroded.[72]

Given the similarity between the educational characteristics of partnered parents receiving the Parenting Payment and sole parents receiving the Parenting Payment, it seems clear that the Parenting Payment is likely to encourage partnered parents in low-income households to maintain their roles as homemakers and care providers. Sole parents, on the other hand, are increasingly encouraged to become at least partially self-sufficient. Although partnered parents are officially no longer simply dependents of a male breadwinner, but persons temporarily engaged in carework, the acute public concern about the increasing welfare dependence of sole parents does not extend to partnered parents despite evidence suggesting a significant minority of individuals move back and forth between partnered and unpartnered status, cycling on and off benefits.

Clearly, the policy agenda is ambivalent. Within the traditional family, the breadwinner homemaker bargain is reinforced, although lip service is paid to a dual breadwinner family where there are no young children. Also reinforced is a division of labour in which men are primarily responsible for wage work and women for care work, despite the fact that women are no longer officially classified as 'dependents'. Sole parents are different. While low-income two parent households exemplify the tradition of the Aussie battler, the dependence of female sole parents is portrayed as pernicious and as undermining the social fabric. In theory, however, it should be easier rather than harder for a partnered parent to move into waged labour, either on a part-time or full-time basis, given that there are two adults to share domestic responsibilities. Nonetheless, this has not been a policy priority in the same way as is reducing the welfare dependence of sole parents, not least because of the pull of the 'traditional family' in family policy and the desire on the part of policy makers to uphold traditional role allocation and values.

The ambivalent policy agenda is all the more striking because some American research suggests that:

> One of the ironies of the class configuration of work-family patterns is that blue-collar men do more child care than higher-income men (Cohen 1998). Split care is an economic strategy that works above poverty-level income, but drops off at higher income levels. This bespeaks the powerful impact of the provider role, masculine norms, and the role of economic policy in redefining fatherhood.[73]

It may be that one effect of these policies will be to discourage the development of role sharing in working class families, a profoundly ironic consequence in light of the sustained attempt by government to emphasise the importance of fatherhood and to encourage men to become social as well as economic parents.

It is unrealistic to assume that roles are infinitely fluid, enabling individuals shift between wage work and care work in a relatively seamless fashion. Even in a relatively egalitarian society such as Sweden, research has shown that during an extended period on parental leave the pre-existing egalitarian division of household labour shifts significantly towards a more traditional style, this being perceived as 'fair' during the leave period. Once this pattern has become entrenched it becomes difficult to shift it back towards a more egalitarian division. Some Swedish research has suggested that dissatisfaction with the division of household labour is given as a major factor in relationship breakdown, women finding that their partners are unwilling to resume an equal share when they return to waged labour following parental leave. In Australia, where an egalitarian division of household labour has been slow to emerge, and where women remain eligible for income support until their youngest child is 16,[74] it is unlikely that partnered low income parents will move into waged work in significantly greater numbers than at present. Those who have been exclusively homemakers and care providers for an extended period are likely to have developed no labour market attachment before beginning their families. Their primary identification is as homemakers, not as workers, and this role identification is expected by their partners. Without marketable skills or recent labour market experience, they are only marginally employable, at least without extensive retraining, at a wage that could compensate for their household work. When women with this profile become sole parents, it is unreasonable to expect them to abandon a role that has offered them some rewards in favour of marginal paid employment. Against this background, the mooted changes to eligibility rules for the Parenting Payment are clearly punitive. If there is any actual rather than rhetorical expectation that they will move into the workforce, making benefits available until the youngest child is 16 is self-defeating. European evidence suggests, however, that reducing the age to 12 is not any more likely to encourage women to adopt dual roles. A woman with two children is likely to have been out of the workforce for at least 14 years before her youngest child turns 12, and in many cases she will only have had a few years experience prior to the birth of her first child.[75] In some European countries, for example Sweden, the age of three is the limit, and Swedish mothers, partnered and single, typically return to work well before their youngest child is three.

Social support systems for women seeking to combine parenting and wage work remain minimal. Childcare is frequently difficult to access and expensive, particularly for low-income parents. The absence of paid maternity leave and paid leave to care for sick children minimises the likelihood that many women will develop strong workforce ties, depressing the participation rate for women and perpetuating traditional gender roles. As pressure mounts to increase the participation rate of sole parents, it is often forgotten that this is unlikely to occur unless the participation rate for all women increases. Given that the Australian participation rate is modest compared to some other jurisdictions, it should not be surprising that the participation rate for female sole parents is also modest, particularly since the gap between the participation rate of sole parents and that of partnered parents is not unusually large.

Concluding Thoughts

Ambivalent social policy, a lack of infra-structural supports for working parents, and a history of relatively depressed female participation in the workforce collectively play a significant role in sustaining the earnings gender gap and maintaining high levels of occupational segregation. Against this background, the current strategies aimed at reducing the welfare dependence of sole parents seem curiously inappropriate. The gap between the workforce participation rate of female sole parents with dependents and that of partnered women with dependents is currently about seven per cent, only two per cent greater than the gap between the participation of sole parents and partnered women without dependents. The figures suggest that female sole parents, unlike male sole parents, are almost as economically active as are their partnered sisters. If, as has been suggested, the government desires to maximise the participation of lone parents, even if only on a part-time basis, workplace supports for all parents are critical. If the pattern in Australia follows that in much of Europe, the essential supports include paid parental leave and maternity leave, family friendly hours, and a workplace culture that allows parents to reconcile domestic responsibilities and parenting, a truly family friendly workplace, not merely a 'flexible workplace'.

The alternative is to travel further down the route taken by the United States. In the USA, as in Australia, paid maternity leave does not exist for the majority of working women.[76] Historically, working women have used available holiday and sick leave during the period following birth to avoid damaging career prospects and to ensure that their position is available when they return. Because of the stigma associated with the welfare program, many low-income women with young children work at two or three jobs to provide an adequate income. The social welfare system is punitive and increasingly tied to workfare programs, even for parents with very young children. No income support is available to low-income intact families with children. In this context it is significant that Esping-Anderson classifies the welfare system in Australia as 'liberal'. According to Vogel:

> Esping-Anderson identified three distinctive welfare state regimes, representing different ways of "decommodification" of labour in a capitalist economy, empirically measured by the replacement rates and contribution periods of benefits, and the financial arrangements. The *Liberal Welfare State Regime* is market oriented in the distribution of resources and social protection benefits. Public provisions are typically modest, flat-rate, and needs/means tested, producing a residual and stigmatised group of beneficiaries. The state encourages market solutions by private welfare schemes. The decommodification effect is limited, and the distribution of living conditions is closely related to the stratification created by market forces. USA is the archetype in this category, as well as Canada and Australia. In Europe the UK is moving in this direction.[77]

Vogel compares the liberal regime with the conservative, characterised by status-preserving intervention aimed at supporting family and motherhood, and the social democratic, with high levels of transfer payments and high standards of material living conditions. Catholic conservative countries such France and Italy exemplify the former, while the Scandinavian countries exemplify the latter. Each is characterised by its own politics, the liberal regime failing to address class conflict, while the conservative creates an underclass of outsiders not covered by social protection including the new surplus population of the unemployed. While the social democratic avoids both of these patterns, Vogel suggests that the politics is one of gender, in which 'equality by redistribution becomes a foremost female interest, moving the gender cleavage into the political arena'.[78]

Despite the absence of the supports commonplace in European social democracies, in 1997 in the US 68.3 per cent of married mothers and 65.9 per cent of single mothers were employed in families with children aged between birth and 18. Only in households with children younger than six does the rate drop significantly. In such households, 61 per cent of married mothers are employed and only 55.2 per cent of single mothers, closely approximating the overall Australian participation rates. The comparable figures for men are 96.5 per cent of married fathers and 84.7 per cent of single fathers in families with children between birth and 18 years and 96.6 per cent of married fathers with children under six and 82.2 per cent of single fathers.[79] One similarity does emerge. The gap between the participation rate of married mothers with pre-school children and that of single mothers with pre school children is relatively small in both jurisdictions, on the order of 5.8 per cent. The gap between the participation rates of married fathers with pre-school children and single fathers is much greater, 14.2 per cent in the US and 20.2 per cent in Australia, perhaps because single fathers have been compelled by circumstances to acknowledge that children must be cared for as well as about.

The US pattern is of particular interest for two reasons. First, it suggests that while the participation rate of female sole parents is somewhat below that of partnered parents, it tracks it quite closely. One possible interpretation of this parallelism suggests that both sole parents and partnered parents respond to similar cultural, social and economic stimuli. If this is the case, as seems quite plausible, it is unlikely that the sole parent participation rate can be independently increased without active efforts to increase the overall participation rate or punitive measures likely to be unpalatable to a significant proportion of the community. Second, there is some evidence that current government policies hope to shift the overall social welfare structure some way towards the US model. Such a shift would have a number of implications for women. While basic workplace supports for women such as paid maternity leave and parenting leave are sorely lacking, financial assistance is available for sole parents and for low-income families. This enables women to choose between full time and part time employment in a way that US sole parents currently cannot. Lacking, in both jurisdictions, are policies that facilitate combining carework and waged work, for both men and women. Lacking as well is any sign that the model of the unencumbered worker is losing its potency. Despite the rhetoric of the family friendly workplace, the reality is of workplaces that are largely structured in traditional ways. The distinction between the core workforce of committed, career track, full time employees and the contingent workforce of casual and/or part-time women workers continues to set the agenda, reminding us that the breadwinner homemaker bargain is as embedded in workplace structures as in family life.

Looking at the trade offs, and the more or less punitive alternatives currently mooted, it is instructive to return once again to the model provided by the Swedish welfare state. Daly suggests that the Swedish welfare state is less tolerant of male-female income inequalities ... [T]he Swedish taxation system has the effect of not only cutting women's poverty rate in half but of reducing it to a level below the male rate. A high level of wage equalization also exists. Sweden's policy configuration also means that married women are less dependent on men for their income, that women already have a job and access to day-care facilities when they become (lone) mothers and that the poverty rate of lone-mother families is among the lowest in the developed world. A number of policy features set this type of welfare state apart. First, entitlement to many benefits and services is granted on the basis of citizenship or residence rather than need or family status. Second, the establishment of a fairly generous flat-rate grant to all mothers and an extensive system of leaves for parental and other purposes spells a recognition of the principle of care. Work in the home qualifies for (some) entitlement to social benefits in a policy framework that derives, at least in part, from a concern with the accommodation of work and family. Third, the Swedish tax system, especially as reformed in the 1970s, entails neither a single-parent penalty nor a dual-earner marriage penalty. Fourth, the provision of 'collective goods in kind' has been a strong feature of the Swedish welfare model, especially since the 1960s, with economic policies organized around the goal of stimulating the labour supply of married women. All of these measures ... weakened the influence of the breadwinner ideology.[80]

Elsewhere, the shadow cast by the unencumbered citizen continues to dominate the political agenda. Whether in the implicit message sent by anti-discrimination law in its identification of discrimination as exceptional and as a deviation from an otherwise efficient and competitive market or in the message sent by social welfare law, the ideal citizen, like the ideal worker, remains the incorporated male family self. In social welfare law, in particular, as the legislative framework shifts from one explicitly acknowledging the normative status of the breadwinner homemaker bargain, to one seeking to accommodate, albeit ambivalently, the dual income household while targeting the single income family for additional support, lines of tension appear. The persistence of the dependent spouse rebate, which will be discussed at greater length in chapter 7, stands in stark contrast to the increasing pressure on predominantly female sole parents (and, to a lesser extent) women with low income or unemployed partners to participate in the paid workforce, almost always as contingent labour. In classical liberal fashion, the political response is fragmented, responding, almost in knee-jerk fashion, to the crisis of the moment, while disregarding the inconsistent messages sent by partial reforms, messages that, as we have seen in the widespread concern over the number of sole parents who are not economically active, encourage precisely the behaviour that is subsequently identified as a serious social problem. In the next chapter, we will examine the structure of waged labour and of industrial relations law and policy in more detail. Like equal opportunity law, family law and social welfare law, industrial relations law and policy both shapes and is shaped by particular social environments and assumptions. Those matters defined as core have much to tell us about its underlying values and its social and legal role. They guide social understandings of the normative worker and of the relationship between equal opportunity law, employment and industrial relations law. In an environment in which, as we have already seen, equal opportunity law is perceived by employers as an externality and in which the supports essential for the participation of women are relegated to family policy, it is hardly surprising that industrial relations law has resisted any attempt to move beyond formal equality and any challenge to existing structures.

Notes

1   Clearly, the 'wrong' women are working!
2   Until 1966, female Commonwealth public service employees were required to resign upon marriage.
3   Stoltz, Pauline, 'Single Mothers and the Dilemmas of Universal Social Policies' (1997) 26(4) *Journal of Social Policy* 425, 438.
4   I am not saying that the educational system in the 1970s and early 1980s served the needs of boys in an exemplary fashion. Young men who were disruptive or who lacked academic aptitude were often encouraged out of the educational system at 15. Those were times of full employment, although it is not unreasonable to think that at least some of these young men, now in their late thirties and early forties, are among the casualties of deindustrialisation and the shift from a manufacturing to a service base.
5   While the gendered formulation that preceded the principle of equal pay was a crude tool, in that it was based upon the biological fact of sex rather than the social fact of dependents, in practice it was a status-based system acknowledging the normative worker as an 'incorporated male family self'.
6   See the discussion of the 'family wage' in chapter 1.
7   Mitchell, Deborah, 'Family Policy and the State' in Hancock, Linda, ed, *Women, Public Policy and the State*, South Yarra, Vic, Macmillan Education, 1999, 73, 75.
8   The *Maternity Leave Act* 1973 introduced maternity leave for Commonwealth public servants.
9   While single women were expected to apply for unemployment benefits, married women were eligible for a spouse's allowance where the breadwinner was unemployed and were not independently eligible for unemployment benefits. Widows with young children could elect either the supporting parent's benefit or the Class A widow's pension, while childless widows and those without young children received the Class B widow's pension.
10   This assumption was built into the *Family Law Act* 1975. Section 75(1)(f) directed the court to have regard to 'the eligibility of either party for a pension, allowance or benefit ...' in setting maintenance and child support. This approach was abandoned with the introduction of the Child Support Scheme.
11   Mitchell, 77.
12   *Maternity Allowance Act* 1912. The maternity allowance was not means tested, however indigenous and Asian women were excluded. This was relatively generous, however, the £5 payment being roughly equivalent to 4 weeks wages.
13   *Child Endowment Act* 1941. While the late thirties and early forties had been marked by extreme pronatalism and this undoubtedly provided part of the ideological underpinning for the introduction of child endowment, it is noteworthy that it was not available for a first child, but only for subsequent children. Despite fears that extension to single mothers would encourage immorality, single mothers did not benefit greatly as a majority had only one child and the payments were not large enough to enable a supporting single mother to care for her children unless she was fortunate enough to have a well-paid job.

14   Those not covered by Commonwealth provision were forced to rely upon patchy state
     provision and upon private charitable organisations. Poor relief was seen as charity, not
     as an entitlement.
15   This was largely because of Constitutional difficulties. Initially, s 51 (xxxiii) authorised
     the Commonwealth to legislate in respect of old age and invalid pensions, but outside
     of this welfare provision was the responsibility of the several states. The *Child
     Endowment Act* 1941 was its first major foray into broadly based social welfare
     provision. The *Widows' Pension Acts* of 1942 & 1943 and *Unemployment and Sickness
     Benefits Act* 1944 followed.
16   For a discussion of Australian attitudes towards single mothers since Federation see
     Howe, Renate & Shurlee Swain, 'Saving the Child and Punishing the Mother: Single
     Mothers and the State 1912-1942' in Howe, Renate, ed, *Women and the State:
     Australian Perspectives*, Bundoora, La Trobe University Press, 1993; (1993) 37
     Journal of Australian Studies 31 (a special issue). The authors note that about 17% of
     applications were rejected.
17   Where a child over 16 was in full time schooling, the benefit was available where the
     child was 21 or under.
18   Howe & Swain, 43.
19   This amendment was passed in 1946. For a comprehensive discussion of the historical
     position see, Sackville, Ronald, 'Social Welfare for Fatherless Families in Australia:
     Some Legal Issues' (1972) 46 *ALJ* 607.
20   A deserted wife was defined as one who had been deserted by her husband 'without
     cause' for a period of 6 months or more.
21   Sackville, Ronald, 'Social Security and Family Law in Australia' (1978) 27 *Int &
     Comp Law Quarterly* 127, 136.
22   This was nothing new, such requirements having been a part of State legislation and
     embedded in the requirements imposed by private charities. In practice, good character
     was often interpreted to mean that the widow was already supporting herself and two
     children by her own efforts and required assistance only because she was unable to
     support a large family. Evidence that she had male companionship, that she frequented
     places where liquor was served or that her conduct while on the street was 'riotous' or
     unseemly would also disentitle her to relief.
23   Sackville, 'Social Welfare for Fatherless Families', 613.
24   The training available was strongly gender stereotyped and included commercial
     courses such as typing, shorthand and bookkeeping, trades such as hairdressing and
     dressmaking, and, for the academically inclined, teacher training.
25   The constitutional amendment giving the Commonwealth government authority to
     provide, inter alia, child endowment was approved by referendum in 1946. Section 51,
     placitum xxiii(A) allowed: 'The provision of maternity allowances, widows' pensions,
     child endowment, unemployment, pharmaceutical, sickness and hospital benefits,
     medical and dental services (but not so as to authorize any form of civil conscription),
     benefits to students and family allowances' and provided the basic foundation for the
     Australian welfare state.
26   Dex & Joshi note that European research suggests that 'generous non-means-tested
     allowances for children depress mother's [workforce] participation'. See Dex, Shirley
     & Heather Joshi, 'Careers and Motherhood: Policies for Compatibility' (1999) 23
     Cambridge Journal of Economics 641, 645.
27   Originally, the maternity allowance seems to have been introduced at least in part in a
     response to the 'moral panic' attending falling birth rates, an issue of significant
     concern at the turn of the century (as it is today). Australian feminists welcomed it as

affirming women's citizenship: the image being of the 'citizen mother' and of bearing children as service to the state equivalent to military service. See Berns, Sandra, 'Law, Citizenship and the Politics of Identity: Sketching the Limits of Citizenship' (1998) 7 *Griffith LR* 1.

28 *Social Security Act* 1947, Part IVAAA.

29 Charlesworth, Stephanie, 'Monitoring Income Maintenance Policies for Single Mothers' (1982) 17 *Aust Journal of Social Issues* 135.

30 The waiting period was finally abandoned in November of 1980. See Charlesworth, 139.

31 Sackville notes that the cohabitation rule has been a source of complaints since its introduction. See Sackville, 'Social Security and Family Law', 156-7.

32 Effectively, the *dum sola et casta* rule which characterised family law prior to the enactment of the *Family Law Act* 1975 was reproduced in social security law. The state was available as surrogate breadwinner only where the original male breadwinner had not been socially replaced.

33 Zanetti, 94.

34 The illegitimacy rate does not provide accurate information in this area since it discriminates insufficiently between children born to women who were not in a long term marriage-like relationship at the time of conception and women in *de facto* relationships.

35 Hannon, Kate, The *Daily Telegraph*, 16 March 1999 cites research done by the Department of Family and Community Services which indicates that nearly two thirds of female sole parents had failed to complete high school. As a group they are both significantly less well educated than other mothers and tend to have fewer children, with 50% having only one child and a further 34% two children. Only 5% had four or more children. According to Zanetti, the average age of female sole parents is 33. See Zanetti, 94. See further Carberry, Fiona, Kate Chan & Alex Heyworth, 'Sole parent Pension and Parent Allowance – A Comparison' (1996) *Social Security Journal* 108, 114-115. They indicate that married mothers and fathers are better educated than their sole parent counterparts, although the discrepancy is greater for women. They also found (116) that among partnered parents, those in receipt of the Additional Parenting Allowance tended to be less well educated than other married women, although better educated than their sole parent counterparts.

36 Against this background it is worth noting that on international measurements of literacy some 17-18% of Australians tested on the lowest level, and about 27% on the second lowest across all three measures. Comparable statistics for Sweden are between 6-7% and 19%. Comparators for the highest two levels are approximately 18% (Australia) and 34% (Sweden). 'Australians' literacy skills: How do they rate internationally?' (Year Book Australia, 1999) accessed at http://www.abs.gov.au/ on 14 February 2000. Given that statistical evidence also suggests that older female sole parents are less likely to have completed high school than the female population as a whole it seems likely that many of these women are among those who are marginally literate. Zanetti notes that studies have shown that long-term dependency is most likely where the pension is granted to a young woman with a poor education and marginal attachment to the workforce. See Zanetti, 101.

37 *Social Services Amendment Act* 1977 s 3. Prior to the introduction of the *FLA* the crude divorce rate was 1.0. By 1976 it had risen to 4.5. It remained high during the late 70s as the backlog was gradually cleared before stabilising in the range 2.5-2.8. Australian Demographic Statistics (3101.0); Marriages and Divorces, Australia (3310.0) accessed at http://www.abs.gov.au/ on 14 February 2000.

38 Parliamentary Debates, 1977, House of Representatives, Vol H of R 107, Canberra, Commonwealth Government Printer, 1977, 2908, 4 November 1977. Needless to say, this curious bit of puffery did not become a reality.

39 Unemployment statistics disregard the potential 'hidden' unemployment of married and cohabiting women, some of whom may well have sought employment unsuccessfully.

40 Dex & Joshi, 645 have found that 'where the system of unemployment benefit means-tests against a wife's earnings it is likely to have a depressing effect on her participation, in part-time if not full-time work'.

41 In the United States, divorce law is a state rather than federal responsibility.

42 Gardiner, Jan, 'Putting Sole Mothers in their Place: The Normalising Discourse of Social Policy' (1999) 34 *Australian Journal of Social Issues* 43, 43.

43 Gardiner, 52. This thrust is, of course, in accord with the largely conservative tenor of Australian values regarding parenting and the propriety of employment for women.

44 While about 23% of JET clients obtain employment, and about 19% are in further education or training, the dearth of family friendly practices means that those who do gain employment often cycle back onto benefits. See Zanetti, 98-99.

45 The participation rate includes both those currently employed and those available to start work within 4 weeks.

46 Carberry, Chan & Heyworth, 108. In some other jurisdictions, the proportion of female sole parents in the workforce is much higher: 87% in Sweden, 84% in Denmark, 66% in the United States and 52% in Canada. See Baker, Maureen, 'Parental Benefit Policies and the Gendered Division of Labour' (1997) 71 *Social Service Review* 51, 61 and Siim, Birte, 'The Gendered Scandinavian Welfare States: The Interplay between Women's Roles as Mothers, Workers and Citizens in Denmark' in Lewis, Jane, ed, *Women and Social Policies in Europe: Work, Family and the State*, Aldershot, Hants, Edward Elgar, 1993, 25, 39.

47 Data for 1998-1999 comes from Australian Bureau of Statistics, Australia Now – A Statistical Profile, Characteristics of the labor force, accessed from http://www.abs.gov.au/ on 16 March 2000. The upward trends undoubtedly reflect increasing employment levels, particularly among women. UK statistics sourced from http://www.statsbase.gov.uk/ on 18 March 2000 suggest that the participation gap is much wider in the UK where the participation rate for sole parents is about 30% lower than that for married parents.

48 Carberry *et al*, 113. While the Carberry figures are somewhat dated, and employment rates for female sole parents are rising, the gap between the participation of female sole parents and that of male sole parents remains substantial, substantiating her original point.

49 As we saw in the last chapter, given the significantly higher rate of repartnering for male sole parents, in many cases a new partner steps into the maternal role, freeing the father to devote his time and energies to employment.

50 This is not surprising. In Sweden, for example, non-residential fathers access parental leave to a significantly greater extent than married fathers and the evidence suggests that parenthood increases, rather than decreases hours of wage work for married fathers.

51 The classic example is that in the banking sector. While this sector was among the first to make permanent part-time employment available, the mature-aged women in these positions were explicitly excluded from career paths within the banks. See Junor, Anne, 'Permanent Part-Time Work: Win-Win or Double Whammy?' in *Current Research in Industrial Relations, Proceedings of the 125th AIRAANZ Conference*, eds Raymond Harbridge, Claire Gadd and Aaron Crawford, Wellington, NZ AIRAANZ, 1998.

52 Furst, 36.

53 Hannon, above, cites FaCS research suggesting that the average age of male sole parents is over 38.

54 Furst, 38-41.

55 Haas, Linda, 'Gender Equality and Social Policy: Implications of a Study of Parental Leave in Sweden' (1990) 11 *Journal of Family Issues* 401, 416. The study also found that where the father claimed the 'daddy month' his participation in child care was greater throughout the pre-school years than that of fathers who did not claim the 'daddy month'. It also found that the greater the amount of parental leave taken by the father during the child's first year, the greater his participation in child care on an ongoing basis.

56 Haas, 419-420.

57 Given the limited skills of many women in this age group and the prevailing climate of ageism, older workers being the first to be retrenched, this is probably reasonable.

58 The government is currently seeking to encourage disability pensioners to access part-time employment, and a concerted effort is being made to replace the aged pension with private provision in the long term. It remains to be seen how successful these efforts will be.

59 Carberry *et al*, 125.

60 This change was effective on 20 March 1998 and followed the return of the Maternity Allowance on 1 January 1998. See *Social Security Act* 1991 s 4.4-4.5 and s 4.3 (MAT).

61 Haslem, Benjamin, 'Thousands caught in welfare trap', The *Australian*, 22 February 2002.

62 Dex & Joshi, 643.

63 See, generally, Zanetti.

64 Dex & Joshi, 647.

65 Australian data from ABS, 'Australia Now – A Statistical Profile: Labour & Employment, Unpublished Data, Labour Force Survey' at http://www.abs.gov.au accessed on 22 February 2000. Swedish data from Nyberg, 85, Diagram 2A.

66 Given the cultural similarities it seems unlikely that a greater proportion of students are economically active in Australia than in Canada and the US. Rather, it seems likely that these figures reflect a residual tendency for Australian girls not to pursue any form of post-school qualification. Part-time work for high school and tertiary students is a long established tradition in the US, and almost certainly in Canada. It therefore seems unlikely that the entire difference can be attributed to a tendency for more Australian students than US students to participate in part-time work.

67 Given youth unemployment rates, a significant number of young men also have marginal attachment to the workforce.

68 About 17% of Australian working women have access to paid maternity leave.

69 Undoubtedly this is correlated to the scope of the EEO legislation.

70 *Bogle v Metropolitan Health Service Board*, Western Australia Equal Opportunity Tribunal, No. 3 of 1999.

71 Gunn, Michelle, The *Australian*, 30 August 1999 accessed on 14 March 2000 at http://www.mensrights.com.au/.

72 Baker, 66.

73 Dowd, 211.

74 Eligibility for the Family Tax Benefit Part A extends these ages further, covering dependent children until age 20 and dependent full time students until age 24. The Family Tax Benefit Part B is more restrictive, covering dependent children only until age 16 and dependent students until age 18.

75 The underlying assumptions are that she would have completed school at 17 and borne her first child at 21 or 22. If, instead, we assume that her first child was born when she was 26 or 27, she might well have had nearly 10 years of workforce experience, however she would be in her forties when she sought to return, confronting both out of date skills and the prevailing climate of ageism.

76 Once again, the public service is an exception, as are corporate workplaces seeking to retain highly qualified staff.

77 Vogel, Joachim, 'The European "Welfare Mix": Institutional Configuration and Distributive Outcome in Sweden and the European Union. A Longitudinal and Comparative Perspective' (1999) 48 *Social Indicators Research* 245, 252.

78 Vogel, 252.

79 US Census Bureau, *Statistical Abstract of the United States*, 'Labor Force, Employment and Earnings' accessed on line at http://www.census.gov/ on 16 March 2000.

80 Daly, 218-19.

Chapter 6

Workplaces and Women: An Uneasy Relationship

Introduction

This chapter will focus on three 'moments' in Australian industrial reform. While their particulars are locally specific, they have profound resonances with similar changes in other countries. They are the equal pay decisions of the Australian Conciliation and Arbitration Commission (ACAC) in the late 1960s[1] and early 1970s, the move to enterprise bargaining in the early 1990s and the introduction of the *Workplace Relations Act* 1996 and the dismantling of the arbitral system in the mid 1990s. Only one of these moments focused upon women directly yet all of them have arguably had a profound impact upon the gender gap and upon workplace structures. In this chapter we will not be concerned with these shifts in industrial relations policy as a matter of labour market policy in the narrow sense. Rather, they will be examined as elements within two overarching constructs, the unencumbered citizen introduced in Chapter 2 and the male breadwinner family and the family wage.[2] While these constructs have much in common, a part of the argument of this chapter is that they both can be and should be separated. The male breadwinner family[3] is historically specific, linked to particular conditions in a Fordian capitalist environment. In all of the countries we have examined the male breadwinner family in its strongest form reached its apogee in the 1950s. It was sustained both by a policy environment which rewarded it and by the growing hegemony of the ideology of motherhood, an ideology reinforced by the work of Bowlby and others who postulated full time maternal care within the traditional family as essential to normal child development. Maternal defalcations were linked with underachievement, with gender identification difficulties and with other forms of deviance.

The construct known as the unencumbered citizen is subtler and more persistent. The notion of the unencumbered citizen often coexists with the strong male breadwinner family in liberal democracies, but is typically not eliminated when that model decays into the weak male breadwinner family or, in Sweden, the dual worker/carer family. It exists as a mindset and is not attached to any specific family form. Thus contemporary liberal theorists such as Ronald Dworkin[4] and John Rawls[5] argue that their particular forms of egalitarian liberalism are 'political' merely. The equality of which they speak is specifically as citizens and can and does coexist with private inequality, for example, within the family.

The same compartmentalisation is present in the organs of capital. In Sweden, for example, despite more than three decades of policies designed to entrench the worker/carer model as the exemplar for both men and women, men routinely attribute their reluctance to fully avail themselves of the available parental leave to the 'fear' that their careers will be damaged.[6] This is particularly true for those working in the private sector, where very few men take all the parental leave for which they are eligible. Researchers have concluded that their fear is, at least in part, justified.[7] Further evidence of the allegiance of private sector employers to the notion of the unencumbered worker (citizen) may be found in the evidence that during times of economic recession and unemployment, employers are reluctant to hire sole parents because of the fear that their parenting responsibilities will render them unreliable as workers. There is some evidence that this reluctance extends to partnered women with family responsibilities. The model of the worker is egalitarian on one level, with employment based on merit, stringent equal opportunity laws and generous parental leave. On another, more subtle level, it is profoundly inegalitarian. To be fully a worker, particularly in the private sector, is to eschew responsibility for care work.[8] In every jurisdiction we have examined, this model has persisted long after the strong male breadwinner family has decayed.

Because the male breadwinner family remains archetypal, and because existing institutions have been shaped by the assumptions underlying it, it is there that we will begin. Writing in the UK context, Creighton says of the male breadwinner family:

> There were five main ways in which the state could promote the [family wage]. One was to exert a direct influence upon the operations of the labour market by embedding the FW more firmly within collective bargaining procedures, legislating for minimum wage rates in particular industries, or instigating bars on the employment of married women. A second was through welfare policies which privileged the [male breadwinner family] by providing benefits to working men and their families based upon the labour market record of the male head of household. A third was through taxation policies which encouraged married women to remain out of paid employment. A fourth was the provision of subsidies, for example, housing, which made it easier to support a family on the wages of the man alone. Finally there could be direct payments to families with children to encourage mothers to remain at home. To these might be added more negative inducements, such as the lack of support for individuals who fell outside the MBWF (e.g. never-married, divorced, separated or deserted mothers) or the failure to provide childcare facilities to enable women to combine paid and domestic work.[9]

In Australia, as in many other jurisdictions, many of these features were, by the 1950s, deeply embedded in legal and social structures and had become normative. Departure was synonymous with deviance. Not until the 1960s did these structures begin to break down, in Australia as elsewhere. As increasing numbers of women moved into the labour force, either from choice or from necessity, pressure grew to eliminate formal barriers to participation.

The 'Equal Pay' Cases

In earlier chapters, we have seen some of the ways in which Australian law and policy supported the male breadwinner family and entrenched the family wage. While the most obvious was undoubtedly the *Harvester* case in 1907 that established the 'female wage' at 54 per cent of the male wage, it was by no means the only mechanism.[10] Bars on the employment of married women were normative both in the public service and the private industry. Margaret Gardner notes that by the early 1900s:

> Australian states and the federation had systems of arbitration. For the next eight decades arbitration shaped employer and union behaviour as well as creating a forum for determining wages and conditions in ways that influenced broader economic and social policy.[11]

The social policy aspects of the arbitral system were critical in shaping the Australian industrial relations environment. In this social policy role it first entrenched and subsequently demolished the family wage as part of an institutional system that has been broadly characterised as 'integrative'.[12] Labour market policy was one element in a broader social vision. Institutionally, the ACAC sought to advance the public interest 'through impartial deliberation on the basis of expertise' and to identify and further 'the public good'.[13] Under this broad mandate, it played a key role in wages settlements and award conditions within the parameters set by prevailing economic and social conditions. While it was only one player in this vision, it and other agencies such as the Prices Justification Tribunal helped to create an economic environment in which the male breadwinner family was both economically viable and socially sustainable.

Equally important, although less obvious, were the introduction of child endowment in the early 1940s and the way in which matrimonial law and social welfare law combined to ensure that divorce was untenable for many women. Unwed motherhood was vigorously censured. This censorious attitude manifested itself both in the pressure upon unwed mothers to surrender their children for adoption and the absence of real options for women who wished to keep their children and to support themselves and their children. As we saw in the last chapter, when the widow's pension was introduced in the early 1940s unwed mothers and deserting wives were excluded as they had been under the various state regimes and under those developed by private charitable organisations. By limiting eligibility to those circumstances where a wife was left without means either through the death of her partner or because she had been unjustly abandoned, a sharp distinction between legitimate and illegitimate dependence was drawn. The state would act as surrogate breadwinner in case of death or unjustified default, but not otherwise.

While the Australian taxation regime treats the individual rather than the family as the unit of taxation, the rebates available for a dependent spouse and for children further entrenched the normativity of the male breadwinner family, as did the rebate formerly available for a 'daughter housekeeper'.[14] Although the Australian social welfare system never fully underwrote the male breadwinner by adopting an insurance based approach to unemployment benefits rather than one based upon needs, the benefit structure reinforced the social vision of the male as productive and the female as reproductive. This was accomplished through the distinction between married and single rates and through the absence of any requirement that the wife of an unemployed breadwinner seek employment, irrespective of the presence of children.

The social settlement in which the male breadwinner family and the family wage were key elements was weakened by ACAC decisions affirming equal pay for equal work, and by the abolition of legal barriers to the employment of married women. While this was not the intention underlying these decisions, in the long term the family wage can only be sustained in the context of the artificial inflation of male wages and concomitant restrictions on female employment. When the family wage was abolished, male wages in Australia were significantly higher and less dispersed than in many other countries, a factor that contributed to the viability of the male breadwinner family while depressing female employment and entrenching traditional gender roles.

Paradoxically, however, the compressed male pay structures that characterised the Australian labour market were critical in the rapid narrowing of the earnings gender gap during the 1970s. According to Gregory:

> When the male pay structure is combined with the fact that women are disproportionately represented among low paid workers, a clear prediction emerges. Where the male pay distribution is wider, and low paid men are particularly disadvantaged, the gender pay ratio will be lower. Where the male pay distribution is narrower, and low paid men receive pay close to the male median pay, the gender pay ratio will be higher ... In Australia, the compressed male pay structures meant that low paid men were better paid and hence women could gain more from Equal Pay decisions.[15]

Gregory makes a further and telling point in comparing the impact of the equal pay decisions on Australian wages with the impact of similar changes in the US and UK. Relying upon work by Blau and Kahn, he notes that measuring the gender gap by reference to the gender pay ratio only tells part of the story.

> Blau and Kahn ... rank 10 OECD countries according to the gender pay ratio. The United States is placed third from the bottom. They then calculate the average position of women in the male pay distribution of each country. The United States is then placed second from the top. Within the US male pay distribution US women do very well. In an OECD context the main source of their disadvantage is the dispersed nature of the US male pay distribution. All low paid workers fare badly in the United States.[16]

Gregory draws two significant conclusions from the comparative studies, conclusions that we will return to later. First, he suggests that labour market deregulation is likely to seriously disadvantage low-income women. Second, he argues that while low income women in jurisdictions such as the US and UK are moving up the male pay distribution, the increasing dispersion has meant that their earnings have not increased relative to the male median.[17] In short, the labour market is becoming less equitable, for both women and men. At the bottom of the heap are the working poor, unskilled men and women who are able to earn no more than they could receive in benefits. The persistence of workplace sex segregation and the historic under-valuation of the work performed in the services sector, which remains predominantly female, means that a disproportionate number of those workers are women.[18]

From Male Breadwinner to Sole Parent

When, in 1972, the Supporting Mother's benefit was introduced, a second blow was delivered to that social settlement. Single mothers, deserting wives, and others who would not have qualified for the widow's pension were eligible for support outside the framework of the male breadwinner family. Although the retention of the six-month qualifying period undoubtedly caused considerable hardship, an alternative structure was beginning to emerge, one that gained considerable momentum when the *FLA* introduced no-fault divorce. These changes went some way towards establishing the dyadic mother/child relationship as a sustainable and acceptable family unit. While there is some evidence that the equal pay cases simply drove the family wage underground, particularly given the failure of the ACAC and the unions to prosecute comparable worth vigorously, the social changes wrought by the rapid increase in female sole parenthood are obvious.

The emerging social settlement was constructed around two separate phenomena. First, while female employment gradually increased through the 1970s and 1980s, the increase was neither as rapid nor as heavily weighted towards full time employment as in jurisdictions such as the US and Sweden. Female sole parents, in particular, were less likely to be in either full or part-time employment than their married counterparts, in part, perhaps because the social welfare structure enabled the majority of sole parents to maintain a traditional female lifestyle centred around domestic duties and carework.

Second, the prevalence of different family forms has changed markedly since the 1970s. Ann Harding tracked the demographic changes between 1982 and 1993 and suggests that:

> In November 1982, there were 170,000 sole parents with children aged between 0-14 years; eleven years later the number had more than doubled to 365,000. As a result, while sole parents with children aged less than 15 made up 1.5 per cent of the adult population in 1982, by 1993 the proportion had almost doubled to 2.7 per cent.[19]

During the same period, the number of couples without children under 15 increased by four per cent, to 33 per cent of the adult population while the number of couples with children under 15 decreased by four per cent to 24.7 per cent. During the same period, women's labour force participation increased by eight per cent, to 53 per cent.[20] If we take a slightly different approach and look at the characteristics of households the figures are even more revealing. In 1976, sole parents headed only 6.5 per cent of households with dependent children; in 1996, a sole parent headed 9.9 per cent of households. The number of couple only households has increased from 28 per cent to 34.1 per cent, while the number of couple households with dependent children has fallen from 48.4 per cent to 40.6 per cent. Since 1993, however, the female participation rate has increased only marginally (to 53.9 per cent), perhaps because structural supports in Australia are lacking in comparison to many other jurisdictions and the social welfare system has not required female participation, unlike that in the United States. It remains low by international standards. These changes in family form have been accompanied by a marked increase in income dispersion, caused both by increasing wage dispersion and an increase in the number of dual income households.[21]

Second, until very recently, other aspects of the benefit structure also reinforced traditional family forms and affirmed the normative status of the male breadwinner family. Because, until very recently, the benefit structure imposed no obligation upon wives and widows to engage in waged labour, active encouragement of sole parents seemed untenable. Thus, paradoxically, the cultural primacy of the male breadwinner family provided a powerful rationale for the structure of the sole parent's pension (now Parenting Payment) when changing social attitudes compelled its introduction. If wives in couple families with unemployed breadwinners were not expected to seek employment, sole parents surely should not be.

Increasingly, however, reality was at variance with this second social settlement. The increasing numbers of couple families without dependent children, the continuing although gradual rise in women's workforce participation, and the economic fragility of the sole breadwinner family in the absence of the family wage, have led to further changes in the social welfare system. These second wave changes are aimed at encouraging both sole parents and wives in couple families with unemployed or underemployed primary breadwinners to re-enter the labour market. Where this will lead and the shape of the new social settlement is, however, far from clear. These changes have been accompanied by the gradual scaling back of childcare provision by the Commonwealth government, a sustained attempt to make the EEO regime more 'business-friendly'[22] and by the continued reluctance of successive governments to push for universal paid maternity leave and parental leave.[23] The mantra of the 90s has been flexibility, but the evidence suggests that this flexibility is largely employer driven and unlikely to benefit men and women attempting to balance work and family life.

It seems likely, on the evidence to date, that Australia will follow Britain's lead and attempt to buttress the weak male breadwinner family as the preferred social form. In the absence of the family wage, economic necessity is likely to compel increasing levels of workforce participation by women, although in a discrete secondary market dominated by part-time and casual labour. Because most such positions are poorly paid and insecure, participation of this kind will not destabilise the gendered allocation of household labour. In turn, the gendered allocation of household labour will, as has happened in Sweden, reinforce the embedded structural assumption that to be a worker is to be an unencumbered citizen and further entrench the distinction between primary and secondary labour markets. Furst notes that even in Sweden with more than three decades of political and social programs designed to entrench the worker-carer family as normative:

> There are an increasing number of reports of employers trying to avoid employing parents of young children ... If such a trend continues, it will inevitably have a greater impact on women than on men. Probably the more uncompromising attitude of the employers in this respect contributed to the fact that parental leave taken by men for the care of sick children declined between 1980 and 1996. Men adjust to the demands of the job and consolidate their position as stable, reliable labour.[24]

Hard won gains, even with a history of strong government backing, are both fragile and easily undermined. In Australia, which lacks that extended history, and which has, for the most part, relied upon EEO law to redress structurally embedded disadvantage, the signs are not promising. OECD[25] statistics suggest that between 1987 and 1995 'the gender pay ratio for part-time work dropped substantially from 85% to 75%, while women in full-time work improved their relative position slightly'.[26]

The rapid fall in the gender pay ratio for part-time workers is largely responsible for a two per cent drop in the total gender pay ratio.[27] The magnitude of this trend coupled with the high levels of part-time and casual employment among Australia women highlights a further risk: that women who work part-time, either from choice or necessity, will become increasingly marginalised. While the total gap is not particularly large by OECD standards,[28] it is disturbing, particularly given that Australia, uniquely, showed an increase in the gender gap during the study period. While the increase in the level of the earnings penalty applying to part-time work is worrying, Australia was also unique in another respect. According to Grimshaw & Rubery:

> this trend does not apply to average full and part-time earnings among the top five occupational groups where women's employment is concentrated ... [T]he gender pay ratio for female part-time workers remains higher in comparison to the pay ratio for full-time workers.[29]

Higher it may still be, but in the Australian context, the worsening position of part-time workers signals a significant change. The gap between average hourly earnings of part-time and full time workers expressed as a percentage of the average male hourly wage has been substantially eroded. In most occupational areas other than primary teaching and nursing,[30] part-time workers earn on average only about two per cent more per hour than full time workers, down from an average of about seven per cent in 1987. Part-time cashiers fare worst of all, earning more than two per cent per hour *less* than full-time cashiers.

If one looks more carefully at the statistics, and considers the ten areas with the greatest female domination, two features are of interest. First, two occupational categories which ranked among the top ten in 1987, secondary school teachers and 'other clerks', have been replaced by cashiers and 'child care, refuge and related workers'. This change has undoubtedly had a significant impact on the overall gender gap, given that secondary teachers earned substantially above the average male wage and 'other clerks' earned over 85 per cent of the average male wage in 1987. The occupations that have replaced them, childcare and refuge workers and cashiers, are both economically marginal, with cashiers at 55.7 per cent and child care and refuge workers at 63.4 per cent of the average male wage. Much of the growth in women's part-time employment has been in economically marginal areas of employment, and in the case of cashiers, in an area where part-time workers earn significantly less than full-time workers on an hourly basis. Equally significant are the drops in parity with the average male wage in other areas. The part-time wages for sales assistants dropped by almost ten per cent, for accounting clerks more than seven per cent, those for receptionists by nine per cent and those for cleaners by a staggering 15 per cent. Part-time primary teachers, while remaining above the average male wage, experienced a drop of almost 20 per cent. Clearly, the traditional loading for casual work has been significantly eroded. Its erosion suggests that during the period between 1987 and 1995 employers had already achieved much of the flexibility they are currently demanding, at least in traditional female occupations. While there were some drops during this period in the parity of full time wages, the largest drops were those for primary teachers at 13 per cent and cleaners, at 12 per cent. In all other cases, the fall was less than five per cent.[31] With award restructuring well under way by 1987 the arbitral structure was already beginning to weaken, eroding the loading traditionally applicable to casual rates (as compensation for the absence of benefits such as holiday leave and sick leave). It also highlights a significant failure of the arbitral structure, one we shall look at in the next section.

Occupational Segregation, Enterprise Bargaining: A Failure of Nerve

Despite the 1972 Equal Pay decision, the ACAC did not prosecute its apparent mandate to entrench comparable worth principles in the award structure. Instead, despite trade union efforts in the 1980s, it adopted the view that to do so would jeopardise 'traditional wage fixing principles'.[32] The hallmark of the arbitral structure was its centralised wage-fixing regime. While the centralised regime played an essential role in entrenching the family wage, it also played a key role in demolishing it and moving to equal pay for equal work. As we have seen, this had a number of consequences, including a rapid narrowing of the gender gap following the equal pay decisions. One legacy of the 'family wage' has, however, proved resilient, a significant level of occupational segregation. The persistence of occupational segregation is significant for two reasons. First, in Australia, as in most other OECD countries, women are 'clustered' in a limited number of occupations in a secondary employment market characterised by high levels of casualisation and truncated or non-existent career paths.[33]

Second, ILO research suggests that of the remaining gender gap in OECD countries, about one third is directly attributable to occupational segregation, and the balance to direct or indirect discrimination and residual differences in human capital. Because these phenomena are interdependent, effecting further change is likely to prove difficult. In Australia, the impact of occupational segregation is particularly critical. While the 1972 'comparable worth' decision should have levelled the playing field, Barbara Pocock argues that:

> The institutional actors choked on the implications that revaluing feminised jobs had for long established, masculinist traditions of work value and comparable wage justice. As the AIRC put it in rejecting the Australian Council of Trade Union's (ACTU) claim for a comparative worth reassessment of nurses' work in the mid-1980s, sex-based comparative worth criteria 'strike at the heart of accepted methods of wage fixation in this country and would be particularly destructive of the present Wage Fixing Principles'. The institutional alarm prompted by notions of comparable worth is striking.[34]

This chapter will argue that while changes in family law, in social welfare law and industrial relations law joined with changing social attitudes in undermining the male breadwinner family as a viable social and economic unit, the organisation of capital and the structure of industrial relations law and policy still take the model of the 'unencumbered citizen' as normatively given. The structural organisation of waged labour, the industrial relations regime and key supporting institutions are predicated upon this model. As a consequence, employers have not, as a group, provided the infrastructure needed to support dual breadwinner families – paid parental leave, workplace based childcare, family friendly hours – while the government has insisted that such measures are a matter for private enterprise to consider on ordinary business principles. While there are exceptions, particularly where they are needed to retain the services of highly qualified staff, in general the institutional response has been to further entrench the dual labour market. In the dual labour market, core positions are typically full time, often with significant paid overtime available, relatively generous conditions including sick leave, long service leave and permanency. In some of these positions, career paths are available, although the Australian labour market has not been as diligent as many OECD countries in providing structured on the job training. In the blue-collar sector, primary labour market workers enter as apprentices, gradually moving up the ranks to become master tradesmen. Increasingly, workers in these core positions have been able to achieve some gains through enterprise bargaining. Supporting this core market is a secondary market of predominantly service-based employees. In the secondary market, positions are more likely to be casual or part-time. Many of these workers are not unionised and they have often been deemed almost impossible to unionise. The fragile nature of their employment means that their bargaining power is extremely limited. In many cases, these employees are among those who have not yet registered any enterprise bargaining agreements and who are covered only by the minimum wage safety net provided by the awards system.

By the 1990s a new category of flexible permanent part-time positions had appeared. These are characterised by a substantially lengthened span of hours and the employer's unilateral ability to alter times and hours of work at short notice. While these positions have substantial benefits for employers in utilisation of plant and equipment and access to trained staff, they impose significant burdens on working women, many of whom find it extremely difficult to access child care at short notice and to meet family commitments. They also have contributed to the rapid increase in the gender gap for part-time workers in feminised categories, a phenomenon that we noted in the last section. In many of these positions, career paths are absent, and hours and days of work are likely to change with minimal notice, under the guise of flexibility. This is particularly significant in Australia where many casual workers have had regular hours and days of work.[35] While many of the workers in the secondary market are both mature and experienced (and these characteristics are sought after) for the most part these workers are seen as substitutable. In this market, apprenticeships are atypical and the opportunities for on the job training non-existent.

When, in the late 1980s and early 1990s Australia moved from a centralised wage-fixing regime to enterprise bargaining, the potential for the Australian Industrial Relations Commission (formerly ACAC) to adopt comparable worth and substantially revalue typical female occupations against their male counterparts was eroded. Although there was some early optimism that this revaluation would occur as part of the award restructuring process, progress has been glacial. In the services sector the early signs were that female service workers were losing ground, both in the failure to secure meaningful wages outcomes through enterprise bargaining and in a general deterioration of conditions. Kathy MacDermott suggests that 'early industrial precedents were not promising for service delivery workers-particularly where those workers were isolated in subsections of manufacturing workplaces'.[36] During the first few years of enterprise bargaining, according to a survey conducted by the Department of Industrial Relations, productivity gains in male dominated workplaces were likely to yield agreements ratified by the AIRC and to be linked to wage increases.

In female workplaces, productivity gains were less likely to be ratified and to be linked to wage increases. Among the potentially deleterious changes were significant increases in the span of 'ordinary hours'. In such workplaces, 'the emphasis was on conditions matters such as working time arrangements and the more flexible use of casual, contract and part-time labour'.[37] Equally significant was the decision of the AIRC in the 1997 Living Wage claim. For those employees, primarily women, who are unable to access the new bargaining regimes, the former award system became a residual safety net establishing a de facto minimum wage for those unable to access the claimed benefits of enterprise bargaining. The Living Wage claim sought an increase in this 'minimum wage' safety net. The AIRC clearly stated that while the *Act* directed it to ensure that awards provided fair minimum standards,[38] it was also directed to act so as to encourage enterprise agreements.[39] As a consequence, the safety net increase was lower than the AIRC deemed fair as it felt that it was legislatively required to leave space for a subsequent productivity increase through enterprise bargaining.

Given this, it is hardly surprising that a 1997

> study of work intensification in a Brisbane hospital found that during a period of reduced hospital funding by government, admissions increased by 8.5 per cent over a two-year period to 1994, inpatients increased by 6 per cent and hospital occupancy rates rose from 86 to 92 per cent. Labour productivity during this time for nurses rose by 22 per cent, accompanied by an increase in staff counselling for depression, stress and anxiety from five per day to eleven per day. Similarly, the quit rate rose from twenty per month in January 1992 to fifty per month in December 1994. Allen concluded that managerial measures of labour utilisation implemented to increase hospital throughput significantly intensified the work effort and severely affected employees' health and wellbeing.[40]

Unless one assumes that nurses are infinitely substitutable, one has to assume that lower productivity due to stress, illness and the need to train and integrate replacement staff were the price of the 'increases' in productivity, making the level of the actual as opposed to apparent productivity gain illusory. This highlights the difficulty in measuring productivity in the delivery of services, and the need to ensure that the 'price' of apparent productivity increases is offset against the apparent gains.

During the balance of this chapter we will explore the interaction between the industrial relations regime, the social welfare regime and broader issues of social and economic policy in shaping the current gender settlement in Australia. In particular, we will examine the role of these forces in first entrenching and subsequently undermining the strong male breadwinner family while retaining the 'unencumbered' worker as normatively given.

Classifying Labour Markets: Where Does Australia Stand?

Substantial work has been done in OECD countries on the typological classification of labour market structures and assumptions. While this work is officially gender neutral, and gendered impacts are not considered in any detail, a part of the argument of this section will be that different labour market structures have significantly different and gendered impacts. In the Australian context, we will be particularly interested shifts in labour market policy during the period between the equal pay cases and the present and the implications of those shifts in the wider policy arena, as well as in the overall typology that emerges.

Vogel cites work by Kohlberg and Esping-Anderson on the typological classification of employment regimes:

> They identified a Nordic model with low levels of early exit, high levels of paid absence, and high rates of public employment. The Continental model has high levels of early exit, moderate levels of paid absence, and low levels of public employment. The Anglo-Saxon model is characterised by low levels of paid absence and early exit, as well as public service employment, but high levels of private social service employment.[41]

At the time the equal pay cases were decided, the employment regime in Australia was, on this schema, clearly hybrid. While levels of paid absence were relatively high by world standards,[42] and levels of private social service employment relatively low, public employment was high.[43] Women's employment was marked by early exit, typically upon marriage or upon the birth of the first child, while men remained in the waged labour force until retirement age. Following the equal pay cases, although female employment gradually increased, the structure of the social welfare system and the increasing dispersion of wages tended to depress its levels, particularly for working class women and those who had not taken out post-secondary qualifications. The absence of universal paid maternity and parental leave weakened women's attachment to the labour force by making it impossible for families to rely upon a wife's earnings in their financial planning. This, in turn, ensured that her wage remained a secondary income and reinforcing the existing division of domestic labour. It is not unreasonable to suggest that this has had spin off effects, among them depressing the inclination of girls and women to amass human capital and making it uneconomic for parents to invest in human capital development for their daughters.

For sole parents, the supporting mother's benefit provided a viable alternative to waged labour for many women, especially those without high level skills, and the married rate of the unemployment benefit had the same effect for economically marginal couples. Depressed wages for unskilled female workers in an increasingly dispersed labour market made unlikely that a working class woman could earn enough to replace the value of the benefit and the Health Care card, even if she worked full time. The absence of subsidised childcare and the relative inaccessibility of childcare acted as a further barrier to employment for many women. It was not until the mid-1980s that a major expansion of subsidised child care places at the Commonwealth level made it possible for families to obtain affordable child care of high quality, making it possible for many women to enter or re-enter the labour force and the cost remains prohibitive for many families.

In 1982 the Family Income Supplement was introduced in response to fears that social security entitlements provided a better income alternative for large families than waged labour.[44] Shortly thereafter the Family Allowance became means tested.[45] The income test became progressively tighter and in 1992 the program was re-named the basic family payment. The introduction of the JET scheme in 1989 was a response to the low participation rate of sole parents and designed to encourage them to enter or re-enter waged labour as their children grew older. It was followed by the elimination of the married rate of the unemployment benefit in the late 1990s. At much the same time, substantial cuts to the public sector deprived many women of the security of permanent positions with access to paid maternity leave and other critical benefits, including the possibility of permanent, career track part-time work. By the late 1990s public sector cuts had been followed by the privatisation of many services that were formerly publicly owned, for example the replacement of the Commonwealth Employment Service by privately owned employment agencies competing for government business.[46] While the period between the late 1980s and 2000 saw significant job creation, many of the new positions were casual positions in the services sector and, as we saw earlier, often with less favourable wage rates than in the past. Although the labour market moved closer to a pure Anglo-Saxon model, with rates of early exit for women diminishing, they remain relatively high. During the same period, the decline in the manufacturing sector saw increasing numbers of men in their forties and fifties reliant upon unemployment and/or disability benefits and unlikely to obtain further employment. An ambivalent social policy aimed simultaneously at supporting the male breadwinner family and encouraging sole parents, most of them female, to enter the labour market continued to depress levels of female employment.[47]

Rhetoric and Reality

When the equal pay cases were decided in the late 1960s and early 1970s the Australian labour market was characterised by essentially full employment, a well developed manufacturing industry supported by high tariff barriers and a strong trade union movement affiliated with the Labor party. Wage dispersion was relatively low by international standards. Many young people left school at 14 or 15 and had little difficulty obtaining employment. Public sector employment was substantial. Most employees enjoyed four weeks annual leave, long service leave after 15 years continuous employment and a holiday leave loading of 17.5 per cent. Other benefits associated with paid employment were also significant and were entrenched in industrial awards registered with ACAC. These included significant levels of paid overtime and generous loadings for holiday and weekend work. Benefits such as paid maternity leave and parental leave were absent from the great majority of industrial awards although they became available within the public sector during the 1970s and early 1980s.[48] Structurally, the labour market provided significant support to the male breadwinner family even after the introduction of equal pay for equal work both because pay rates were generous by international standards and because of the availability of various loadings. The practice, common in many male dominated industries, of providing substantial overtime for skilled employees rather than expanding the workforce also supported the male breadwinner family.[49]

At the time of these reforms, the Australian social settlement, despite some anomalous features, fell clearly within the strong male breadwinner typology. Although the unit of taxation was the individual rather than the family, the allowable deductions for dependents were relatively generous and child endowment provided a valuable supplement to household income. Given that the Commonwealth public service bar on the employment of married women had not been lifted until 1966,[50] and maternity leave was largely unavailable, childcare within married couple families was strongly supported. Divorces were relatively difficult to obtain and the absence of social welfare supports for women who left their husbands and for unmarried mothers discouraged female independence and reinforced the normativity of the male breadwinner family. Informally, a wide range of commercial practices also discouraged female employment and economic independence. The income of married women was not taken into account for loan and other credit applications, effectively minimising the benefits otherwise available from a dual breadwinner family. Most women left the labour market upon marriage and, in normal circumstances did not re-enter although there is some anecdotal evidence that women sometimes concealed marriages, often until pregnancy became apparent, to retain public service positions. Commercial childcare was both expensive and difficult to obtain, making it difficult for those who could not command a substantial income to combine work and family. At the policy level, little attention was given to the structural supports required by the dual breadwinner household, and the absence of these supports lessened the immediate impact of the equal pay decisions outside the public service.

The equal wage cases marked the first departure from this model, producing an immediate increase in women's wages in occupations where they were employed alongside men, but leaving wages unchanged in female dominated sex-segregated workplaces. The introduction of the Supporting Mother's Benefit in 1973 began to erode the normative status of the male breadwinner family. While basic supports such as maternity and parenting leave were still unavailable to most working women, the Supporting Mother's Benefit made it possible for women and their children to maintain an adequate lifestyle without financial support from a husband or de facto. This process was accelerated by introduction of no fault divorce in 1975. While the *FLA* attempted to have it both ways, simultaneously affirming 'the family' as the fundamental unit of society and promising protection to those women who sought to continue their roles as 'wives and mothers', its enactment signalled the emergence of a new gender compact in Australia. Both the Supporting Mother's Benefit and the *FLA* directly challenged the strong male breadwinner model. While the social welfare model that prevailed at the time of the equal wage cases was largely liberal in its orientation, it had elements of a conservative welfare state regime. Features such as child endowment and maternity benefits bolstered the resources available to the family unit, contributing to continuing low levels of female employment. Greatly enhanced access to divorce and the availability of resources enabling women to maintain a full time parenting role following separation and divorce marked a shift from the mixed liberal/conservative regime to a model recognising the dyadic mother-child relationship as an independent family unit. While benefit levels were not generous, the absence of any activity test and relaxed social attitudes towards sole parenthood created a uniquely Australian hybrid. Despite the elimination of formal barriers to employment, labour market participation by Australian women increased only gradually during the 1970s.

During the 1980s women's participation began to accelerate. The partnership between the Labor Party and the trade union movement reached its apogee during the Accord years, a period which saw significant wage restraint acceded to by the ACTU in exchange for substantial benefits through the social wage, chiefly in the form of child related payments to the primary carer. While this was an inherently unstable alliance, it endured because of the coercive powers of the ACAC and its ability to craft solutions where the parties could not agree. During the latter part of 1980s, following a political decision to allow the Australian dollar to float and the deregulation of financial markets, the centralisation within the industrial relations framework began to break down. While the industrial agenda and wages outcomes were still set nationally, award restructuring introduced decentralised bargaining and outcomes at the enterprise level. The introduction of enterprise bargaining and the disappearance of nationally set wage outcomes followed in October 1991.

As we saw in earlier chapters, other changes also marked the 1980s. The Commonwealth government, relying upon international treaties introduced EEO and sex discrimination legislation as increasing numbers of women entered the workforce. While New South Wales, South Australia, Victoria and Western Australia had introduced sex discrimination legislation during the 1970s, the enactment of Commonwealth legislation put it firmly on the national agenda.[51] At much the same time, the nature of employment in Australia began to change as deregulation captured the political imagination of both political parties and tariff barriers were lowered. As a consequence, Australia began the transition from a manufacturing economy to a services economy. Against this background and faced by falling membership and the need to re-establish relevance, the trade union movement intensified its campaign for equal pay in the 1989 National Wage Case Decision.[52] At much the same time, the Labor government continued its expansion of funded childcare places to meet the needs of working parents, although this was addressed, not as a labour market issue but as a matter of family policy. During the period between 1983 and 1995 child care places increased from about 50,000 to 234,000.[53] Mitchell notes that during the early 1990s maternity benefits, parental leave provisions and opportunities for part-time work were also introduced under Accord VII.[54]

In retrospect, this choice has had several significant consequences. The first was discussed in the last chapter: the institutionalised competition between the interests of working mothers and those who were full time parents. The second, perhaps more significant consequence, was the way in which gender issues were marginalised. Like the EEO regime, the support structures essential to reconciling work and family were characterised as externalities, as a barrier to competitiveness and an undesirable interference with market forces. This both naturalised existing policies and practices, denying their situated and contingent character, and ensured that the responsibility for change lay elsewhere. Equity issues were thus officially characterised as interest group politics, rather than as foundational, facilitating the development of competing demands by, among others, men's groups.

Perhaps presaging the shift from an integrative industrial relations model to an aggregative model, the fluid boundaries that had characterised industrial relations policy for much of the century were becoming circumscribed. While the male breadwinner family was no more, the unencumbered worker that replaced it, while ostensibly androgenous, had neither financial responsibility for partners and children nor care work obligations. Workers were detached from their family circumstances, from the reality of their lived experiences and were simply bundles of skills and attributes capable of commanding a particular price. As Thomas Hobbes had said centuries before:

> The *Value*, or WORTH of a man, is as of all other things, his Price; that is to say, so much as would be given for the use of his Power: and therefore is not absolute; but a thing dependant on the need and judgment of another.[55]

In a very real sense, in a society in which industrial relations policy had, for most of the century, served a critical social policy role, its role was increasingly relegated to the margins. Broad questions of the public good, whether conservative or progressive were to be abandoned in favour of a very different agenda, one that emphasised competitiveness and productivity as exclusive public sphere values and as constitutive of the public good. A Benthamite vision of social ordering had been replaced by a Hobbesian.

Collectively these changes, together with the introduction of the JET program to encourage sole parents to enter the waged labour force, the abandonment of child endowment and the maternity benefit and increasing emphasis upon women's economic role marked a shift away from the strong male breadwinner model. This shift was not, however, accompanied by the introduction of universal benefits intended to sustain women's attachment to the waged labour force. Instead, paid maternity leave, parental leave and other infrastructural supports facilitating a dual role were benefits that might be incorporated in individual awards or enterprise agreements. Because they were funded by individual employers rather than funded through a universal levy upon all employers (as in Sweden where employer contributions cover 85 per cent of the cost of parental leave) coverage was extremely patchy. The continued contraction of public sector employment, an area where benefits such as paid maternity leave were available, and deepening economic recession continued to dampen women's employment prospects, although there was significant growth in casual employment in the services sector.

By the mid 1990s with a change of government and changed government policy, massive changes were under way in industrial policy, in social welfare policy, in family law and in the overall attitude of the government to women's issues. Following on from the shift to enterprise bargaining, the Liberal government introduced the *Workplace Relations Act* 1996. While the *Workplace Relations Act* incorporated universal, albeit unpaid, maternity leave[56] and made provision for unpaid parental leave, it also removed the obligation to consider the equity aspects of enterprise agreements which had been incorporated in the *Industrial Relations Act* 1988. The Commission was, however, directed to have regard to the covenant on family responsibilities in its deliberations[57] and to Australia's obligations with respect to equal pay for work of equal value.[58] Most disturbing from the perspective of disadvantaged workers was the introduction of individual contracts, styled Australian Workplace Agreements. These allowed employers to negotiate individually and directly with employees and placed a premium upon individual bargaining power. While AWAs, as they are known, remain comparatively uncommon, they are subject to minimal scrutiny and there is no requirement that they be scrutinised on equity grounds. Other changes were underway as well, most significantly an employer driven push for increased 'flexibility' in hours of work and a push for the abolition of penalty rates. While flexibility, in particular, was promoted as helping to realise the family friendly workplace, as we saw in chapter 3 the reality of flexibility was often increasingly family unfriendly hours of work. For 'casual' and part-time workers, primarily women, many of whom had worked for the same employer for an extended period of time, flexibility often means greatly increased variability of working hours causing significant difficulties with child-care arrangements and increased travel costs.

Flexible, family unfriendly hours, erosion of the hourly pay of part-time workers in female dominated occupational categories, both relative to full-time workers in the same category and to the average male hourly wage sees Australia move closer to the classical liberal settlement predominating in the US and UK. Van Gramberg notes the accelerating shift from standard to non-standard forms of employment and comments:

> The proportion of employees who are casual in their main job rose from 13 per cent in 1982 to 26 per cent in 1996. Part-time employment increased from 15 per cent to 25 per cent over the same period. This employment shift has been highly gendered, with women making up the majority of non-standard job holders. In 1990, 28.2 per cent of women workers were employed on a casual basis compared to 12.7 per cent of men. By 1997 the proportion of women in casual work had risen to 31.7 per cent compared with 29.9 per cent of men.[59]

Against this background increasing government pressure upon sole parents and wives in couple households where the principal breadwinner is unemployed to enter or re-enter waged labour, euphemistically termed 'mutual obligation' in the Interim Report of the Reference Group on Welfare Reform released in March 2000, flags a new social settlement.[60] Australia, at the beginning of the 21st century is clearly aligned with the Anglo-Saxon model. Levels of paid absence are at best moderate;[61] early exit is diminishing as economic realities dictate that increasing numbers of women maintain, however precariously, labour force attachment; and a decade of economic rationalism has radically slashed public service numbers and diminished wages equity for those who remain. Increasingly, social welfare provision is shifted to the private sphere as the increasing demands upon charitable organisations demonstrate. In Australia as elsewhere, equity is seen as an impediment to efficiency. Wage dispersion is increasing as well. While much has been made in the media of the emergence of 'family friendly' workplaces, in the private sector these can also be interpreted as a symptom of the increasing stratification of the workforce. Where workplaces desire to retain the services of highly qualified workers whose services might be lost if family needs are not accommodated signs of flexibility are undoubtedly beginning to emerge. For women in marginal casual and part-time employment, flexibility means something very different.

Therese MacDermott argues that many of the structural features identified earlier in this chapter mean that women are unlikely to fare well under the new legal framework. According to her:

> Factors that compound the difficulties faced by women in bargaining include weaker industrial strength, high numbers of part time and non-unionised workers, and concentration in industries where productivity is comparatively more difficult to measure, such as the child care industry.[62]

The overall problems are exacerbated in the case of AWAs. MacDermott notes that:

> Addressing discrimination issues is not a stated aspect of the approval process undertaken either by the Employment Advocate or the Commission, unless these issues were to be taken into account in applying the no-disadvantage test. The main avenue for redress where an AWA is discriminatory appears to be an individual complaint. AWAs do not come within the exemption that applies to awards and certified agreements under the *Sex Discrimination Act* 1984 (Cth). Therefore the process of referring complaints regarding discriminatory provisions in awards and agreements from the Sex Discrimination Commissioner to the Commission does not apply. The shortcomings of a complaints-based system include the burden on individuals in identifying the systemic nature of the discrimination involved, and the willingness of individuals to take action against their employer. These problems are likely to be magnified in the new industrial relations environment of individualised bargaining.[63]

An increasingly difficult and family unfriendly labour market has been coupled with a social welfare policy with a substantial (and continuing) history of predicating women's entitlement to social benefits on their status as mothers. Lewis suggests that states typically recognise women either as mothers or as workers, and argues that

> where the male breadwinner model still has major purchase, then women find that their position as paid workers is, at best, a matter of secondary concern ... and, at worst, actively discouraged.[64]

In Australia, while we have moved from a strong male breadwinner regime to a weak one, women's position as paid workers remains a matter of secondary concern, particularly for those women who are not well educated, and who form part of an increasingly casualised secondary market. The evidence suggests that women have, over the last decade or so lost some of the ground that they gained prior to the 1990s. Structural supports for women attempting to combine waged work and parenting remain under-developed, providing little real incentive for women to invest extensively in their human capital. The overall picture is remarkably similar to that in Britain in that

> women have been left to 'choose' whether to engage in paid employment, without government providing very much in the way of systematic aid to their labour market integration, but where it is also assumed that they will provide unpaid labour in the home.[65]

While efforts were made to entrench publicly funded childcare during the 1980s, the support available in Australia for women seeking to combine waged work and family work remains substantially below that available in the UK. In the UK, women with two years continuous service are entitled to 11 weeks leave prior to the birth of a child and 29 weeks after. Six weeks of that period involves income replacement at 90 per cent of prior earnings and the legislation provides for guaranteed reinstatement to the position held. While this is hardly generous by European standards, it is substantially better than the unpaid parenting leave provided by the *Workplace Relations Act* 1996, even with the maternity benefit now available as part of the parenting payment package.[66] After they have children, women are constructed primarily as mothers. The existing social and infrastructural supports reflect this primacy, firmly locating women within the family and giving priority to their family roles, even while acknowledging that a majority of mothers are also in the waged labour force and encouraging those on benefits to become economically active.

The general relegation of policy issues concerning infrastructural support for working women, including the provision of child care, to family policy rather than industrial policy highlights the symbolic primacy accorded motherhood and the secondary status of women as workers in waged labour.[67] This, in turn, mirrors the labour market construction of men as core workers and women as secondary workers in a narrow range of female ghettos. Both reinforce the underlying model of the worker as unencumbered, as fully committed to the waged labour market and free to meet its demands. Both also reinforce the prevailing division of family labour and legitimate the earnings gender gap. Whether the gender gap is attributed to women's failure to amass human capital, to employment histories interrupted by full time parenting, or to discriminatory practices reflecting employer predictions about women's commitment to waged labour, its continued existence discourages the reallocation of family labour. Against this background, a conservative government with a history of cutting programs designed to assist working women and 'redirecting expenditure to breadwinners with a non-working partner'[68] continues to pursue policies aimed at supporting what it sees as its core constituency, the traditional male-breadwinner family.

In this context, Yvonne Hirdman's elaboration of dual systems theory is particularly suggestive. She argues that gender, democracy and capitalism form interlocking systems which, collectively, govern the relationship between women and men. Sites of tension between these independent, but interlocking, systems power social change. Within the gender system, two basic principles are primary: gender segregation and the primacy accorded the male norm. As a system, gender is maintained by socialisation practices, by cultural traditions, and by its universal social integration into institutions at every level of society.[69]

While this elaboration was developed in the context of historical trends in Sweden, it offers substantial insights into the forces driving the current Australian settlement. At Federation, Australia was among the first countries in the world to extend full suffrage to women and the site of a prolonged feminist campaign for recognition of women's contribution in child bearing and rearing as equivalent to men's contributions as soldiers. Within democratic institutions the citizen mother was portrayed as the counterpart of the citizen soldier and the maternity allowance (available to all white women without distinction as to marital status) was a first step in providing economic independence for women as citizens. While the initial arguments were for a formal equality of citizenship and produced significant advances (for some women), in practice maternalist conceptions of citizenship entrenched two gendered settlements: that of the valorised 'good mother' within the confines of the breadwinner homemaker bargain, and that of the threatening 'independent woman' seeking to survive outside its constraints. Within the dynamic formed by the interaction of capital and labour, the family wage sustained the breadwinner homemaker bargain while utilising 'outsider women' – those who remained single and those who struggled to support children both inside and outside of marriage – as contingent labour which could be exploited as required, particularly during wartime. Between the first and second World Wars, waged labour and motherhood were ideologically mutually incompatible, and mothers who sought or were forced to be economically independent were at risk of being seen as 'bad mothers'. Child welfare laws, divorce laws and the strength of maternalist conceptions of citizenship meant

> that motherhood, rather than providing women with a new basis for independence and public recognition, was being invoked as reason to confine women to dependence and degradation in the private realm of the family. In a patriarchal context, the maternalist emphasis on the importance of child welfare rebounded on mothers as citizens, serving only to curb their rights and limit their freedom.[70]

Despite the early appearance of the maternity allowance, the nascent social welfare system was resolutely paternalistic – benefits for women were, at Commonwealth level, exclusively for 'deserving widows' and 'deserted wives'. As workers, even those single women with dependents to support were denied a 'family wage'. Status as a mother was incompatible with status as a worker.

When, during the 1960s social attitudes began to change and notions of human rights and egalitarian aspirations captured the political, if not the cultural, imagination, two critical shifts occurred within democratic institutions. First, it no longer seemed necessary to use government power to maintain a discriminatory wages regime. Within one of the most sex segregated employment markets in the OECD, wages could be left to a market that had already set 'appropriate' wage levels for the majority of women.

Second, changing social attitudes towards divorce and towards unmarried mothers paved the way for a broadening of social welfare provision and a liberalisation of family law. Formal equality had attained a kind of hegemony, both within democratic institutions and within market institutions. Neither touched, or was intended to touch, the culturally embedded realm of gender relations. Within the family as within the market, separate spheres and separate lives remained the rule, a rule initially elevated and subsequently undermined by the quasi-egalitarian *FLA*.

Conclusion

In all of the areas thus far examined, the policy picture represents a classically liberal each way bet. The rhetoric of 'choice', specifically the choice to be a full time parent, together with a social welfare system predicated upon the male breadwinner family have discouraged women's investment in their human capital despite evidence that such investment provides higher returns for women than for men. While, on one level, the emergence of the supporting mother's benefit marked a significant break with the male breadwinner model, on another level it reinforced its normative status through the tacit presumption that wage work and care work were largely mutually exclusive. Against the background of a high level of sex segregation in the workplace, and a history of female concentration in casual part-time employment, the traditional male breadwinner metamorphosed almost seamlessly into the unencumbered worker.

Despite relatively early attempts at implementing equal pay for equal work[71] and significant public sector success during the 1980s by the so-called 'femocrats', it remains fair to say that there are at least four distinct labour markets in Australia and these deliver very different outcomes for women. Within the private sector, women predominate in casual, predominantly service sector employment at marginal rates. Despite the contraction of the manufacturing sector and the predictable increase in structural male unemployment and casual employment, men continue to predominate in skilled trades and in the higher levels of managerial and professional work. Within the public sector, the picture is somewhat different. While women are still under-represented in senior managerial work, and over-represented in clerical and secretarial work, women have successfully moved into middle management and made inroads into senior positions at both State and Commonwealth levels. Here, to a far greater extent than in the private sector, women have access to permanent part-time career track positions while their children are young although managerial positions have, until recently, been excluded on the basis that they cannot be shared by two employees. Here, as well, equal opportunity and sex discrimination laws appear to have had a measurable impact, with organisations routinely implementing EEO practices and adhering to the merit principle. Private enterprise has proved much more resilient. EEO monitoring applies only to organisations employing more than 100 workers and exemptions were granted in a number of critical areas. Perhaps more significantly, the failure of the ACAC to fully implement the comparable worth decision has allowed private enterprise to shelter behind the legacy of occupational segregation, making depressed wages in largely female areas of the labour market difficult to challenge without direct government intervention. Because many of these workers are not unionised, and most do not have the bargaining skill to negotiate beneficial AWAs, they seem unlikely to advance their position significantly.

The figures usually relied upon to measure the earnings gender gap compare the ordinary weekly earnings of full-time female workers to the ordinary weekly earnings of full-time male workers. In Australia, women currently earn about 81 per cent of male average ordinary weekly earnings. While this is respectable by international standards, it is sobering to note that if the calculation is based upon total weekly earnings for full time workers the gender gap increases by almost 5 percentage points. Where the comparator is total weekly earnings for all workers,[72] the gap increases to almost 18 percentage points. While this reflects the concentration of women in part-time positions (43 per cent of women workers are employed part-time) it also reflects the worsening conditions for workers in these categories. Significantly, a paper prepared by the National Federation of Australian

Women using OECD figures suggests that between 1986 and 1995 the level of occupational segregation increased. In 1986, women were under-represented in 34 of the 52 occupational categories studied. In 1995, that figure had increased to 36 of the 52 occupational categories studied.[73]

Against a background of institutionally embedded conventions, the introduction of equal opportunity and sex discrimination legislation was perceived as doubly threatening: to the family as the core institution of society, and to the workplace, as anti-competitive and threatening. The structural reform principles embedded in equal opportunity law and sex discrimination law were central to the equality push of the 1980s. While these reforms have had an impact and have significantly enhanced the position of some women, the most significant gains cannot be attributed to these legal changes but to the equal pay decisions of the late 60s and early 70s. As wage dispersion increases it is precisely these gains that are at risk. Against the background of increasing emphasis upon workforce participation by (female) sole parents and by women in economically marginal couple families, it is difficult to be optimistic about the likelihood of further gains. Instead, Australia appears to be moving in the direction taken by the UK and by the US. While well-educated professional and managerial women may continue to narrow the gender gap, those in marginal employment are likely to fall further behind as wage dispersion increases. Gregory notes that the gender gap for women earning high salaries[74] has decreased since 1983. In 1983, well-paid women earned almost 1.3 times the male average wage. In 1997, that figure had risen to mid-way between 1.3 and 1.4 times the male average wage. A similar gradual increase also applies to those earning in the 70th and 80th percentiles. Wages for low paid women[75] after some limited initial gains during the 1980s have remained stagnant at about 55 per cent of average male earnings. Gregory suggests that labour market deregulation in the UK was accompanied by a sharp fall in the wages of this group, from 42 per cent of the average male wage to less than 38 per cent, a fall of almost five per cent. While, in Australia, low paid women are improving their position relative to that of low paid men, the increasing dispersion and inequality in the male pay distribution has meant that they have lost ground against the average male wage.[76] As the government weakens its stance on equity issues and increasingly subordinates them to employer led concerns regarding productivity and international competitiveness, further progress on comparable worth and further reductions in the gender gap seem illusory.

These failures, particularly against the background of a stated intent by government to curtail welfare dependence by sole parents, signal a potent reaffirmation of the breadwinner homemaker bargain. While highly trained professional women can be allowed (but not supported) to seek positions commensurate with their ability and some are able to negotiate relatively favourable working conditions, impoverished sole parents are increasingly told that they must become part of the contingent labour force and reduce their welfare dependence. Women remain not quite halfway to equal, whether positioned as underpaid and undervalued workers, as sole parents increasingly stigmatised for their reliance on public provisions, or as dependent wives.

Notes

1   The 1969 decision entrenched equal pay for equal work; the 1972 decision permitted claims based on equal pay for work of equal value. These decisions were followed in 1974 by a decision establishing a non-discriminatory minimum wage.

2   As we saw in chapter 2, Fraser calls this construct the 'incorporated male family self'.

3   This family form is sometimes termed the strong male breadwinner family to distinguish it from the various hybrid forms that emerge, as dual income families become the norm.

4   Dworkin, Ronald, Cambridge, MA, Belknap, 1986.

5   Rawls, *Political Liberalism*, exemplifies this approach.

6   A second reason often given is that that they would prefer several shorter parenting breaks but this is not acceptable to their partner because multiple breaks might jeopardise her career.

7   Furst, 35-37.

8   Like gender, race, ethnicity and class are simultaneously obscured and stigmatised. Officially, the unencumbered citizen is raceless, classless and genderness. Unofficially, in the countries we are examining, deviance from a white male middle class norm becomes a lack of merit, a failure to comply with putatively objective indicators.

9   Creighton, Colin, 'The rise and decline of the "male breadwinner family" in Britain' (1999) 23 *Cambridge Journal of Economics* 519, 523.

10 In the long term, the 1912 *Fruitpicker* case was probably more damaging. In it, Higgins J held that the lower 'female wage' applied only in areas where only women were employed. Where women worked alongside men, they must be paid at the same rates. Otherwise employers would have a powerful incentive for using women to displace men by undercutting their wages. The *Fruitpicker* case provided a powerful incentive for occupational segregation. The National Wage Case of 1949-50 increased the basic female award rate to 75% of the male wage.

11 Gardner, above, 6.

12 Because the award system operated at both the Commonwealth and the State level, the system was one of considerable complexity. While the state Industrial Relations Commissions generally followed the lead of the Commonwealth, there was often a considerable lag. While the Equal Pay decision was handed down by the ACAC in 1969, some of the states did not adopt equal pay for several years.

13 Gardner, 18.

14 The rebates available for a dependent spouse and children often made it uneconomic for women to enter the waged labour force. The institutionalisation of the 'female wage' and the bar on the employment of married women in the public service lowered their earning capacity and made it unlikely that a majority could earn enough to compensate for the loss of the rebate, given the expenses involved in participation. The daughter housekeeper rebate was available where the male breadwinner lacked a wife to provide domestic services, either through ill health or death. It was available only where the daughter housekeeper devoted herself on a full time basis to providing for his needs. The rebate was unavailable if the daughter housekeeper sought to participate in waged labour or education, even on a part-time basis. The rebate continues to exist, rendered gender neutral and termed child-housekeeper.

15 Gregory, Bob, 'Labour Market Institutions and the Gender Pay Ratio' in 'Policy Forum: The Equal Pay Case – Thirty Years On' 32(2) *The Australian Economic Review* 273, 274-275.

16 Gregory, 277.

17 Gregory, 277. More recent statistics from the US Department of Labour tell a somewhat different story. For those aged 16-24, women's median weekly earnings were 91.3% of men's, while for those 25 and over, women's median weekly earnings were 75.9% of men's, an all time high. While the latter figure is distorted somewhat by the comparatively low earnings of older women, it also highlights the cost of childbearing. Statistical information downloaded from 'Monthly Labor Review', US Dept of Labor at http://stats.bls.gov/ on 7 April 2000. Independent Women's Forum data downloaded on the same date notes that women aged 27 to 33 who have never had a child earn 98% of the earnings of men with identical characteristics. See IWF at http://www.iwf.org/. The statistics are taken from the National Longitudinal Survey of Youth. Childless women and men are not, of course, necessarily comparable in other ways. It is becoming increasingly common for career-oriented women to postpone childbearing until they have established themselves professionally. Given that this is not necessarily the case with men, it is difficult to know how similar the two populations are. In Australia, for example, childless men are more likely to be unemployed and to never have formed a long term relationship where as childless women are more likely to be upwardly mobile career women in secure positions. The same is true in the US.

18 In this context, it is worth remembering that Adam Smith distinguished sharply between the labour involved in manufacture, which he characterised as productive, as adding value, and the work done by 'menial servants', which added no value. See Smith, Adam, *Wealth of Nations*, New York, Random House, 1965, 14.

19 Harding, Ann, 'Income Inequality in Australia from 1982-1993: An Assessment of the Impact of Family, Demographic and Labour Force Change', Discussion Paper No. 4, November 1994, NATSEM, University of Canberra, 1994, 4.

20 Harding, 4-5.

21 These figures are taken from ABS, 'Australia Now: A Statistical Profile: The Labour Force' and ABS, 'Australia Now: A Statistical Profile, Population, Households and Families', accessed on 30 March 2000 at http://www.abs.gov.au.

22 See the discussion of the changes to EEO in chapter 3.

23 International statistics suggest that only 17% of female workers in Australia are covered by awards or by enterprise agreements providing for paid maternity leave although they are entitled to unpaid maternity leave subject to certain conditions. See Bertelsmann Foundation, 'International Reform Monitor Country Info: Australia Family Policy' accessed on 19 April 2000 at http://www.reformmonitor.org/.

24 Furst, 95-96.

25 Organisation for Economic Co-operation and Development.

26 Grimshaw & Rubery, 17.

27 Grimshaw & Rubery, 17.

28 Grimshaw & Rubery, 16-17. In the UK and West Germany, women in the five areas with the greatest female employment earn (as a percentage of male earnings) 55% and 61% respectively, compared with ratios for all remaining occupations of 77% and 92% respectively.

29 Grimshaw & Rubery, 18

30 Part-time primary teacher's hourly earnings, expressed as a fraction of average male hourly earnings are 10% higher than those of full-time teachers, while part-time nurse's hourly earnings are about 4% higher than those of full-time nurses.

31 See Grimshaw & Rubery, Table 14, 61.

32 While the ACAC affirmed the equal pay principles of the 1972 equal pay case in 1985-6, it rejected the comparable worth concept. Only now, some 15 years later, are there

concrete signs of progress in this area with the decision of the New South Wales Industrial Relations Commission in the Equal Remuneration and Other Conditions of Employment Test Case. The decision, which was handed down on Friday 30 June 2000, took on board the concept of 'comparable worth' and provides that it may be revisited in awards. While awards serve only a residual safety net function, this chink may put upwards pressure on certified agreements in areas where women's labour is clearly undervalued.

33   For a discussion of the issues associated with contingent work see Hall, Harley & Whitehouse, 55. Sweden is a partial exception here. While it has high levels of sex segregation, the gender gap is exceptionally low by world standards and it has been suggested that the 'female market' is parallel and on the whole equally paid.

34   Pocock, Barbara, 'Equal Pay Thirty Years On: Policy and Practice' in 'Policy Forum: The Equal Pay Case – Thirty Years On' 32(2) *The Australian Economic Review* 279, 281-282.

35   In many cases, casual workers have worked for the same employer for an extended period and enjoyed largely regular hours of work.

36   MacDermott, Kathy, 'Women's Productivity: Productivity Bargaining and Service Workers' (1993) 55(4) *The Journal of Industrial Relations* 538, 549.

37   MacDermott, 551.

38   *Workplace Relations Act* 1996 s 88B.

39   *Workplace Relations Act* 1996 s 88A(d). See AIRC, *Safety Net Review-Wages* 1997, 18 for a discussion of the dilemma the Commission perceived.

40   Van Gramberg, Bernadine, 'Women, industrial relations and public policy' in Hancock, Linda, ed, *Women, Public Policy and the State*, MacMillan Education, Victoria, 1999, 99, 107-108.

41   Vogel, 257.

42   Given that four weeks annual leave and long service leave after ten or 15 years was becoming the norm, levels of paid leave were higher than in the US where annual leave was typically two weeks and long service leave was not available to a majority of workers. Australian workers also enjoy a significant number of paid holidays. Sick leave and similar benefits were also available, although paid maternity leave was not available.

43   The federal structure and the relatively low population base significantly boosted public service employment.

44   Mitchell, 1997, 7.

45   Mitchell, 1997, 7.

46   It is unlikely that the employees in the private providers that have replaced the former CES enjoy equivalent benefits.

47   According to comparative data accessed through Statistics Canada on 25 March 2000 at http://www.statcan.ca/english/ the participation rate for Australia is 63.9%, for Canada 69%, for the US 70.7%, for New Zealand 68% and for Japan 59.8%. Figures for the UK were comparable, with 70% of women economically active, however, while the participation rates shown for the other jurisdictions are for all women 15 and over, those for the UK are women 15-64 suggesting that the UK participation rate is likely to be closer to that of Australia.

48   *Maternity Leave Act* 1973 made maternity leave available to Commonwealth public servants while the 1979 ACTU Maternity Leave test case set the standard in all awards for 52 weeks unpaid maternity leave.

49   In some industries, overtime boosted the pay of some employees by $15,000 or $20,000 above award rates. Overall, women were unlikely to receive over award payments and

much less likely to work overtime on a regular basis, although women in some sectors were expected to work extra hours without overtime payments.

50   The States followed suit rather later.

51   Sex discrimination legislation was not introduced in Tasmania and Queensland until the early 1990s. See *Sex Discrimination Act* 1991 (Qld) and *Sex Discrimination Act* 1994 (Tas) now repealed and replaced by the *Anti-Discrimination Act* 1998.

52   See ACTU, 'Women's Pay: 1989 Strategy Statement', ACTU Women's Employment Strategy 1989 accessed on 23 March 2000 at http://www.actu.asn.au/.

53   Mitchell, 1997, 12.

54   Mitchell, 1997, 12.

55   Hobbes, Thomas, *Leviathan*, ed by CB MacPherson, Harmondsworth, Middlesex, England, Pelican, 1968, 151-152.

56   *Workplace Relations Act* 1996 s 170BB. See also s 170KB covering parental leave.

57   *Workplace Relations Act* 1996 s 93A.

58   *Workplace Relations Act* 1996 s 161.

59   Van Gramberg, 103-104. Two patterns are emerging here. While almost one-third of working women are casual in their main job, and the number increased steadily between 1990 and 1997, the acceleration in the number of male workers who are casual in their main job has been even more dramatic. Since 1990, the proportion of men in casual work has more than doubled.

60   'Participation Support for a More Equitable Society', downloaded from Department of Family and Community Services on 3 April 2000.

61   The absence of universal paid maternity leave, even for a minimal period, aligns Australia firmly with the USA and sets it apart from most European countries.

62   MacDermott, Therese, 'Bargaining Under the New Industrial Relations Regime and its Impact on Women' in Cass, Bettina & Rowanne Couch, *Divided Work Divided Society: Employment, Unemployment and the Distribution of Income in 1990s Australia*, Sydney, Research Institute for Humanities and Social Sciences, University of Sydney, 1998, 101, 102.

63   MacDermott, 105.

64   Lewis, 15.

65   Lewis, 18.

66   The recently reinstated maternity benefit is $750.

67   The advertisements for JET mirror this construction, encouraging women to become part-time waged workers while 'not neglecting your most important job'.

68   Mitchell, 1997, 20.

69   Hirdman, Yvonne, *Women – from Possibility to Problem? Gender Conflict in the Welfare State – The Swedish Model*, Stockholm, Swedish Centre for Working Life, Research Report No. 3, 1994.

70   Lake, Marilyn, 'Childbearers as Rights-bearers: feminist discourse on the rights of Aboriginal and non-aboriginal mothers in Australia, 1920-50' (1999) 8 *Women's History Review* 347, 357.

71   Many other jurisdictions had moved to formal equality in the 1960s. I can still recall my disbelief (and absolute fury) when I arrived in Melbourne in 1972 to work for the Education Department and discovered that my salary was 75% of my partner's despite identical qualifications and experience. I was even more furious when I discovered that as a 'married woman' I could not become permanent despite having been imported at some expense by the government!

72   This includes casual, part-time and junior wages.

73 The figures in this paragraph are taken from National Federation of Australian Women, 'Raising Women's Economic Standing – Breaking Through the 80¢ in the Dollar Barrier', prepared for the Australian Women's Roundtable 1998, Canberra, 19-20 August 1998 accessed on 2 May 2000 at http://www.dpmc.gov.au/osw/. The paper also notes that men are increasing their concentration in masculinised occupations.
74 Those in the 90th percentile and above are characterised as high pay.
75 Those in the 10th percentile and below are characterised as low pay.
76 Gregory, 276-277.

Chapter 7

The Family as Signifier: Tax and Families

Introduction

Like social welfare law and industrial law, taxation law[1] and policy both transfers resources and rewards particular ways of living while penalising others. Family, and our understandings of its social and cultural significance, is a central signifier within taxation law and policy. Because different family forms are treated in different ways by the taxation system, the transfer payments extracted by the taxation system and reallocated through the social welfare system as well as through rebates directed to the 'taxpayer', make powerful normative statements. Miranda Stewart notes that:

> Tax and transfer laws rely fundamentally on a distinction between private and public. However, the division of public/private is not clear-cut or uniform. Transfer law in particular is ambiguous, as it seeks to characterise women both as 'private' carers in the home and as 'public' workers in the market and requires surveillance of 'private' family finances. Even in tax law, however, the ideal family is not always a site that is private in the sense of being unregulated; indeed it may be subject to considerable investigation, although not so intrusive as the surveillance of recipients in the transfer system. Paradoxically, tax and transfer laws may exert greater normative or disciplinary power over those who could conform to the ideal family, such as heterosexual couples, while limited freedom from regulation – some privacy – may be allowed, through the very silence that surrounds them, to lesbian, gay and other non-normative families.[2]

In the last chapter, we saw some of the ways in which social welfare and industrial law and policy were bound together in a complex web. We saw this in the affirmation of the strong male breadwinner family that prevailed until the Equal Pay cases. It was also apparent in the strengthening and targeting of the social welfare transfer system in an effort to replace the family wage during the 1980s. Against the background of falling real wages under the wage restraint policies of the Accord years and the inevitable impact upon the male breadwinner family, the social wage increasingly provided targeted support to single income families, primarily though not exclusively, families with a male breadwinner. In this chapter, we will be particularly concerned with the ways in which the taxation system continues to reinforce the normativity of the male breadwinner family and with its increasing interaction with other legislative programs.

Taxing Families: Winners and Losers

Unlike Sweden, for example, where the family was the unit of taxation until the early 1970s, Australia has used the individual as the official unit of taxation since the first Commonwealth income tax legislation was introduced in 1915.[3] This was not, however, as straightforward as it seemed. When the first Commonwealth income taxation statute was enacted, the male breadwinner family had already been entrenched by the *Harvester* case.[4] The 'living wage' became the tax-free threshold for a single taxpayer. The threshold was increased where a dependent wife and one or more children were present, for all practical purposes affirming the 'incorporated male family self' as the basic unit of taxation. During this period most wage earners did not earn enough to exceed the threshold and most income taxes were, in fact, collected by the states. The states, with the exception of Tasmania, also adopted the individual as the basic taxation unit. Through time, the Commonwealth taxation base expanded to include almost all wage earners, and the threshold represented an increasingly tiny proportion of the average male wage.

As the tax-free threshold diminished in real terms, rebates became increasingly important as a mechanism for taxation relief for taxpayers with dependents.[5] All rebates for which the taxpayer is eligible are deducted from the tax payable. When they were introduced in 1975, undoubtedly the most significant were those for a dependent spouse and for dependent children. Historically, these included the dependent spouse, child-housekeeper (formerly daughter-housekeeper), parent maintenance and invalid relative rebates. The level of the dependent spouse rebate depended upon whether the household also included children under 16 years or full-time students under 25 years. The 'notional' rebates for children were only used to establish the level of the spouse rebate and could not be claimed independently.

The symbolism of these measures is significant. No rebate is available for dependent children and students where a taxpayer does not qualify for a dependent spouse rebate or a sole parent rebate. The fact of dependence is, therefore, less significant than the question of status: specifically the status of a wife in the male breadwinner family.[6] The explicit tension between the refusal to recognise the cost of childcare as a legitimate deduction against the income of the taxpayer and its recognition as a legitimate expense against the earnings of a 'dependent spouse' affirms the conventional image of a middle class wife working for 'pin money'. In this way, taxation law rewards legitimate dependence and affirms the normative status of the unencumbered worker.

Cogent arguments against such rebates had already been put as early as 1920. These arguments suggested that marriage did not reduce the ability of the taxpayer to pay but provided the taxpayer with the valuable unpaid services of another individual, thus enhancing that capacity by freeing time that would otherwise be required to perform household tasks.[7] The economic value of these services is recognised by the availability of both child-housekeeper and housekeeper rebates. Within the private sphere, at least in the case of the child-housekeeper, domestic services are exchanged for food and shelter. Under normal circumstances, a housekeeper rebate is only available where the housekeeper cares for the spouse of the taxpayer and provides household labour that the spouse would otherwise provide. The animating force depends upon a particular model of the worker and of a particular division of labour within the family and not the desirability, strictly speaking, of providing relief for taxpayers who are required to provide for dependents. As Claire Young comments:

> Provisions such as the dependent spouse rebate affirm that women's dependency on men deserves tax relief, which in turn undermines the autonomy of women. Furthermore the tax rebate is delivered to the economically dominant person in the relationship (usually the man) and not to the 'dependent' who needs it. This manner of delivery assumes that income is pooled and wealth redistributed equitably in the relationship. Studies have shown that this assumption is simply false and that, in reality, such pooling and redistribution of income and wealth does not occur in the majority of relationships.[8]

Other taxation provisions reinforce the positive value of dependence for minimising taxation. Under Australian law, the splitting of property or investment income is also allowed. Where the economically dominant person in the relationship, usually the husband, has significant income from personal exertion, notionally allocating half of all investment income to a spouse can impact significantly on the taxation payable. What it does not do, of course, is actually transfer resources to the dependent spouse. Because income assignment is ineffective if it endures for less than seven years, during which time the lower income spouse must remain economically inactive, it discourages any potential move back into the workforce and encourages prolonged dependence. Since many women with affluent partners are themselves well educated and capable of earning an above average income, it encourages them to significantly depreciate their human capital and imposes artificial limits upon choice, in particular, the choice to return to part-time employment, by making it economically counterproductive.

More recently, in the lead up to the introduction of a goods and services tax, the *Family Tax Assistance Act* 1996 established 'a family tax unit for a modest amount of wage earner income'[9] by raising the tax-exempt threshold by $1,000 per dependent child. The income ceiling for this benefit was set at $70,000 where there is one dependent child. Significantly, the higher threshold is available to only one parent and cannot be shared in a dual wage earner household. An additional flat exemption of $2,500 was made available where at least one child was under five provided that the primary carer earns less than the income cut-off for the basic Parenting Allowance, currently $4,573 pa and the breadwinner earns less than $65,000.[10] The income ceilings for both forms of assistance increase by $3,000 for each additional child. For a family with four dependent children, one being under five years, the total tax relief available through this avenue is about $1,300 per year. The underlying normative model remains that of the male breadwinner family and the need to provide taxation relief for that family form in the absence of a family wage. In 1999, the *A New Tax System (Family Assistance Act)* 1999 consolidated taxation benefits for families and, in addition to the family tax benefit introduced by the 1996 legislation, provided for a maternity allowance of $780 per child, a maternity immunisation allowance of $208, and a child care benefit where children are in approved or registered care.

With the introduction of the *A New Tax System (Family Assistance Act)* 1999 the dependent spouse rebate for families with children became part of the Family Tax Benefit Part B[11] providing additional help for single income families. Where the spouse does not qualify, for example, because his or her separate net income exceeds the allowable level, currently $8,079 where the youngest child is over the age of five and $10,853 where the youngest child is under five, no rebate is available for children. The separate net income of a spouse includes earnings and benefits such as the parenting allowance as well as income from other sources. Once it exceeds $1,679, the rebate is reduced by $.30 for every $1 of additional income. In calculating a spouse's separate net income, non-deductible outgoings incurred in deriving that income, including the cost of childcare, entertainment expenses, and the cost of driving to and from work may be taken into account.

While the above measures provide tax advantages to the primary wage earner in low and moderate-income families, they do not impact upon the marginal rate of taxation to the same extent as would treating the married couple as the unit of taxation. Unlike the parenting payment, they reinforce traditional gender role allocation. The critical relationship is one of dependence. Effectively these provisions seek to cushion the alleged hardships facing low and moderate-income families in which gender roles remain traditional and reinforce that model as normative.

In jurisdictions that treat the married couple or family as the unit of taxation, a number of very different approaches have been taken. That used in the United States allows couples to opt for either joint or individual filing, and the scale used is determined by that choice. Where joint filing is adopted, the income of the spouses is aggregated and the tax payable is calculated on their combined income. When joint filing was introduced in the late 1940s, the tax schedule adopted for married couples electing joint filing had brackets twice as wide as the schedule for individual taxpayers. Effectively this created a form of income splitting or pure averaging. It imposed a substantial cost on the revenue and penalised single taxpayers and couples who elected to file as individuals. In 1969, a new tax schedule was introduced which attempted to keep the tax burden on singles and married couples within 20 per cent of each other, a change which instituted a marriage penalty for dual income couples, one which increases as incomes become more nearly equal. Moving from a tax system using the individual as the unit of taxation to one using the couple effectively imposes a higher marginal rate on the earnings of one member of a couple. The level of this 'penalty' increases as the incomes of the parties become more nearly equal, effectively discouraging dual career households by reducing the benefits available from the 'second income'.

In the UK, aggregation was used until the mid-1990s. The scale used for couples was the same as for an individual taxpayer, although allowances partially offset the harshness of the result for dual income couples. The UK has since moved to an individual system, although it retains a married couple allowance that will be phased out for younger couples in the near future, perhaps in recognition of the increasing workforce participation by married women. Although most EU countries now treat the individual as the unit of taxation, France and Germany continue to use the family as the basic unit. France has adopted a complex system in which all family members represent tax units. Each adult counts as one unit, the first child counts as half a unit, and each subsequent child as one unit. The total income for all family members (including children) is aggregated, and then divided by the number of units in the family. The tax burden on the notional income for each individual is then calculated and multiplied by the number of units to reflect the taxation owed by the family as a whole. Germany has adopted an income splitting regime somewhat similar to that in the US.

In Australia, populist pressure groups continue to advocate some form of family unit taxation to relieve the tax burden on the single income household.[12] There is no concrete evidence that the present government is contemplating moving fully to treating the couple as the tax unit, despite ongoing flirtation with the concept for electoral gain, although the *A New Tax System (Family Assistance) Act* 1999 moved some way in that direction. Its history of 'fiddling at the margins' and ongoing efforts to replace the 'family wage' with a social wage suggests that we should be mindful of the implications of policy changes. Bruce Bartlett, Senior Fellow at the National Center for Policy Analysis in the US emphasises that:

> It has long been known that a tax system cannot simultaneously do three things: (1) have progressive tax rates, (2) have equal tax treatment of couples with the same income, and (3) be marriage-neutral.[13]

Despite increasing synergies between social welfare and taxation, the propriety of using the individual rather than the family unit as the foundation has been affirmed by several reviews of the taxation system. A partial exception was the Report of the Asprey Committee in 1975 which recommended that the 'government prepare, for public examination ... a detailed scheme for elective family unit taxation'.[14] The question was revisited by the Labor government in the mid-1980s and advocated by John Howard as Leader of the Opposition in a speech given in 1994.[15] Cooper notes that such proposals ignore the substantial increase in non-deductible expenses (travel, clothing, child care, and homemaking services) incurred by the two-income family and the 'disincentive' to workforce participation for the 'secondary income earner'. While such proposals retain their attraction and their populist appeal, a majority of OECD countries have moved away from family unit taxation. Joyce Crago suggests that the original choice of taxation unit was far from accidental. According to Crago:

> The initial choice of taxation unit in most European countries (Britain, France and Sweden) was the family, based on the assumption that the tax unit should correspond to property rights under the civil law or marital property law. Most European countries introduced income tax systems much earlier than the New World; Britain in 1799 and Sweden at the end of the sixteenth century. These systems started at a time when marital property rules treated the couple or family as a unit under the control of the male head of the household.[16]

Crago emphasises the recurrent bickering in the US over the fairness or otherwise of the four scales currently in use there.[17] She suggests that all attempts to treat the married couple as the unit of taxation raise profound equity questions but notes that while the Canadian system does not currently aggregate income for taxation purposes it increasingly recognises the marital unit for certain purposes.

Yet this simplistic model ignores other, equally efficient, avenues for supporting and rewarding particular family structures. These include rebates for 'dependent' spouses and children, as well as the definition of income and the relationship between the earning of income and the expenses that can be deducted as necessary to the realisation of that income. The most obvious example is the distinction between expenses that are private or domestic in nature and not deductible, and those that are deemed essential to the realisation of the income stream. In this way, to give but one example, books, computers and other 'tools of the trade' may be deductible for an academic or teacher, but replacement services, such as child care, in a dual income household are not deductible, being 'private' in nature. In this way, not only is the 'essential' nature of replacement services denied, but also the economic value of non-market production is collapsed into 'leisure', defined as useful uses of time for purposes other than financial reward or consumption. As Miranda Stewart has argued,

> This favours the breadwinner-homemaker family in which the wife can specialise in child rearing and caring, supported by the husband's market income, in contrast to a family in which both spouses work in the market, both are taxed and they must pay for childcare and homemaking services (which are non-deductible).[18]

Similarly, s 26-40 of the *Income Tax Assessment Act* 1997,[19] disallows a deduction for expenditures necessary to maintain the spouse or children of the taxpayer. Even where the payments are necessitated by a court order or administrative assessment by the Child Support Agency they are neither deductible in respect of the payer nor subject to tax in the hands of the payee. In this way their 'private' nature is reinforced. Even more remarkably, as we saw earlier in this chapter, childcare is taken into account in determining the net income of a dependent spouse for rebate purposes, and where the taxpayer's spouse is disabled, a rebate is available for a housekeeper or child-housekeeper. The taxpayer, like the worker and the citizen bears a startling resemblance to the incorporated male family self. Australian taxation law explicitly recognises both that others may depend upon the taxpayer for their subsistence and that their services enable him to devote himself to the market in an unimpeded fashion.

Perhaps equally remarkable, and typically overlooked or avoided as populist suggestions of the desirability of a family tax emerge, is the economic value of the domestic and caring services provided by the wife in a male breadwinner family. Because these services are 'private' in nature, rather than secured in the market as commercial surrogates for private services, they are assigned no value by existing economic arrangements. Services of substantial commercial value are provided at no cost to the taxpayer, and arguably represent an unacknowledged supplement to family income. Individual taxpayers, and taxpayers in families in which both adults are fully engaged in waged labour must either provide these services themselves and thus carry a second shift, or secure replacement services in the market.

Other family forms, gay and lesbian families, extended families and so on escape, in part at least, this 'web' of regulations.[20] For purposes of comparison, it may be useful to consider the likely treatment of a lesbian couple with two children. The biological parent would, on the face of it, be eligible for a sole parent rebate; despite the existence of what would be deemed a *de facto* relationship were the couple heterosexual. She would also be eligible for an enhanced threshold under the *A New Tax System (Family Assistance) Act* 1999 provided that her income (including any parenting payment received) did not exceed the applicable ceiling. Unlike a married couple or heterosexual *de facto* couple, her partner's income would not be considered when determining whether the ceiling had been exceeded, since her partner does not exist within the frame of reference of taxation law.[21] Such a family could benefit significantly from its ambiguous status under current laws, being eligible for the increased rebate available to all families with dependent children that qualify under the income limit in the Family Tax Benefit Parts A and B. A similar result would obtain under social welfare law. Eligibility for the parenting payment and additional parenting payment would depend entirely on the income of the primary carer – the income of her partner would not be taken into account.[22] For taxation purposes, as for social welfare purposes, the relationship becomes invisible when it does not conform to the heterosexual norm. For other purposes, of course, including the intervention of child welfare agencies, the relationship may be highly visible and have deleterious consequences.

In other jurisdictions, this invisibility is gradually being broken down. Sweden has gone further than most by allowing homosexual couples to register their relationship and to adopt children. In Australia, registration is not available and adoption is restricted to heterosexual couples. In the US, in most jurisdictions, legal barriers to adoption exist and while laws restricting marriage to heterosexual couples have been challenged, thus far despite an initial success in Hawaii, the challenges have not borne fruit. On the other hand, in New Jersey, the state Supreme Court recently allowed visitation rights to the former partner in a lesbian relationship, holding that she had acted as a parent since the child's birth and therefore visitation was in the best interests of the child.[23] While other US states have rejected applications for visitation rights in such circumstances, such permission is becoming more common. The bounds of family are, in this way, in the process of being legally rewritten although the process is uneven. In some areas, such as family law, change has a way of forcing itself into consciousness, sometimes in battles over children. In other areas, such as taxation, even in its newer and gentler guise as a vehicle for family assistance, those who benefit from their invisibility have little reason to emerge from the closet although in other circumstances they may actively seek equivalent status to married couples.

The Iconic Family

As a signifier, family continues to have iconic status and in conservative jurisdictions such as Australia its potency underwrites legal measures that undermine the public egalitarianism that prevails in other areas. Effectively, measures such as the *A New Tax System (Family Assistance Act)* 1999 both support the male breadwinner family by substituting a social wage for the family wage and indirectly undercut economic equality for women. By effectively discouraging women with young children from maintaining their labour market attachment before their children reach school age, attempts to maintain their human capital are also discouraged. Such measures reinforce a number of critical social decisions.

First, they implicitly reject a dual worker-carer model within families. Families in which both parents curtail their labour market participation while their children are young would be eligible for the basic increase in threshold. They would not, however, be able to claim the additional increase available to families earning under $60,000 in which the primary carer has income below the threshold for the additional parenting payment. This would be true even if their combined income fell below the $60,000 threshold and they provided essentially full time parenting between them. It is not difficult to imagine a family in which both parents worked constricted hours with a combined income falling below the threshold – say a husband earning $30,000 pa and a wife earning $20,000 pa while reducing their employment to a 75 per cent fraction. Such a couple, if reasonably flexible hours were available, could easily restrict the need for child care to three hours per day (or even less if days of work were staggered rather than hours being reduced). It is not immediately obvious why the additional increase in the threshold is available only where the income of one individual falls below the cut-off for the Additional Parenting Payment. Surely a couple in which the parents are attempting both to provide effectively full-time parental care while maintaining workforce participation is, if anything, in greater need of assistance than a couple in which one individual specialises in household and caring labour while the other specialises in market labour. The 'hidden' economic benefit of the household labour of the spouse in the male breadwinner family more than compensates for the impost created by the higher marginal rate. Legal structures such as these discourage experimentation in the division of household labour and parenting and encourage couples to shape their behaviour in ways that maximise total cash income.

Second, and perhaps more significantly, the provision of family assistance in a form that discourages workforce participation by one parent significantly increases the likelihood that, should the relationship fail, that parent will become dependent upon the additional parenting payment for support. Restricted or non-existent labour force participation for an extended period has a significant impact upon the maintenance of human capital. Research in the European Union has shown that women who are out of the workforce for extended periods are less employable than are those who maintain workforce participation at a significant level. Their skills have diminished through lack of regular use and, increasingly, are likely to be dated, given the pace of technological change. Against this background, the provision of family assistance in a form which discourages rather than encourages workforce participation can be seen as fostering the growth of welfare dependence, given that more than one-third of all relationships are likely to break down.[24]

Third, such policies either deliberately or inadvertently, particularly coupled with social welfare policies increasingly designed to discourage long-term welfare dependence, foster the formation of a cadre of marginally skilled 'disposable workers'. Workers who have been out of the workforce for substantial periods are unlikely to be employable without substantial retraining. Even where such workers have developed significant skills prior to withdrawal from waged labour, upgrading is likely to be essential, and, unlike further education and training for those in waged labour is not tax deductible. Re-entry, therefore, is likely to be in the unskilled or semi-skilled category and in casual or part-time positions targeting mature aged women. Such policies also contribute significantly to sex segregation in the workforce and thus to the maintenance of the earnings gender gap, given the failure of comparable worth to make real headway. The absence of paid maternity/parental leave also encourages dual career families to postpone child bearing, perhaps indefinitely. This is particularly true where both are relatively equal in earning capacity. In families where the income differential between husband and wife is significant, the knowledge that the wife's income will be unavailable for a significant period before and after childbirth discourages reliance upon this income in planning. For this group, this weakens labour force attachment and discourages significant investment in the human capital of the secondary earner. Together with taxation and social welfare structures that effectively replace the family wage with a social wage, this constellation of policies tends to perpetuate the very problem it seeks to eradicate, that of long term welfare dependence.

As discussed earlier, current statistics suggest that female sole parents are less well educated and have more limited workforce skills than married mothers. While some of this is undoubtedly due to the number of migrants who become sole parents, many sole parents are Australian born and educated. This, in turn suggests that a significant number have assumed that workforce connection will cease when they have children, and that their independent income before children arrive is for 'extras' rather than core household expenditure. When their relationships break down, their lack of skills and the presence of family responsibilities make them relatively unattractive employees outside of a defined casual female market at low wages. As we saw earlier, this market is one that is undergoing rapid change, under the guise of flexibility and productivity, and one in which exploitive practices are increasingly common. A particularly telling example was reported recently and has led to a formal complaint of indirect discrimination to HREOC. A major Australian bank, the ANZ, has restructured the work hours of 6,000 part-time female tellers. In one case, a part-time teller was told that her 19.5 hours were to be spread over four rather than three days, significantly increasing the costs involved. When she refused, she was transferred to a branch one hour from her home.[25] When practices such as these are combined with a taxation system intended to support the male breadwinner household and indirectly discourage women from maintaining an independent income, the underlying message is clear. The income of the 'secondary wage earner' remains 'pin money'. This, in turn, has certain side effects, not least that there is little incentive for the secondary wage earner to devote time and resources to developing her human capital and extending her workforce participation.

Choices and Realities

While these are, of course, choices, they are choices whose sustainability depends upon certain assumptions that are no longer wholly realistic: that relationships will endure, the breadwinner will be able to earn enough to provide for the needs of the family, and that part-time work will be structured in a way that is compatible with other responsibilities. All of these choices are reinforced and implicitly supported by policy decisions in taxation, in social welfare law, and in the structure of industrial relations. Given the embedded character of these policies, it is hardly surprising that OECD evidence suggests that the gender gap is once again widening in Australia and that this widening is largely a consequence of the increasing economic marginality of casual employment. In a policy environment in which the worker and the taxpayer are essentially indistinguishable from the unencumbered citizen it is hardly surprising that the paradigmatic subject of social security law and welfare policy is, increasingly, both encumbered and seen as an undesirable drain on the resources generated by the unencumbered citizen. Private dependence is both acceptable and rewarded by taxation law and policy. Public dependence is both undesirable and threatening.

The young unemployed are threatening, both because in the public (and political) mind they are at once 'dole bludgers' and potential delinquents, and because their presence gives the lie to the rhetoric of increasing economic well being. Sole parents are seen as 'choosing' both sole parenthood and dependence, and as breeding a new generation of unemployed (and unemployable) youth – the stereotype of children who have grown up without adult role models in the waged labour force. Increasing, older Australians who would once have viewed the old age pension as an entitlement are being told that unless they have made private provision they will, at best, be economically marginal.

At every level, perceptions are gendered. Young unemployed men are stereotyped as potential or actual delinquents, young women as potential or actual sole parents. Despite the statistical reality that most sole parents become such following the breakdown of a long term relationship, in the popular mind sole parents are both female and 'choosing' to 'breed' to sponge off the state in preference to engaging in productive work. The increasing policy emphasis upon private provision following retirement disregards the reality that superannuation is a relatively recent phenomenon and one that is both classed and gendered. The vast majority of those able to rely upon private provision are male (and in some cases, the dependent spouses of those men) and from business and professional backgrounds. Working class men and women, and women from all backgrounds, even those with relatively uninterrupted participation in waged labour, are unlikely to be able to rely upon private provision. Women whose working lives have been interrupted for extended periods by family responsibilities, and who, through divorce or other misfortune are unpartnered, will end their days as they have lived them, as economic dependents in a world in which this form of dependence is seen as a symptom of social disorder. The work they have done for most of their adult lives: caring for children and aging parents, providing services for partners, volunteer work in schools and other community organisations increasingly reliant upon their services is, as it has been throughout their lives, invisible. They are simply those who have failed to provide for their retirement.

A Fairer Tax System or More of the Same?

As Australia follows other Western nations such as the UK and Canada with the introduction of a broadly based goods and services tax (GST), is anything likely to change? By its nature, even with the exclusion of most food,[26] the GST is regressive, falling most heavily upon those with lower incomes. Claire Young notes that:

> Unlike an income tax, the GST is not based upon ability to pay. All consumers pay at the same rate of tax regardless of their income. This means that the cost of a particular transaction is more burdensome for the taxpayer with the low income than the taxpayer with the high income, if that burden is measured by the percentage of income spent on the transaction.[27]

While the government made much of its claim that no one will be worse off under a GST,[28] it is clear that this is not true. Those whose incomes fall below the current tax-free threshold and who do not benefit from the proposed tax cuts will undoubtedly be worse-off. Their earnings will lose in purchasing power, and, since they currently pay no income tax on their earnings, this loss will not be compensated in other ways. Predictably, the great majority of these low-income earners are women, specifically women in casual work. While those who are sole parents or partnered secondary earners in households with children will make up some of this loss through family assistance, the increased tax free threshold (the mechanism through which the benefit is provided) is available only to one income earner in the family, thus reinforcing the dependent status of the secondary earner and the prevailing distribution of resources within the household. Claire Young notes that the Canadian experience has been that:

> The tax mix has shifted inexorably towards more reliance on the flat rate GST rather than progressive income taxes, and I would speculate that the same will happen [in Australia]. Changing the tax mix in this manner will ... have an especially negative impact on those with low incomes, the majority of whom are women.[29]

Thus far, little reason has emerged to doubt this view. Perhaps more significantly, the dynamic relationship between taxation policy (which has almost unambiguously reinforced the male breadwinner family) and social welfare policy (which transferred resources to female headed households and to women in couple families through the now abandoned child endowment) has altered significantly. Increasingly, taxation policy is being harnessed to achieve family policy goals, specifically to support the increasingly marginal male breadwinner family and those families that clearly differentiate between the primary and secondary earner. Because the mechanism adopted has been through the modification of the tax-free threshold to take account of dependants and because the tax savings thus generated are returned to the primary breadwinner, the effect is to reinforce the existing distribution of economic power within families. This has been accompanied by a further 'redistribution', this time through the mechanism of child support payments, primarily from non-residential fathers to residential mothers. The recent announcement that child support payments will be reduced for those fathers whose non-residential children spend between 10-30 per cent of nights per year with them, effectively disregards both the negative impact on residential parents disposable income, an increasingly significant factor against the background of the GST, and the fact that the costs incurred by residential parents are unlikely to diminish. Rent (or mortgages and rates) still have to be paid; power and telephone bills are unchanged; the need for clothing, toys and funds for school activities continues undiminished. The same may be said of the proposed exemption of overtime wages and earnings from a second job from the funds available for child support and the lowering of the income level at which child support no longer increases proportional to income. The perceived policy need to support non-residential parents who have formed new families, and the increasing view of sole parents as an economic and social liability outweighs the marginal economic status of most female sole parents and the penalty paid by their children for their marginality. While no one disputes the fact that there are costs associated with contact (transportation, food and, perhaps, the more significant expense of ensuring that accommodation is available for one or more additional children), the levels of contact at which this transfer occurs and the rationale given, to encourage non-residential fathers to exercise contact, suggests that the motivation is politically driven rather than directed at the 'elimination of major disparities in people's material resources, well-being, opportunities, and political and social power'.[30]

The ideological agenda underpinning 'reform' was clearly evident in the massive advertising campaign in the lead up to the GST. On 26 May 2000 the Australian Commonwealth government ran full double page advertisements in all major metropolitan daily newspapers emphasising the taxation savings available to families under the 'new taxation system'.[31] When both the tax cuts and the family assistance package are taken into account, 'savings' to single income families are significantly greater at every income level between $25,000 and $70,000 than those available to dual income families.[32] While a part of this difference may be off-set by the Child Care Benefit, both the publicity and the structure of the 'new tax system' makes the social agenda transparent. It completely disregards the fact that two income families are likely to be more disadvantaged by the GST than single income families, since both transportation and clothing are subject to the GST, and, with the exception of approved child care services, replacement services such as household help and prepared meals are also subject to the GST.

Despite the partial elimination of the family wage, its increasing replacement by a social wage structured to ameliorate the hardships experienced by certain favoured social groups, combined with the persistence of the earnings gender gap suggests that fundamentally, Australia remains committed to a form of strong male breadwinner policy. In tandem, taxation and social welfare policy seek to maximise support through the social wage to single income families (including sole parent households) but these benefits are strongly linked to status, specifically the status of wife and/or mother. The gender-neutral language (dependent spouse/sole parent) obscures but does not alter the fact that the vast majority of dependent spouses, like the vast majority of sole parents, are female. The choices offered by the taxation system, like those in the waged labour market and in social welfare are fundamentally illusory. The rhetoric of choice suggests that women are able to choose the lifestyle they prefer, whether as full time carers, as part-time workers and full-time carers, or as full time participants in waged labour. It does not, however, highlight the disincentives to choice that operate at all levels. In the concluding section of this chapter, we will examine some of these disincentives and their interaction.

Conclusion

As we saw in the last section, official rhetoric seeks to emphasise the 'family friendly' nature of the 'new taxation system', promising a better deal for single income families and the simplification of the current plethora of transfer payments. The rhetoric suggests, inter alia, that this will offer 'real choice' to families, by reducing the tax burden on single income families. Unfortunately, for those women who wish to maintain their human capital by working part-time even while their children are very young, the changes may render this particular choice economically unviable, given the costs attached to maintaining workforce participation, costs which will undeniably increase following the introduction of the GST.[33] If the intention is to relieve the burdens on families and offer greater choice, it is not clear why single income families should be privileged over dual income families, given the economic value of the services provided by a partner engaged in home work rather than wage work.

In the workplace as well, the gap between family friendly rhetoric and family unfriendly reality remains stark. The 1995 AWIRS survey suggested that approximately one-third of all workplaces with more than 20 employees offered paid maternity leave and a smaller percentage offered paid paternity leave. While these figures are slightly dated, the absence of paid parental leave in the vast majority of Australian workplaces[34] and the reluctance of successive governments to pursue its introduction vigorously makes it clear that no fundamental commitment to women and children exists. While demographic panic and the ongoing 'concern' over declining fertility rates remains live, and much is made of the family friendly workplace, in reality little is done to enhance the ability of Australian women to realise a balance between work and family while pursuing careers rather than merely moving in and out of a series of slots in the secondary labour market. Parental leave, access to permanent part-time career track positions and other policies that enable women to utilise all of their talents fully (and encourage men to do so as well) represent minimum commitments to women and children. That they are not seen as representing minimum commitments to families as well is largely due to the psychic hegemony of one particular form of family and one particular understanding of family life.

Women are still expected to 'choose' between family and career, and men are expected to live out the demands of the breadwinner role and to understand that whatever the earning capacity of the women who become their partners, that earning capacity will effectively vanish when childbearing commences. Paid maternity leave allows women's income to count as 'real' income; as income that may diminish for a time if part-time work is chosen, but as income that may be counted in long term planning and is, therefore, of value, not simply pin money. Despite the increasing 'unreality' of the housewife bargain and the breadwinner bargain, despite statistical evidence of increasing workforce participation by women and a diminishing fertility rate, the popularity of political railing against welfare dependence and the rhetoric of mutual obligation reminds us that sole parents and their children remain popular targets. Yet the patterns and practices of work and childrearing decried among sole parents mirror precisely those rewarded by the taxation system and the transfer system in couple households. Most of the children in sole parent families once lived in couple households whose role allocation was, in part, shaped by both the taxation and the transfer system and by the reality of the gender gap. The levels of economic activity decried among sole parents are those rewarded by the taxation system in couple households and reinforced by the absence of family friendly practices in the labour market as a whole. Attempts to alter this pattern through the rhetoric of mutual obligation are simply punitive, a new rhetoric for an ancient distinction, that between the deserving and the undeserving poor.

Notes

1   The Australian taxation regime involves numerous closely inter-related statutes. For present purposes the most important are the *Income Tax Assessment Act* 1936, the *Income Tax Assessment Act* 1997, and *A New Tax System (Family Assistance) Act* 1999.

2   Stewart, Miranda, 'Domesticating Tax Reform: The Family in Australian Tax and Transfer Law' (1999) 21 *Sydney Law Review* 453, 460.

3   See *Income Tax Assessment Act* 1915 (Cth). Historically, Tasmania represented a limited exception.

4   (1907) 2 CLR 1.

5   See Division 17, *Income Tax Assessment Act* 1936, s 160AD. These were introduced in 1975.

6   While spouse also includes de facto spouse, the underlying imagery is that of the male breadwinner family with the state replacing the breadwinner in the case of sole parents.

7   Professor Lilian Knowles, dissenting in the report of the 1920 Royal Commission on Taxation quoted in Cooper, Graeme S, Robert L Deutsch & Richard E Krever, *Cooper, Krever & Vann's Income Taxation*, 2nd ed, Sydney, LBC, 1993, 2.8-2.9.

8   Young, Claire, 'Taxing Times for Women: Feminism Confronts Tax Policy' (1999) 21 *Sydney Law Review* 487, 489.

9   Stewart, 463.

10   See s 20D(4) *Income Tax Rates Act* 1986 which refers to the 'breadwinner' and breadwinner's partner.

11   See *A New Tax System (Family Assistance) Act* 1999. This legislation also provides for the maternity allowance, the maternity immunisation allowance, and other programs providing support to families.

12   See, for example, Women's Action Alliance, 'Family Unit Taxation' accessed on 14 April 2000 at http://users.bigpond.com/jsmitty/waaFamilyUnitTaxation.html. The Women's Action Alliance favours a variant of the French approach, although limiting the amount of income that can notionally be allocated to any individual to $15,000 to eliminate any windfall for high-income families.

13   Bartlett, Bruce R, 'Testimony before the US House Committee on Ways and Means' 28 January 1998, downloaded 10 April 2000 from http://www/ncpa.org/.

14   Taxation Review Committee, *Full Report*, 31 January 1975, 144 [10-16]. The Chair of the Committee expressed some reservations about this aspect of the report. For a full discussion, see Cooper, 1995, 87.

15   The Honourable John Howard, MP, 'Towards an Economic Policy for the Family', speech delivered to the Council for the National Interest, Sydney 7 March 1994. The proposal was limited to single income families and incorporated an income test designed to exclude high wage earners.

16   Crago, Joyce M, 'The Unit of Taxation: Current Canadian Issues' (1993) 52 *Univ. of Toronto Faculty of Law Review* 1, 3.

17   There are separate scales for single persons, married couples filing jointly, married couples filing separately, and for sole heads of households.

18   Stewart, 462.

19   The *Income Tax Assessment Act* 1936 was supplemented by the *Income Tax Assessment Act* 1997 as part of the government's tax reform agenda.

20   Other forms of regulation proliferate. Sexuality remains a vexed area in family law, particularly in the context of custody battles. Homosexual couples are unable (in Australia) to adopt children; reproductive services including IVF are largely unavailable to lesbian couples (or individuals) seeking to conceive a child. While some recent progress has been made, a family law system that tacitly assumes nuclear family structures has difficulty coming to terms with the child rearing practices prevailing among indigenous peoples who maintain their original cultures.

21   The same would be true in the case of a gay couple.

22   See *In The Matter of: B and J (Artificial Insemination)* No. ML 4677 of 1996 at http://www.austlii.edu.au/ accessed on 17 April 2000. It held that a male person providing sperm for the artificial insemination of one member of a lesbian couple was not liable to pay child support as the 'father' of the children born to that couple and recommended legislative changes to eliminate the ambiguity.

23   See *VC v MJB* cited on GAYLAWNET at http://www.labyrinth.net.au/~dba accessed on 18 April 2000.

24   While the present government is also putting significant sums into services designed to strengthen relationships, no developed jurisdiction has seen a significant decrease in the divorce rate following the introduction of no-fault divorce. It is usual for the rate to stabilise, perhaps at a slightly lower level than the peak.

25   Bachelard, Michael, 'Part-time staff take on "bullying" bank', The *Australian*, 5 May 2001.

26 Broadly speaking, food is excluded from the GST. Exceptions to this general rule include prepared food and restaurant meals.
27 Young, 498.
28 In May 2000 advertisements paid for by the Commonwealth Government on free to air TV during prime time emphasise this claim.
29 Young, 498.
30 Bakan, Joel, *Just Words: Constitutional Rights and Wrongs*, Toronto, Univ. of Toronto Press, 1997, 9-10.
31 See, for example, The *Australian*, 26 May 2000 at 10-11.
32 For families with one child, single income households were to 'gain' $54.77 pw, dual income households, $27.06. At $70,000, single income families were to gain $92.75, dual income families, $54.82. The figures for dual income families presume a fifty-fifty income split, a wholly unrealistic presumption given the earnings gender gap and the propensity of women to work part-time. On a more realistic split, in which the primary worker earned $50,000 and the secondary worker $20,000, the dual income family would fare significantly worse! The figures cited are taken from the government sponsored advertising campaign in the mass media.
33 Transportation, clothing and footwear are all GST liable and these costs are likely to be greater in a dual income household than in a single income household. While approved childcare is exempt, other replacement services are also subject to the GST.
34 OECD statistics suggest that about 17% of Australian working women have access to paid parental leave.

Chapter 8

Making Room for Families: Choices and Realities

Introduction

Inevitably, in a pluralist society, our conceptions of family and family roles are no longer monolithic, but kaleidoscopic, almost infinitely variable. Over the last few decades, the increasing prevalence of ART, high profile litigation involving a dispute between a birth mother and a genetic mother,[1] the voices of gay and lesbian families, and the claims of indigenous families have gained an increasing public profile. An action seeking to deny unmarried women access to ART is now before the High Court, with the support of the Commonwealth Attorney-General. Most recently, a landmark Family Court decision upheld the right of a female to male transsexual to marry a woman.[2]

As we have seen in earlier chapters, despite the political rhetoric of choice, choices are made within a complex social and legal order. Inevitably, these forms of ordering, both legal and communal, shape choices made by individual men and women, often in unexpected ways. Some of these realised choices spill over into waves of apparent moral panic fuelled by media campaigns. Many of these have already been explored as we attempt to separate the mythological dimension from a complex social and demographic reality. Yet the resonance of the mythological dimension, its ability to capture the popular imagination, highlights a profound political and social failure conveniently hidden behind the classical liberal rhetoric of supporting individual choice.

The last 30-40 years have born witness to profound social and legal changes, changes often at odds with the cultural traditions of the peoples making up multicultural Australia. One way of reading these mythological underpinnings is through the persistent cultural myth of the simultaneously castrating and alluring woman.[3] Often figured as the dichotomy between the madonna and the whore, this European cultural myth arrived in Sydney with the First Fleet and retains its potency, despite a complex over weaving of other cultural traditions. Despite apparently progressive legal and political traditions, making Australia one of the earliest western democracies to enfranchise women and a sustained attempt by early 20th century maternalist feminists to entrench the rights of the citizen mother, in practice, maternalist policies valorised dependence and reinforced cultural traditions equating the 'good mother' with the dutiful wife within the patriarchal household. By Federation, policies that were lineal descendents of those entrenched in the *Poor Law Amendment Act* 1834 (UK) constructed single mothers as 'fallen women' who were likely to fabricate accusations of parentage to obtain support from 'innocent' men.[4] Unable to earn a living wage, devoid of support from a welfare system providing minimalist and often grudging support to 'deserving' widows and deserted wives, in reality mothering was valued within the patriarchal nuclear family and condemned outside it.[5]

While this web of patriarchal practices seemingly receded with the introduction of the supporting mother's benefit and no fault divorce in the early 1970s, it retained its cultural potency. Women who rejected the 'homemaker bargain' were, by the late 1980s, castigated for welfare dependence and attacked as castrating demons stealing the children of deserving men by an increasingly politically powerful fathers' rights movement. By the late 1990s, media portrayals of non-residential fathers, including those who murdered their children during contact, romanticised them as unjustly deprived of their children.[6] Residential mothers were often portrayed as castrating bitches, unjustly depriving deserving fathers of their children under the influence of 'radical feminists', perhaps the newest cultural manifestation of the traditional Lilit myth. Equally significantly, mothers who engaged in waged labour, particularly those with pre-school children, were also castigated and their parenting ability and dedication questioned. For many women, a no-win situation emerged. If they were unable to live out the terms of the sexual contract, they were at significant risk. Those who relied on child support payments and social welfare benefits were increasingly targeted as drones rearing a new generation of welfare dependents. Those who sought to maintain themselves through waged labour risked being deemed inadequate parents, simultaneously neglecting their duty as mothers and 'stealing' men's jobs.

Married mothers were also at risk. If they complied with the terms of the housewife bargain, they risked an uncertain future should their relationships fail. If they did not and sought a more egalitarian vision of family life, they risked condemnation from both women and men for their lack of maternal devotion, and confronted a waged labour market in which essential support structures were unavailable. Marooned in a halfway house, neither 'good mothers' nor 'good workers', they negotiated an ostensibly egalitarian but pervasively gendered labour market, one in which family friendly practices were largely absent and in which paid maternity and parenting leave were unlikely to be available. Labour market structures and practices, like those in schools and other institutions, continued to be predicated upon the 'sexual contract'. Men are culturally (and sometimes legally) compelled to live the breadwinner bargain, despite the fact that the family wage was eradicated 30 years ago. Those who themselves wish to participate in family life fully, caring for their children as well as caring about them, confront a set of market practices which grudgingly provide a 'mommy track' for a few fortunate women, and contingent and marginal employment for the majority. Even the minimalist supports available for women are, on the whole, unavailable to men. The dichotomy between 'working mothers' and 'workers', and the ingrained belief that 'working mothers' are somehow seeking special privileges powerfully reinforces the gendered division of labour and ensures that those who might wish to seek alternative imaginings are penalised. As contingent forms of contract and casual labour gradually make inroads into the mainstream labour market, and employment security recedes, for both men and women, social experimentation becomes more dangerous. As Nancy Dowd argues:

> The culture of work must accept and support family responsibilities and value family work ... We have to visualize parenting and working being combined in a variety of ways and in ways that are not gender defined or likely to play out according to gender... If we expect all parents to nurture along some range of conduct, then our planning or structure must reflect all parents.[7]

Dowd makes the critical and radical argument that a core reason for the pervasive failure of existing policies to achieve greater gender equity, within family law, within labour law, and, I would add, within social welfare law, lies in their gendered focus. To the extent that existing policies have focused on women, as they have in equal opportunity law and in efforts to eliminate discriminatory practices, they reinforce the conceptual barrier between woman and worker and the tacit equation of worker and breadwinner. In this way, programs intended to develop more equitable workplaces become programs perceived as pandering to the needs of that increasingly marginalised and vilified special interest group, 'feminists', and thus as programs which penalise men and full time mothers. Similarly, in social welfare law, and for a substantial period in family law, the focus upon women-as-mothers – and as mothers safely contained within the patriarchal family – unshakeably linked mothering with carework, thus privileging the full time mother and potentially labelling women who combined carework and wage work as selfish and neglectful. The focus upon women-as-mothers also reinforced the association between fatherhood and breadwinning. To be a father was to live out the breadwinner role. Nothing more was required or expected. In earlier chapters we have seen how these role patterns played out, in equal opportunity law, in family law, in labour law and in taxation law. We have also seen their consequences played out in demographic indicators, and in the increasing public profile of pressure groups such as the fathers' rights movement. The policy response has been punitive rather than empowering, repackaging failed policies of the past rather than seeking new visions.

Contradiction and Tension: Policy, Social Change and Lost Opportunities

The proclaimed flagships of gender equity, equal employment opportunity and sex discrimination law have, as critics predicted at the outset, largely sought to deliver formal equality packaged as radical social change. Their failures are obvious. Gender segregation remains high by world standards. The unabated flow of sex discrimination complaints highlights employer reluctance to accommodate pregnancy and childcare responsibilities. Perhaps most tellingly, the earnings gender gap was unaffected by legal change in these areas and has once again begun to widen. None of this should be surprising – legal programs to enhance gender equity are peripheral to labour market policy, to family policy, to social welfare policy and, most tellingly, to taxation policy. For more than a decade labour market policy has emphasised deregulation, competition and decreased employment security in the name of flexibility. The signals in these areas are strong and fundamentally incompatible with measures intended to enhance equity.

Like labour market policy, family policy has, except for a brief period in the 1980s, assumed that women's labour force participation is contingent, rather than core, perhaps summed up in the statement that men have careers and women jobs. Despite the increasing participation of married women in the labour market, the assumption is that this participation will be part-time, that single income families warrant support with a 'social wage' to replace the vanished family wage, and that men will continue to be breadwinners and women homemakers. Most recently, the interaction of family policy and social welfare policy has highlighted the tension between the belief that welfare dependence is pernicious and that children raised by parents on benefits will (almost inevitably) themselves be unemployed, and the belief that the mothers of young children ought to be full time parents. While 'mutual obligation' has yet to become fully entrenched and 16 remains the cut-off age for the parenting payment, pressure to lower the cut-off age is mounting and impoverished women with school age children are being encouraged to seek training or part-time employment.

These policies reinforce two separate social norms. First, they reinforce the male-breadwinner tradition that has long been a cornerstone of Australian social policy. Second, because women are still not expected to establish careers before beginning their families and because appropriate employment for mothers is seen as part-time, typically in non-career track service positions, existing labour market patterns are reinforced. Permanent part-time career track positions remain a rarity and are exclusively a matter for negotiation between either trade unions (although these are a waning force) or individual employees and their employers. While mothers are entering the waged labour force in increasing numbers, most continue to work in segregated, contingent jobs, often without career tracks, and in positions which, increasingly, are structured to meet employer demands for flexibility rather than mother's need for predictability.

Against this background, the failure of sex discrimination and equal employment opportunity law to diminish the earnings gender gap and the prevailing levels of occupational segregation is predictable. Also predictable is the evidence that while women are increasing their workforce activity men are not increasing their active participation in unwaged work, particularly housework and active carework, to the same extent. Women have been socialised into a second shift, enabling men to retain many of the benefits of the breadwinner bargain. Yet this is only part of the story. When women's status as secondary workers and primary parents is reinforced, men's status as primary, career track workers and breadwinners is also reinforced. The same policies that have failed to deliver a family friendly workplace for women also ensure that men who seek to become actively engaged in parenting are unable to access the support structures that might make this possible. In Australia, as elsewhere, to seek leave to deal with family responsibilities is (marginally) acceptable for female (secondary) workers and unacceptable for men. The breadwinner bargain, which entitles men to domestic services and relieves them of responsibility for hands-on parenting, carries its own price. Given the existing gender gap, and the historic tendency for women to marry up and men to marry down, the resulting behaviour conforms to that predicted by the theory of rational choice. Women typically have few benefits to trade for a more equal family bargain and men have no incentives to take on a more active family role and valid reasons to recommit themselves to waged labour and eschew parenting and domestic labour.

Taxation law and policy further entrench the status quo, providing rebates for single income households and encouraging the affluent to split investment income to reduce the tax impost on the primary breadwinner. Both these policies discourage even part time work by married women and thus discourage the maintenance of skills and employment capabilities in the longer term. Against this policy background, and against social attitudes and expectations entrenched since at least the 1930s, equal opportunity rhetoric is little more than window dressing.

Social welfare policy sent out unambiguous signals until comparatively recently. Where the breadwinner was unemployed or unable to work due to illness, irrespective of whether there were children in the household, married women were not expected to engage in waged labour, even on a part-time basis. Social welfare policy entrenched the male breadwinner family, unemployment and sickness benefits being payable at the married rate. In the case of sickness benefits, any income earned by a working wife did not affect eligibility until 1977 when the Supporting Mother's Benefit was replaced by the Sole Parent's Pension, eligibility being extended for the first time to custodial fathers.

Equally significantly, the failure to implement comparable worth legitimated the disparity between wages in traditionally female occupations and those in traditionally male occupations, even where the skills required in traditionally female occupations such as nursing were significantly greater than those in many male comparators. Over time, this has had a second effect following the 'law of unintended consequences', crippling efforts to attract men into many 'female' occupations, for example, primary teaching. The results were outlined in chapter 3, an increasing movement by career oriented women into non-traditional occupations and no evidence of a comparable movement by men into traditionally female occupations. Predictably, this development has led to increasingly vitriolic abuse from some segments of the men's and fathers' rights movements, particularly those which identify the breadwinner role as fundamental to harnessing male aggression to productive social purposes.

As Australia continues to reject universal nationally funded paid parenting leave, it is worth noting some of the costs. First, leaving paid parenting leave to negotiation, either through AWAs or through enterprise bargaining will undoubtedly ameliorate the disadvantages traditionally experienced by working women in workplaces where negotiations are successful but will not advance gender equity in the long term. If, as some public rhetoric suggests, as a society we want women to have more equal access to the workplace and want men to play a more active role in parenting and family life, a universal, national policy is essential.[8] Only through national provision of parenting leave is it possible to put provisions in place that both protect women and encourage men to engage in hands-on parenting. While the Swedish model, canvassed in earlier chapters, is among the world's most progressive, it lacks flexibility in several respects. An optimal model would make it possible, after a period of full time leave, for both parents to undertake part-time work while supplementing their income with their remaining parental leave. Such a policy might also encourage more fathers to access leave than has been the case in Sweden, since both they and their partners would be able to maintain workforce ties. Similarly, it would accommodate the needs of women who may wish to return to the workforce on a part-time basis while their children are young, rather than take an extended period of full-time leave. There are very few jobs that actually need to be done on a full time basis and even fewer which require the kind of hours that are the norm in many professional workplaces. Only where provision is national, rather than workplace based, is it possible to structure leave provision to reserve a part of the leave period for fathers (as in the Swedish 'daddy month') and thus to encourage greater involvement by fathers in hands on parenting. Making room for families in this way is critical. While, undoubtedly, attitudinal change is slow, such changes would recognise the fact that most men and women are likely to have family responsibilities at some point in their lives and would begin to dismantle existing assumptions about the nature of the worker – or incorporated male family self – and assumptions about the gendering of carework.

As Nancy Dowd has argued in the American context, every limitation on the opportunities of women to participate fully in wage work is also a limitation on the opportunities of men to become equal parents and active nurturers. Until the gender gap is closed, until the tacit distinction between worker and woman worker disappears, any attempt to encourage equal nurture by men will founder on economic reality.[9] A workplace which sees family friendly policies as policies providing limited flexibility for women workers, typically in support roles, and configures professional and managerial roles in which ways which equate commitment with 'putting in the hours' is not a family friendly workplace. A family friendly workplace would recognise that all workers, men and women, are likely, at some time in their lives, to have both family obligations and professional obligations and that if they are to be productive as workers these must be accommodated. Egalitarian programs are not programs designed to meet the 'special needs' of the woman worker, but programs that begin from the assumption that both men and women have a right to participate fully in nurturing and both have a right to function fully as economic parents. The division between social parenting and economic parenting, and the assumption that the ideal worker is an economic parent and not a social parent is a profound barrier to change, just as is the assumption, played out in other areas, that normative fatherhood is economic parenting.

Family law is an accurate barometer of the vagaries of policy in this area and of the social distance that remains to be travelled. While restrictive fault based divorce regimes provided critical support for the breadwinner housewife bargain, reinforcing the social prejudice against unmarried mothers (and separated and divorced women), the shift to no fault divorce did not reject that bargain outright but merely sought to remedy its perceived injustices. When the *Family Law Act 1975* was enacted, the legislation explicitly sought to protect the position of a woman who wanted only maintain her role as 'wife and mother', that is, to continue with the role she had enjoyed during marriage, including the absence of any obligation to engage in economic parenting. While that provision has since been amended, and is now gender neutral and substantially broadened, the legislation continues to pay lip-service to protecting the position of one who wishes to be a full-time parent. In this way, the affirmation of traditional roles and the separation of economic and social parenthood remain entrenched, albeit buried beneath gender-neutral rhetoric. Other changes to the *Family Law Act* 1975 also send mixed signals. During the 1970s and much of the 1980s, the legislation explicitly encouraged judges to consider the availability of the Supporting Mother's Benefit (later the Sole Parent's Pension) in setting child support levels. That role ended with the enactment of the *Child Support (Assessment) Act* 1989 in the late 1980s, and under current laws even unemployed fathers are required to provide some support. For legal and genetic fathers, economic fatherhood remains the acknowledged norm, although affluent fathers who are able to conceal their income through companies or other legal devices remain out of reach. Social fatherhood, caring for children as opposed to caring about them, is paid lip service. While it is nominally reinforced by provisions specifying that children have a right to contact with their biological parents and with significant others, no attempt has yet been made to compel fathers to comply with contact arrangements (although mothers can be compelled to facilitate them). In this way, the traditional model is reaffirmed, that of the social mother and economic father. Economic incentives are provided to encourage fathers to increase contact with their children, incentives that, in practice, reduce the resources available to residence mothers and which have, in some cases, exposed residence mothers to significant taxation liability.[10] These enticements begin with contact levels that fall far short of co-equal physical parenting, as little as 36.5 nights a year of overnight contact.

Perhaps most tellingly, where fathers seek residence through the courts, the focus is often upon the parenting capabilities of the father's new significant other or female relative (often described as a mother figure), rather than upon the father's capabilities as caregiver. Judicial attitudes are very different where the mother's parenting capabilities are evaluated. While the courts are concerned with the impact of any new partner upon the children, the emphasis reflects underlying assumptions about gender roles. Sometimes the concern centres on the role her new partner plays in the household and whether he is a suitable influence on the children. At other times, there is a clear concern that he will become a 'substitute father', replacing the absent father in the children's lives. A residence father is often expected to provide a 'substitute mother', a replacement for the mother's labour in caring for her children. A residence mother may secure an alternative breadwinner, a man to provide her and her children with support, but must not allow him to become a 'substitute father'. These differences reflect a profound difference in perception. A substitute mother is acceptable precisely because a distinction is made between the necessity of caring for, and the relationship between mother and child. Because caring about is understood as feeling rather than practice, and because the actual practice of fatherhood is often episodic, becoming a 'substitute father' is seen as replacing the absent biological father in the children's emotional and social lives, rather than simply providing the necessary care.[11] Fatherhood, it seems, is fragile and in need of protection, motherhood is not. Implicitly, a 'substitute mother' is preferable to a nanny or day care centre, and, in some jurisdictions a working mother is at a significant disadvantage in a parenting dispute with a father whose new partner is a suitable substitute mother. While the economic role of the father can be wholly or partially supplanted, his 'social role', however limited, remains sacrosanct although difficult to define with any precision.

Counting the Costs

The costs are clear. Some are highlighted by the demographic indicators explored in earlier chapters, the declining birth rate, low levels of workforce participation by sole parents, the failure of many fathers to maintain contact with their children following relationship breakdown and widespread anger over compulsory child support. Others are reflected in the inflammatory rhetoric in the mass media, in which women are accused of 'stealing' men's jobs, in which men are pitted against women and 'feminists' demonised both by the media and by pop psychologists and the fathers' rights movement. Other costs are more subtle, but worth highlighting. Existing legal and policy structures marginalise equity agendas. Equal opportunity programs are persistently portrayed as harmful to business and the economy, and sometimes as antithetical to family welfare. One cost (perhaps deliberate) has been the artificial competition generated between 'full-time mothers' and working mothers, so that programs which benefit employed mothers are seen as depriving full-time mothers of essential support. More insidious is the increasing prominence given claims that men are somehow discriminated against by programs seeking to enhance opportunities for women: in education, in employment and in participation in the wider community.

These patterns are precisely what ought to have been expected from the legal and policy positions of the past 30 years. Falling fertility rates are consistently linked with increased education for women and with the social failure to implement programs which support women's workforce participation and facilitate combining parenthood and career opportunities. During the period examined, Australia has successfully enhanced educational opportunities for girls, and while retention rates for both sexes are still below some international comparators, progress has been significant. At the same time, social welfare law and policy, family law and policy and labour market policy have consistently upheld the breadwinner homemaker dichotomy. Workforce participation by sole parents was neither supported nor encouraged from the introduction of the supporting mother's benefit until the introduction of the JET program in the late 1980s. Perhaps more significantly, from the introduction of the unemployment benefit and the commonwealth widow's pension in the early 1940s it was assumed that partnered women would not engage in waged labour, even where the breadwinner was unemployed. From the introduction of the supporting mother's benefit, family law and policy assumed first, that it was appropriate for sole parents to rely upon benefits for support and, perhaps more significantly, that benefit payments could be used to reduce the child support otherwise payable. Sole parents and mothers in low income families are still entitled to the parenting allowance until their youngest child reaches 16, effectively giving social and legal approval to a period of at least 16 years out of the paid workforce. Only recently has universal unpaid maternity leave become available, and universal paid parenting leave (as distinct from maternity leave) has yet to reach policy level in the platform of either major political party.[12] These legal and policy positions send strong signals: mothers ought not to be expected to engage in waged labour and should not expect to find programs facilitating their participation. These signals are clearly understood, not only by ordinary men and women, but also by business groups.

Against this background, it is hardly surprising that complaints under sex discrimination law frequently involve discrimination on the basis of pregnancy or family commitments. Supporting workforce participation often seems limited to occasional high profile programs seeking to retain the services of highly trained professionals; while the complaints often involve workers in service industries and low level managers. The marginal status of equal opportunity law and the core status of labour market policy and employment law send unmistakeable signals. These patterns are not dissimilar to those in European countries such as Greece and Spain where the fertility rate has plummeted to 1.3, well below the replacement rate of 2.1 and far lower than the 1.7 rate which triggered media headlines in Australia.

These same policies have also ratified the cultural perception of motherhood as primarily associated with care giving, rather than with the provision of economic support and of fatherhood as almost exclusively associated with the provision of economic support. Men whose roles during relationships were largely limited to the provision of economic resources and whose hands on participation in nurturing was limited to 'helping with the children' on weekends and after working hours, increasingly found themselves unmoored by failed relationships, resentful of a legal and policy system that demanded child support but neither could nor would guarantee that they could 'parent' as they had while their relationship endured.

In order to remain viable, the breadwinner homemaker bargain requires a particular legal and policy environment, and that environment has, since the 1960s, been significantly eroded. The sexual contract is not a natural phenomenon, but one constructed by specific background conditions. In Australia, these background conditions included the family wage, a social welfare structure that maintained the breadwinner homemaker bargain during unemployment, during illness or disability, and following retirement, and a family law regime that restricted access to divorce and penalised women who did not comply with the terms of the homemaker bargain. Other necessary background conditions included a punitive attitude toward unmarried mothers, women who left their partners and towards widows, deserted wives and divorced wives who had behaved in ways deemed inconsistent with the sexual contract. The stigmatisation of illegitimate children, or as they were once termed, filius nullius – no man's child – was a critical element in these background conditions. All of these supporting structures have gradually been eliminated, perhaps because they could not be sustained in the face of increasing education, increasing access to health care, including effective means of birth control, and the changing social expectations of girls and women, including the expectation that careers would be available which were commensurate with the expectations generated by increasing education and with talent.

Predictably, perhaps, in a liberal state and one without strong social welfare traditions, the legal changes were incremental rather than proactive, chipping away at the foundations supporting the sexual contract, beginning with the rejection of the family wage. This was closely followed by family law reform and by the 1973 changes to the *Social Security Act* 1947 providing the supporting mother's benefit. Yet even while the supporting mother's benefit made it possible for women to choose whether or not to remain in relationships without the strictures imposed by the widow's pension, taxation policy and the broad thrust of social welfare policy continued to support the sexual contract, for example by retaining the married rate for unemployment benefits.

While some of the provisions of the *Family Law Act* 1975 contained a strong equity focus, for example those directing the court to count non-financial contributions equally with financial contributions in the division of marital property, it did not disturb existing roles, but merely ratified the broader social changes that had undermined the viability of the fault based system. The dichotomy between breadwinning and caretaking roles was entrenched, albeit in somewhat altered form, through statutory affirmation of the need to protect a woman who wanted only to 'continue' her role as wife and mother.

Many of the features now identified as urgent social problems, the relatively low workforce participation rates among sole parents, the failure of many fathers to maintain contact, intense hostility over child support and a tendency among some fathers to see child support as payment for contact, are precisely the features that were structurally encouraged, given the laws and policies in force between the early 1970s and the mid-1990s and given the continuing attitudes about working mothers and the association of masculinity with the breadwinner role. Given a social welfare system and labour market structured to reinforce the breadwinner bargain, and a family law regime that acknowledged its legitimacy, as well as the difficulty of raising one or more children alone, sole parents could hardly be expected to 'volunteer' for a second shift, when partnered parents in families with unemployed breadwinners were expected not to do so.

Under the terms of the breadwinner homemaker bargain, economic support is the currency used to purchase domestic services and the pleasures of childrearing without the associated labour. Following the collapse of relationships, the benefits no longer exist for either party. Against the background of a tacit social agreement in which economic support was exchanged for services, including the labour of caring for children rather than simply caring about them, there were few incentives for many fathers to maintain contact with their children, especially where contact involved caring for children as well as caring about them. Likewise, there were few incentives for women, particularly women whose relationships had been difficult and sometimes dangerous, to facilitate contact, since it could be seen as providing a former partner with some of the benefits of the breadwinner homemaker bargain while receiving nothing in return. The persistent demand of some fathers' rights groups that child support be directly linked with contact is simply a reiteration of part of the breadwinner homemaker bargain, as is the sometimes expressed desire for 'unfettered contact', that is, contact at any time convenient for the father. Even those apparently radical men's groups who are demanding a return to automatic father custody, or, somewhat more moderately, shared physical parenting, do so within the context of the sexual contract, the argument being that these changes will reinforce the breadwinner homemaker bargain by deterring women from abandoning relationships and may prevent women from competing with men in the labour market. The presumption is seldom that the father will physically care for the children. Either former partners will be forced back into relationships to retain care of their children, or care will be provided by a new partner. Either way the terms of the sexual contract remain unchallenged.

On a very different level, the background reality of the breadwinner homemaker bargain provides the context against which the contributions of both partners to parenting are evaluated, both in judicial determinations and where parenting arrangements are negotiated by the parties' legal representatives or through ADR. It provides the baseline for 'normal fathering', just as it does for 'normal mothering'.[13] Thus a father who is involved in hands-on parenting, particularly with young children, is often described as an exemplary parent, even where (as in most cases) it is clear that his involvement is best described as 'helping his partner' rather than assuming primary responsibility for parenting himself. Similarly, a mother in full time employment continues to be judged against the background standard set by the breadwinner homemaker bargain and thus is expected to assume full responsibility for parenting. It also sets the ground rules for the distribution of property, that is, provides the baseline against which contributions are evaluated precisely because background social expectations are normative.

These norms are legally reinforced in two very different ways. For marginal families, families which cycle on and off benefits or in which the breadwinner is among the long term unemployed, the structure of social welfare benefits continues to uphold the breadwinner homemaker bargain despite recent changes encouraging partnered women to participate in education or training. For wealthy families, the structure of the taxation system, and, in particular, the rules governing income splitting and trust arrangements also reinforce the sexual contract. Among middle class families, the structure of the *A New Tax System (Family Assistance) Act* 1999 (which allows the cost of child care to be deducted from any income earned by the dependent spouse in determining eligibility) and the contradictory treatment of child care as a 'private' expense for women who engaged in waged labour on a full time basis serve the same function. Income earned by married women is, where participation in waged labour is minimal, defined as pin money and it is seen as only fair that only her profit from this extra exertion is used to determine eligibility. Where income is more substantial, whether from full time employment or from substantial part-time employment, the terms of the sexual contract demand that her status be assimilated to the worker norm. By definition, a worker is one who can rely upon the unwaged services of others. The current structure of the GST also entrenches this model, exempting fresh food and imposing a GST upon the partially or wholly prepared meals often purchased by time-poor families seeking to minimise the impact of the second shift (typically borne by the woman).

Given the powerful messages sent by the taxation system and the social welfare system, it is hardly surprising that business groups are largely hostile to any proposal for paid maternity leave, just as it is hardly surprising that equal opportunity requirements are regarded as an imposition. The hostility is not simply about cost and about efficiency. Rather, against the background of a law and policy environment which explicitly upholds the sexual contract while paying lip service to equal opportunity, the perception is that business is unfairly required to bear the cost of an 'equality agenda' which is not sustained in other areas. Rightly or wrongly, these programmes are perceived as externalities, as extrinsic to the broad social and economic agenda.

Lessons Learned

Perhaps the critical lesson from the Australian experience is the inadequacy of the classic liberal assumption that equity failures are symptomatic simply of a legacy of prejudice and discrimination, and its logical corollary, that they are best tackled by proscribing discrimination and seeking to promote equal opportunity. The evidence suggests that the reasons equity agendas fail are entrenched in laws and policies that initially seem far removed from the remit of equal opportunity law. While at least some of their origins are cultural, and thus emerge from forces within civil society that seem far outside the reach of the liberal state, the permeable membrane separating the state and civil society means that these cultural phenomena form the background assumptions for law and policy in diverse areas.

While chapter 2 identified the industrial revolution as a central force in creating and subsequently entrenching the breadwinner homemaker bargain by isolating work from home, within Australia (often in response to pressure from a variety of interest groups) it was entrenched and reinforced by industrial relations law and labour market policy, by family law, by taxation law, and by social welfare law and policy. Although the industrial relations framework enforcing the breadwinner homemaker bargain has been partially abandoned, their legacy has been almost untouchable in two critical areas: the level of gender segregation and absence of the political will to prosecute comparable worth vigorously during the period before the arbitration system was abandoned. Without countervailing programs this virtually guarantees that these features will be reinforced by enterprise bargaining and the push towards AWAs, and it is clear than equal opportunity law is not equal to the task and cannot be made so. Equal opportunity law is designed to redress breakdowns in an otherwise equitable system and not to compensate for the failure to dismantle inegalitarian structures entrenched by law.

The failure to eradicate the legacy of the breadwinner homemaker bargain in the labour market reinforces its persistence within the family. Most women simply do not have the bargaining power to seek a more equal family bargain and their residual bargaining power is further eroded by the tax benefits available to single income families across the spectrum and the absence of concessions for services needed by dual income households.

Endemic discontent persists on both sides of the gender divide with the administration of family law. Against the background of legal structures attempting to sustain the breadwinner homemaker bargain the attempt to honour both monetary and non-monetary contributions in property allocation remains a source of ongoing discontent. The sexual contract itself identifies the provision of resources as the price for services rendered, as, in other words, a quid pro quo. From the perspective of the sexual contract, the 'contributions' in question have already been paid for, in full, and it is, therefore, unjust that they be paid for again upon divorce, especially since the specified services have been withdrawn. Within its frame of reference, more contemporary understandings, such as partial compensation for opportunity costs are wholly foreign.

Even more interesting are the persistent allegations that decisions in disputes over residence and contact are biased against men. The argument often put is that now that women are 'guaranteed' equal opportunity in the workplace, men ought to be guaranteed equal parenting rights, in some versions, joint physical custody. Here, the subtext is formal equality although the coda reveals an economic motive. If joint physical custody were a reality, child support payments would be redundant. Yet these arguments (often no more than assertions devoid of supporting framework) belie the reality of pre-separation parenting in which mothers, overwhelmingly, care for their children, and fathers are typically economic parents, although in many cases no longer the sole support of their children. These battles, whether in the minority of cases that require judicial resolution or in those resolved by mediation and counselling, are classic 'he said she said' battles in which each party has every reason to maximise his or her own contributions and minimise those of a former partner. They are also disputes in which there is unlikely to be evidence from a disinterested third party.

In Australia, as in a number of other jurisdictions including Sweden, the law provides for joint parental responsibility as the norm, not joint physical parenting or, as it used to be termed, physical custody. Dowd suggests that a legal requirement for joint parental responsibility devoid of any mandatory duty to nurture children or even sustain a relationship with them not only reflects the hegemony of the breadwinner role but also constructs 'fatherhood as chosen and voluntary, not a matter of obligation and responsibility'.[14] She also suggests, and this is borne out by Australian research into the impact of the 1995 reforms to the *Family Law Act* 1975, that the move to shared parental responsibility significantly weakens the position of the residence parent without ensuring greater parental involvement by the contact parent.[15] Men are sanctioned for failing to act as economic parents where they have the resources to contribute while women are sanctioned for interfering with contact. Men are not sanctioned for failing to maintain connection and assume a nurturing role; indeed the law assumes that it is necessary to entice them to do so, as with the current reduction in child support for fathers whose children have overnight contact for between 10-30 per cent of the time. Only where women are contact parents are they sanctioned for failing to provide support and the available evidence, both in Australia and elsewhere, suggests that mothers are much more likely to maintain contact with non-resident children than are fathers.

These outcomes, like the demographic indicators discussed earlier, are precisely what should have been expected from a legal and policy regime that superimposes a formal equity agenda on a framework affirming the breadwinner homemaker bargain. Also predictable is endemic discontent with family law outcomes. That bargain, in its classic form, encourages women to overcommit to their children (as their only reliable source of power and status) and encourages men to believe that provision of resources carries with it certain entitlements. Where relationships break down, the underlying belief systems persist, sometimes generating a desperate battle for control following divorce.

Concluding Thoughts

In Australia, as elsewhere, the critical lessons to be learned from more than 30 years of equity agendas highlight the folly of assuming that a focus on 'women's inequality' and the implementation of programs designed to ameliorate particularly glaring inequities has the potential to eliminate (or even modify) the underlying causes. Over the last 30 years, egalitarian policies have largely focused on highly specific disadvantages. Sometimes the focus has been on eliminating overt discrimination against women in the workforce, whether based on marital status, on pregnancy, or on presumed family responsibilities. At other times, it has been on supporting women who have been victimised by family violence, or who are attempting to raise children on their own. Sometimes business has been encouraged to adopt flexible programs to assist women to balance family responsibilities with workplace commitments. More recently, the focus has shifted to men, whether as the casualties of deindustrialisation or as victims of failed relationships. All of these programs have, despite their differences, a common core. They view society and social change through gendered lenses, focusing now on this gendered disadvantage, now on that, seeking to redress disadvantage without attention to the structural factors linking apparently independent sources of disadvantage.

In earlier chapters, I have identified two related theoretical constructs that form the structural foundation for these clusters of disadvantage. The first and the most pervasive is the notion of the unencumbered citizen. The unencumbered citizen is fundamental to liberal understandings, although it is not limited to societies such as Australia, the UK and the USA where the political and social frameworks are explicitly liberal. The second is that of the breadwinner homemaker bargain, the sexual contract.

In the second chapter, the dangers inherent in attempting to disestablish the hegemony of the unencumbered citizen were highlighted. Women have much to gain from dismantling the construct of the unencumbered citizen, but may have even more to lose. The core argument made by chapter 2, that citizens could be understood as encumbered in specific and limited ways, specifically by the understanding that all citizens, male and female, should be understood as having actual or potential responsibility for carework and in that way encumbered, is not without risks. Some of those risks were identified in that chapter, most particularly the space such arguments might make for the voices of others who wish to encumber the citizen in gender and race specific ways.

The sexual contract, in the form I have discussed, is a relatively recent construct, but one which is deeply embedded in all of the legal regimes we have examined. I would argue that we have nothing to lose from eradicating all provisions either tacitly or overtly functioning in ways that seek to shore up the sexual contract. Indeed, a part of the argument made in previous chapters is that as a society we have a great deal to gain. Perhaps the most obvious gains lie in the areas of family and social welfare law.

Much of the pervasive discontent with family law stems from its inherent tension with the dominant form of the breadwinner homemaker bargain, specifically that portion that understands financial provision, both for the homemaker and for children, as the price to be paid for sexual, domestic and child rearing services. Within the terms of the sexual contract as understood by both men and women, there are no 'contributions' within the terms of s 97 *Family Law Act* 1975. Rather, the provision of resources during a relationship purchases services. This understanding cannot be reconciled with legal provisions suggesting that, following dissolution, the distribution of marital property should take into account both financial and homemaking contributions in allocating resources with an aim of ensuring an equitable division of property. From the perspective of many aggrieved men, the division of property that often results is inherently unfair, requiring them to pay twice for the services received in the past and now unavailable. With child support as well, the sexual contract suggests that the payment entitles them to access and to ultimate control over its expenditure and over the child's life more generally.

Women also understand the sexual contract as a bargain, one in which they are entitled to resources (and, perhaps, protection) in exchange for services. Where those resources are not forthcoming, or are not sufficient or sufficiently reliable to meet needs (and expectations) or where another kind of 'price', one outside the terms of the bargain is attached, some women see themselves as entitled to withdraw from the bargain. Because the sexual contract effectively compels women to over invest in their children, some women find it difficult to relinquish control. Where this is the case facilitating the father's relationship with the children is too great a reminder of the sexual contract. As Nancy Dowd notes:

> Men are more likely to be 'serial fathers' parenting a succession of children as they enter and leave households. Mothers are more often 'linear mothers'. Men are more likely to nurture the children with whom they share a home. Third, there is a strong correlation between male nurturing and the strength and health of men's relationships with the women with whom they share children. Men rarely parent alone.[16]

As part of the sexual contract, women facilitate the fathering of the men with whom they share their lives. After its end, such facilitation is supererogatory, as much a lingering reminder of the sexual contract as is the provision of support by men.

These parallel understandings of the sexual contract are deeply rooted and the source of many of the perceived injustices in family law outcomes. Unless the grip of the sexual contract and the perception of its legitimacy is weakened they cannot be eradicated. Measures to enhance the justice of outcomes from partial and gendered perspectives only give rise to new grievances, some of which are legitimate enough from the perspective of those who hold them. While the existing legal regime has faults, the perceptions of injustice stem, not from its real and imagined faults, but from the entitlements generated by the sexual contract.

Earlier in this chapter, I alluded to the tendency for perspectives to be partial and to the all too human tendency to overrate one's own contributions and underrate those of others. Nowhere is this more obvious than in time-use surveys seeking to evaluate the participation of men and women in household labour and parenting. Over time, one of the advantages of universal provision for paid parenting leave for both men and women would be the availability of an objective measure (albeit limited) of pre-separation involvement in parenting, one that could assist negotiating parenting arrangements post-separation. As Dowd argues, joint parental responsibility without co-equal parenting reinforces the breadwinner homemaker contract and encourages men to regard active parenting as non-obligatory. So does legal permission to delegate post-separation carework to a new partner or relative. So long as active nurturing remains optional for men, both pre and post divorce, and no meaningful sanctions are brought to bear upon those who voluntarily forego contact with their children or delegate active parenting of those children, the understanding of fatherhood as optional in a way that motherhood is not is reinforced.

In an environment in which both the social welfare system and the taxation system tacitly reinforce the breadwinner homemaker bargain, neither of these changes is likely to occur. Within a social and legal environment that continues to reinforce the sexual contract, confronted by a labour market whose structures consistently profit from the status quo, it is hardly surprising that progress is slow. What is, perhaps, surprising is that, increasingly, survey evidence suggests that men and women are gradually coming to acknowledge more egalitarian ideals. The survey evidence cited earlier, in which a majority of people both acknowledged that mothers had an obligation to support their children and fathers had an obligation to nurture their children suggest that many in the community are willing to relinquish the benefits of the sexual contract and pursue more egalitarian ideals. Perhaps they too are coming to recognise that the problems generated by our awkward stance, not quite half way to equal, are precisely what could and should have been expected. The question is how we address them, how we build legal and social structures that encourage experimentation with more equal ways of living rather than reinforce conventional patterns of social organisation. Equal opportunity is insufficient. Changes in family law, in social welfare law and policy, in taxation law and in industrial relations law will all fail unless they are animated by a consistent social vision. To the extent that, intentionally or otherwise, some provisions reinforce aspects of the breadwinner homemaker bargain, these features will undermine more progressive provisions in the same statute and fatally undercut equal opportunity law itself. Every provision that rewards the breadwinner homemaker bargain encourages its persistence, and encourages the disorders that attend it in a changing world. We cannot expect men or women to behave as egalitarians following divorce if their marriage was conducted according to the terms of the sexual contract and this behaviour was rewarded by the legal system. The evidence of this failure is readily visible, in newspaper headlines and in the family court. Similarly, we cannot expect business to comply willingly with the formally egalitarian regime imposed by sex discrimination and equal opportunity law in a society in which the background reality is governed by the sexual contract. Perhaps most tellingly, we cannot expect mothers whose partnered lives demanded adherence to the homemaker role to be self-sufficient following the end of a relationship. While they can be compelled to become so by a harshly punitive welfare regime like that in the United States, they could, quite legitimately, complain that they are being punished for behaviour for which they were formerly praised and rewarded. An attempt to roll back the clock, to reinscribe the formal gender roles of the 1950s, while appealing to some, could, quite easily lead Australia down the path already travelled by Greece and Spain, and to a lesser extent, Italy. Those roles are, quite simply, incompatible with increasing educational opportunities and with the information revolution wrought by the Internet. The society to which they belonged has vanished. As young men and women are encouraged to prepare themselves for an egalitarian world that does not yet exist, we need to build on those expectations and create an environment in which egalitarian changes are supported and in which outworn practices are not rewarded by the legal and institutional structure.

In the past, a complex web of legal and cultural supports nurtured the breadwinner homemaker bargain and constructed a context in which it seemed both natural and inevitable. Central among these were legal restrictions on divorce that mirrored the terms of the sexual contract, restrictions on women's capacity to maintain themselves independently, whether through the family wage and a concomitant assumption that working women had only themselves to support or through restrictions on the employment of married women, and a system of informal and formal social supports for women and children where the breadwinner had either died or abandoned his responsibilities. While these had been slightly weakened by 19th century legislation allowing married women to own and dispose of property and to retain their own wages,[17] they retained their vitality. Within this framework, other legal measures also seemed appropriate, such as separate taxation arrangements for married couples and restrictions on the education of girls and young women.[18] Taken as a whole, this legal and policy framework ensured that the breadwinner homemaker bargain remained stable and could be, if necessary, legally enforced.

Yet the breadwinner homemaker bargain was always on the edge of instability, ironically, instability fostered by the increasing hegemony of notions of the unencumbered citizen. Despite its incompleteness, its radical isolation of the citizen from the attributes of individual citizens, the increasing understanding of the citizen as a political abstraction – devoid of race, of class, of particularity – laid the foundation for a kind of formal political equality. As the vote became increasingly symbolic of the distinction between the citizen and the subject, as the Kantian distinction between the active and passive citizen lapsed into desuetude,[19] suffrage was gradually extended, first to some propertied men, later to those without property,[20] still later to women, married and single,[21] and finally (and perhaps still incompletely) to those who are racially and ethnically different.[22]

The advent of female suffrage, in 1893 in New Zealand, 1902 in Australia, and in the early 1920s in the US, emphasised the formal public equality of men and women. Once the formal public equality of men and women is enshrined in the public sphere, as happened with the vote, the pressure for change begins: education, public sphere opportunities in employment, in political and social participation, and finally, within the family itself. While contemporary egalitarian theorists are careful to insist that the equality of which they speak is political merely, ultimately political equality is incompatible with certain (but not all) forms of private inequality. While change may, and often does, take a long time, and it is worth recalling that in Australia woman suffrage was entrenched in 1902 and it took some 70 years before the family wage was eradicated and another 14 years before sex discrimination was proscribed at the commonwealth level, it is, nonetheless, inevitable. While suffrage did not, as some politicians feared, bring an end to war, to cricket and to other manly games, it did imply an obligation to make educational opportunities available and education opened the door to demands for equal employment rights, for equivalent welfare rights, and ultimately for rights within family law and allied areas acknowledging the equal citizenship of men and women and the incompatibility of that citizenship with certain forms of subordination, including that entrenched in traditional forms of fault based divorce. It is these further changes, even more than formal property rights and suffrage that have destabilised the breadwinner homemaker bargain and it is these changes that are beyond our power to recall without measures so draconian and so regressive that no ostensibly 'liberal' government would attempt them.[23]

The question, in Australia and in other liberal democracies such as Canada, the UK, and the USA, is whether we, as a people, are willing to abandon the remnants of the breadwinner homemaker bargain and the gendered rhetoric that shadows it. We have seen the costs of maintaining it in Australia, and in those jurisdictions in which the birth rate is perilously low, such as Italy, Spain and Greece. Contrary to the rhetoric that portrays changes to existing social arrangements as a form of social engineering, adoption of the 'modest proposals' made earlier would offer a genuine choice. Universal paid parenting leave which could be taken on either a part-time basis or a full time basis and which could be shared by both parents would not deny those parents, male or female, who believe that full time parental care is essentially the option of providing it. Rather, it would simply support experimentation and (hopefully) encourage more men to take an active role as nurturers.

The abandonment of the 'social wage' in its current form, one that reinforces the breadwinner homemaker bargain, would not unjustly deprive low-income families of the resources needed to support their children. Rather, elimination of the provisions disadvantaging households where both parents engage in waged labour and both engage in hands on parenting, a traditional pattern in many working class households, would enable parents to maximise the opportunities available to them without incentives designed to privilege one set of choices over another. Those who argue that such provisions merely adjust for the higher taxation rate of a single income earner fail to acknowledge the economic value of household and child care services provided by a parent specialising in domestic labour and the additional necessary expenditure necessitated by a dual income household. The provision of an 'independent' taxation rebate for children, that is, one not predicated upon the presence of either a dependent spouse or a sole parent, would acknowledge a fundamental reality of the human condition, that an extended period of neoteny demands an extended period of parental or social care, one which, under contemporary conditions has been artificially extended into the late teens.

Similarly, an entitlement for both men and women to follow a period on full time parenting leave with a period combining part-time employment with partial parenting leave (again available to both mothers and fathers) would make it possible for both parents to become active nurturers. If such an entitlement were combined with subsidised high quality child care (essential for children from disadvantaged backgrounds),[24] genuine inroads might be made against the lifelong disadvantages that tend to flow from early deprivation. Maria Montessori proved that early intervention programs work in the early years of the 20th century in Italian slums; Head Start proved that such programs work in the mid-20th century in Afro-American ghettos. Yes, such programs are costly, but our failure to provide them is costlier still, allowing the reproduction of disadvantage in subsequent generations.

While those who are threatened by social change have made much of the rhetoric of choice, in reality existing legal and social provisions curtail rather than enhance choice, and do so in ways that ensure the persistence of the social and demographic problems they purport to ameliorate. They are the remnants of a failed and deliberate experiment in social engineering, one with its genesis among the bourgeoisie in the 19th century, and one which was exported to the working class through the efforts of Evangelical philanthropists and 'lady visitors' during the late 19th century and early 20th century in Australia, in Canada, in the UK and in the USA. Sustained among the middle and upper middle classes by, inter alia, market arrangements presuming the availability of a 'trophy wife' for the upwardly mobile young executive, and by educational structures presuming the availability of teacher's wives and tuck shop mothers to provide costless services, this experiment in social engineering persists, despite the obvious costs.

Notes

1   *Re Evelyn* [1998] FamCA 55 accessed at http://www.familycourt.gov.au/ on 20 October 2001.

2   *Re Kevin (validity of the marriage of a transsexual)* [2001] FamCA 1074 accessed at http://www.familycourt.gov.au/ on 20 October 2001.

3   For a fascinating exploration of this dimension in the context of stalking see Kamir, Orit, *Every Breath You Take*, Ann Arbor, Univ. of Mich Press, 2001.

4   4 & 5 Will IV cap 76. Section 71 provided that the mother of an illegitimate child could not seek support from the putative father herself and that no man could be named the father merely on the uncorroborated word of the mother while s 72 provided that, where the poor law union sought support from the father no part of that support was to be used to meet any portion of the mother's needs.

5   For a discussion of Australian attitudes towards single mothers since Federation see Howe & Swain, above.

6   See Cleary, Phil, 'Let's stop telling blokes it's romantic to kill the kids', The *Age*, 28 August 2001 detailing a series of such cases between 1987 and the present.

7   Dowd, *Redefining Fatherhood*, 224.

8   While some individual companies are making substantial progress, as the 2001 Work and Family Awards show with several companies including Alcoa and Gavin McLeod Concrete Pumping offering paid parenting leave for men and women, the overall picture remains bleak. See Department of Employment, Workplace Relations and Small Business ACCI National Work and Family Awards 2001 web site at http://www.dewrsb.gov.au/ accessed on 25 September 2001.

9   Dowd, *Redefining Fatherhood*, 210-11.

10   This taxation liability arises out of the eligibility of contact parents who contribute as little as 10% of care for a pro rata share of the increased rebate under the *A New Tax System (Family Assistance Act* 1999, thus reducing its availability to a low income residence parent. Perhaps the biggest practical difference between caring for and caring about is that contact mothers are much more likely to maintain connection with their children than are contact fathers.

11   Dowd, *Redefining Fatherhood*, 204-205 emphasises that mothers serve as 'gatekeepers' to men's relationship with their children and that 'when [divorced] fathers maintain a connection with their children they are far more likely to do so either when they share their household with a female intimate partner or when they have established a cooperative relationship with their former partner'.

12   The Australian Democrats incorporated universal paid maternity leave (at a modest rate) in their platform in the 2001 election.

13   Thus, in *Cooke and Stepben* [1998] FamCA 154 a father who travelled a substantial distance for contact with his children in his wife's home and under her supervision was described as an exemplary father because he sought to maintain connection with the children.

14   Dowd, *Redefining Fatherhood*, 139.

15   Dowd, *Redefining Fatherhood*, 139.

16   Dowd, *Redefining Fatherhood*, 21.

17   While there were numerous such statutes, in the UK, in the USA and later in Canada and Australia, the most significant was the *Married Women's Property Act* 1884.

18   In the 19th century, professional training, for example medicine and law, was restricted to men. Education for women emphasised the domestic arts and accomplishments, such as fluency in European languages, drawing, playing musical instruments, and singing, considered appropriate for upper class women. Early reformers in the UK were particularly concerned that 'factory girls' should learn domestic skills else they would be useless as wives and mothers.

19   For Kant, passive citizens included apprentices, all those who worked for wages, and women. Their dependence, the fact that their status compelled them to serve masters

other than their own reason, meant that they could not truly be citizens, men governed by a law they gave themselves.

20 *Reform Act* 1832 (UK) allowed all adult males owning a household worth £10 or more, the *Reform Act* 1867 (UK) extended suffrage to working class men, and the *Redistribution Act* 1885 (UK) extended the vote to most agricultural labourers.

21 *Reform Act* 1918 (UK) extended the vote to all men above the age of 20 and to all women above the age of 30.

22 Indigenous Australians did not gain full voting rights until the 1967 referendum, Native Americans did not gain suffrage until the 1920s, and African Americans living in the southern states remained substantively disenfranchised until the Voting Rights legislation of the 1960s.

23 The steps taken by the Taliban in Afghanistan and those taken earlier by the Ayatollah Khomeini in Iran suggest what is required. Once women's access to education and to public space is destroyed, the rest follows.

24 High quality childcare ought not to be confused with infant and child warehousing services. Many children would benefit from time spent in a high quality facility that was developmentally stimulating and provided early childhood education: the original Montessori program run for disadvantaged Italian housing project children and the American Head Start program come immediately to mind.

Bibliography

'Catalyst, Report on A National Study Of Parental Leaves' 65-66 (1986), reprinted in 'The Parental and Medical Leave Act of 1986: Joint Hearing on HR 4300' before the Subcomm on Labor-Management relations and the Subcomm on Labor Standards of the House Comm on Education & Labor, 99 Cong, 2d Sess 151-228 (1986).

'Children ignored as martyrs go to war', The *Weekend Australian Review*, 4-5 July 1998.

'Delay brings the best of both worlds' The *Courier Mail*, Tuesday 14 December 1999.

'Explaining Trends in the Gender Wage Gap' accessed at http://www.whitehouse.gov/ on 11 November 1999.

'Frequently Asked Questions' on line at http://www.austemb.org/faqs.htm accessed 11 November 1999.

'Harsh Realities', Human Rights & Equal Opportunity Commission, Canberra, AGPS, 1999.

'Social engineering aside, mum is not a dirty word', The *Australian*, 25 August 1998.

'Status of Women: Opportunity and Choice', Authorised by L Crosby, Liberal Party of Australia, Corner Blackwell & Macquarie St, Bardon, ACT 2600. http://www.liberal.org.au/ accessed 5 July 1999.

'Women's Economic Status – Equal Wealth, Output 4', a report prepared for the Australian Commonwealth/State and New Zealand Standing Committee for Advisors on the Status of Women, May 1999, accessed 2 October 1999 on http://www.dpmc.gov.au/osw/.

Abella, Madam Justice Rosalie Silverman, *Human Rights and the Judicial Role*, Ninth AIJA Oration in Judicial Administration, delivered at School of Electrical Engineering and Computer Science, The University of Melbourne, Friday, 23 October 1998.

ABS Cat. 4102 accessed on line at http://www.abs.gov.au/ on 5 July 2000.

ABS Cat. 6302.0 accessed on line at http://www/abs.gov.au/ on 5 July 2000.

ABS, 'Australia Now – A Statistical Profile, Characteristics of the labour force', accessed at http://www.abs.gov.au/ on 16 March 2000.

ABS, 'Australia Now – A Statistical Profile: Labour & Employment, Unpublished Data, Labour Force Survey', accessed on 22 February 2000 at http://www.abs.gov.au/.

ABS, 'Australia Now – A Statistical Profile: Population, Households and Families', accessed on 30 March 2000 at http://www.abs.gov.au/.

ABS, 'Australia Now – A Statistical Profile: The Labour Force', accessed on 30 March 2000 at http://www.abs.gov.au/.

ABS, 'Computing Services Industry, Australia: 1992-93', ABS Cat. No. 8669.0, March 1995.

ACTU, 'Equal Pay: A Union Priority' accessed at http://www.actu.asn.au/ on 11 November 1999.

ACTU, 'Women's Employment Strategy 1989' accessed at http://www.actu.asn.au/ on 12 December 1999.

ACTU, 'Women's Pay 1989 Strategy Statement' accessed on 23 March 2000 at http://www.actu.asn.au/.

Andersson, Gunnar, 'The impact of labor-force participation on childbearing behavior: pro-cyclical fertility in Sweden during the 1980s and the 1990s', Stockholm University Demography Unit, 28 July 1999.

Anker, Richard, 'Theories of occupational segregation by sex: An overview' (1997) 136 International Labor Review accessed at http://www.ilo.org/ on 14 November 1999.

Anker, Richard, *Gender and Jobs: Sex segregation of occupations in the world*, Geneva, International Labor Office, 1998.

Atkinson, Judy, 'Violence in Aboriginal Australia: Colonisation and Gender' (1996) 14 *The Aboriginal and Islander Health Worker* 5.

Bachelard, Michael, 'Part-time staff take on 'bullying' bank', The *Australian*, Friday May 5 2000.

Bakan, Joel, *Just Words: Constitutional Rights and Wrongs*, Toronto, Univ. of Toronto Press, 1997.

Baker, Maureen, 'Poverty, Ideology and Employability: Canadian and Australian Policies for Low-Income Mothers' (1998) 33 *Australian Journal of Social Issues* 355.

Baldock, Cora Vellekoop, 'The Family and the Australian Welfare State' (1994) 29 *Australian Journal of Social Issues* 104.

Barclay, Susan, 'Where There's no Will There's no Way' (1990) 35 *Refractory Girl* 33.

Baron, Ava, 'The Masculinization of Production: The Gendering of Work and Skill in US Newspaper Printing, 1850-1920' in Helly, Dorothy O & Susan M Reverby, eds, *Gendered Domains: Rethinking Public and Private in Women's History*, Ithaca, Cornell University Press, 1992, 277.

Baron, Paula and Elizabeth Barber, *An Evaluation of Australian Academic Performance Measurements*, Report to DETYA, Evaluations and Investigations Program, 1998.

Barrett, Nancy S, 'Comments' in Brown, Clair & Joseph A Pechman, eds, *Gender in the Workplace*, Washington DC, The Brookings Institution, 1987, 299.

Bartlett, Bruce R, 'Testimony before the US House Committee on Ways and Means' 28 January 1998, downloaded on 10/04/00 from http://www/ncpa.org/.

Bejstam, Lars, 'Social Benefits and Families with Children' in Wahlgren, Peter, ed, *Legal Issues of the Late 1990s*, Scandinavian Studies in Law Volume 38, Stockholm, Stockholm University Law Faculty, 1998, 217.

Bell, Derrick, *Race, Racism and American Law*, 2nd ed, Boston, Little & Brown, 1992, 657.

Bender, Leslie, 'An Overview of Feminist Torts Scholarship' (1993) 78 *Cornell LR* 575.

Bennett, Laura, 'Women and Enterprise Bargaining: The Legal and Institutional Framework' (1994) 36(2) *Journal of Industrial Relations* 191.

Berns, Sandra, 'Women in English Legal History: Subject (almost), Object (irrevocably), Person (not quite)' (1993) 12 *Univ. Tas LR* 26.

Berns, Sandra, 'The Hobart City Council Case: A Tort of Sexual Harassment for Tasmania?' (1994) 13 *Univ. Tas LR* 112.

Berns, Sandra, 'Regulation of the Family: Whose Interests does it Serve?' (1994) 2 *Griffith LR*, 152.

Berns, Sandra, 'Law, Citizenship and the Politics of Identity: Sketching the Limits of Citizenship' (1998) 7 *Griffith LR* 1.

Bertelsmann Foundation, 'International Reform Monitor Country Info Australia Family Policy' accessed at http://www.reformmonitor.org/ on 19 April 2000.

Bertoia, Carl & Janice Drakich, 'The Fathers' Rights Movement: Contradictions in Rhetoric and Practice' 1993 (14) *Journal of Family Issues* 592.

Betz, Nancy F & Gail Hackett, 'Manual for the Occupational Self-Efficacy Scale' accessed at http://seamonkey.ed.asu.edu/ on 13 November 1999.

Bluestone, Barry, 'The Inequality Express' 20 (Winter '95) *American Prospect* 5.

Boyd, Susan, 'Child Custody, Ideologies, and Employment' (1989) 3 *Canadian Journal of Women and the Law* 111.

Bradley, David, *Family Law and Political Culture*, London, Sweet & Maxwell, 1996.

Braithwaite, Valerie, 'Designing the Process of Workplace Change through the Affirmative Action Act' in Gatens, Moira & Alison Mackinnon, eds, *Gender and Institutions: Welfare, Work and Citizenship*, Cambridge, CUP, 1998, 107.

Brennan, Deborah, *The Politics of Australian Child Care: Philanthropy to Feminism and Beyond*, Cambridge, CUP, 1998.

Brown, Charles & Shirley J Wilcher, 'Sex Based Employment Quotas in Sweden' in Brown, Clair & Joseph A Pechman, eds, *Gender in the Workplace*, Washington DC, The Brookings Institution, 1987, 271.

Bryson, Lois, 'Women, Paid Work, and Social Policy' in Norma Grieve and Ailsa Burns, eds, *Australian Women: Contemporary Feminist Thought*, Melbourne, OUP, 1994, 179.

Burkett, Elinor, *The Baby Boon: How Family-Friendly America Cheats the Childless*, New York, The Free Press, 2000.

Burton, Clare, 'Merit and gender: organisation and the "mobilisation of masculine bias"', paper presented at the conference 'Defining Merit', Macquarie University, 1985.

Burton, Clare, 'Women in Public and Private Sector Senior Management', Research Paper for the Office of the Status of Women, Department of the Prime Minister and Cabinet, Canberra, AGPS, 1997.

Carberry, Fiona, Kate Chan & Alex Heyworth, 'Sole parent Pension and Parent Allowance – A Comparison' (1996) *Social Security Journal* 108.

Carpenter, Tracey, 'The Regulatory Review of Affirmative Action legislation, and what this means for organisations', 24 February 1999, Equal Employment Opportunity Network (EEON) Victoria accessed at http://www/eeo.gov.au/ on 5 July 1999.

Cass, Bettina, 'Towards a New Australian Model: Social Protection and Social Participation Through Market Wage and Social Wage' ACIRRT Working Paper No. 40, April 1996 in Bryce, Merilyn, ed, *Industrial Relations Policy Under the Microscope*, Proceedings from the Conference, 'Industrial Relations Under the Microscope: A Critical Assessment and Outlook', Holiday Inn, Menzies, Sydney, 7 December, 1995, 71.

Casson, Louise, 'Jobs for Women Campaign' *Refractory Girl*, May 1985, 30.

Castles, Francis G, 'The Institutional Design of the Australian Welfare State' (1997) 50 *International Social Security Review* 25, 35-36.

Charlesworth, Sara, 'Enterprise Bargaining and Women Workers: The Seven Perils of Flexibility' (1997) 2 *Labour & Industry* 101.

Charlesworth, Stephanie, 'Monitoring Income Maintenance Policies for Single Mothers' (1982) 17 *Aust Journal of Social Issues* 135.

Cleary, Phil, 'Let's stop telling blokes it's romantic to kill the kids' The *Age*, 28 August 2001.

Colker, Ruth, *Pregnant Men: Practice, Theory, and the Law*, Bloomington, Indiana University Press, 1994.

Collier, Richard, '"Waiting Till Father Gets Home": The Reconstruction of Fatherhood in Family Law' (1995) 4 *Social & Legal Studies* 5.

Collier, Richard, '"Coming Together?": Post-Heterosexuality, Masculine Crisis and the New Men's Movement' (1996) 4 *Feminist Legal Studies* 3.

Comstock, Gary 'Dismantling the Homosexual Panic Defense' (1992) 2 *Tul Journal of Law and Sexuality* 81.

Cook, Peter, 'Home truths absent in early childcare debate' The *Australian*, 24 March, 1999.

Cooper, Tony, 'Taxing the Family Unit: Income Splitting for All?' (1995) 5 *Revenue LJ* 82.

Cornell, Drucilla, *The Imaginary Domain*, New York & London, Routledge, 1995.

Cover, Robert, 'Nomos and Narrative' in Minow, Martha, Michael Ryan, and Austin Sarat, eds, *Narrative, Violence, and the Law*, Ann Arbor, University of Michigan Press, 1992, 95.

Crago, Joyce M, 'The Unit of Taxation: Current Canadian Issues' (1993) 52 *Univ. of Toronto Faculty of Law Review* 1.

Creighton, Colin, 'The rise and decline of the "male breadwinner family" in Britain' (1999) 23 *Cambridge Journal of Economics* 519.

Daly, Mary, *The Gender Division of Welfare: The Impact of the British and German Welfare States*, Cambridge, UK, Cambridge University Press, 2000.

Dean, Jodi, *Solidarity of Strangers: Feminism after Identity Politics*, Berkeley, University of California Press, 1996.

Delgado, Richard, 'The Ethereal Scholar: Does Critical Legal Studies have What Minorities Want?' (1987) 22 *Harv CR-CL LR* 301.

Delgado, Richard, 'Critical Legal Studies and the Realities of Race – Does the Fundamental Contradiction Have a Corollary' (1988) 23 *Harv CR-CL LR* 407.

Department of Employment and Workplace Relations, 'Executive Summary: Work and Family: State of Play 1998', accessed at http://www.dewrsb.gov.au/ on 19 July 1999.

Department of Employment, Workplace Relations and Small Business, 'ACCI National Work and Family Awards 2001' accessed at http://www.dewrsb.gov.au/ on 25 September 2001.

Department of Family and Community Services, 'Participation Support for a More Equitable Society', downloaded 3 April 2000.

Dewar, John & Stephen Parker, 'Parenting, planning and partnership: The impact of the new Part VII of the *Family Law Act* 1975', Family Law Research Unit Working Paper No. 3.

Dex, Shirley & Heather Joshi, 'Careers and Motherhood: Policies for Compatibility' (1999) 23 *Cambridge Journal of Economics* 641.

Donovan, Dolores & Stephanie M Wildman (1981) 'Is the Reasonable Man Obsolete? A Critical Perspective on Self-Defence and Provocation' 14 *Loyola of Los Angeles LR* 435.

Dowd, Nancy E, 'Stigmatizing Single Parents' (1995) 18 *Harvard Women's Law Journal* 19.

Dowd, Nancy E, *Redefining Fatherhood*, New York, NYU Press, 2000.

Dressler, Joshua, 'When "Heterosexual" Men Kill "Homosexual" Men: Reflections on Provocation Law, Sexual Advances, and the "Reasonable Man" Standard' (1995) 85 *Journal of Criminal Law and Criminology*, 726.

Durkheim, Emile, *Suicide: a study in sociology*, trans. by John A Spaulding and George Simpson, ed with an introduction by George Simpson, Glencoe, Ill, The Free Press, Routledge [1951], 1970.

Dworkin, Ronald, *Law's Empire*, Cambridge, MA, Belknap, 1986.

Eurostat, 'Still a Big Pay Gap Between Men and Women' accessed 11 November 1999 at http://europa.eu.int/en/comm/eurostat/.

Evaline, Joan, 'Heavy, Dirty and Limp Stories: Male Advantage at Work' in Gatens, Moira and Alison Mackinnon, eds, *Gender and Institutions: Welfare, Work and Citizenship*, Cambridge, CUP, 1998, 90.

Faludi, Susan, *Stiffed: The Betrayal of the Modern Man*, London, Chatto & Windus Ltd, 1999.

Fastenau, Maureen, 'Women's Employment in Australia, 1986-1996: A Period of Glacial Change' (1997) 3 *International Employment Relations Review* 61.

Federal Court 8th Circuit, 'Gender Fairness Task Force Report' http://www.wulaw.wustl.edu/8th.cir/ accessed on 10 November 1999.

Fieldes, Diane, 'Women's Wages and Decentralised Wage Fixing: The Australian Experience' in Bramble, Tom, Bill Harvey, Richard Hall & Gillian Whitehouse, eds, Current Research in Industrial Relations, *Proceedings of the 11th AIRAANZ Conference*, Brisbane, Queensland, Australia 30 January-1 February 1997.

Fraser, Nancy, 'Gender Equity and the Welfare State: A Postindustrial Thought Experiment' in Benhabib, Seyla, ed, *Democracy and Difference: Contesting the Boundaries of the Political*, Princeton, NJ, Princeton University Press, 1996, 218.

Furst, Gunilla, *Sweden – The Equal Way*, trans. by Stephen Croall, Stockholm, Swedish Institute, 1999.

Gabel, Peter, 'The Phenomenology of Rights Consciousness and the Pact of the Withdrawn Selves' (1984) 62 *Texas LR* 1563.

Gardiner, Jan, 'Putting Sole Mothers in their Place: The Normalising Discourse of Social Policy' (1999) 34 *Australian Journal of Social Issues* 43.

Gardner, Margaret, 'Industrial Relations Reform and Strategy: If enterprise bargaining is the answer what was the question?' Professorial Lecture delivered on 23 March 1999.

Glendon, Mary Ann, *The Transformation of Family Law: State, Law and Family in the United States and Western Europe*, Chicago & London, Univ. of Chicago Press, 1989.

Gregory, Bob, 'Labour Market Institutions and the Gender Pay Ratio' in 'Policy Forum: The Equal Pay Case – Thirty Years On' 32(2) *The Australian Economic Review* 273.

Grimshaw, Damian & Jill Rubery, Labour Market and Social Policy – Occasional Papers no. 26, 'The Concentration of Women's Employment and Relative Occupational Pay: A Statistical Framework for Comparative Analysis', Paris, OECD, 1997.

Grimshaw, Patricia, Marilyn Lake, Ann Mcgrath & Marian Quartly, *Creating a Nation 1788-1990*, Melbourne, McPhee Gribble, 1998.

Gunn, Michelle, The *Australian*, 30 August 1999.

Haas, Linda, 'Gender Equality and Social Policy: Implications of a Study of Parental Leave in Sweden', (1990) 11 *Journal of Family Issues* 401.

Hall, Richard, Bill Harley & Gillian Whitehouse, 'Contingent Work and Gender in Australia: Evidence from the 1995 Australian Workplace Industrial Relations Survey' (1998) 9 *The Economic and Labour Relations Review* 55.

Hannon, Kate, The *Daily Telegraph*, 16 March 1999.

Harris, Catherine, 'Women, men and work: time for a new dialogue', speech given on 11th August 1998 at The Sydney Institute.

Harris, Neville, 'Unmarried Cohabiting Couples and Social Security in Great Britain' (1996) 18 *Journal of Social Welfare and Family Law* 123.

Hasche, Annette, 'Sex Discrimination in Child Custody Determinations' (1989) 3 *Australian Journal of Family Law* 218.

Haskey, John (Office for National Statistics), May (1996) *Family Law* 301.

Haslem, Benjamin, 'Thousands caught in welfare trap', The *Australian*, 22 February 2002.

Henderson, Ian, 'For women the gender gap doesn't pay', The *Australian*, March 26 1999.

Hirdman, Yvonne, *Women – from Possibility to Problem? Gender Conflict in the Welfare State – The Swedish Model*, Stockholm, Swedish Centre for Working Life, Research Report No. 3, 1994.

Hobbes, Thomas, *Leviathan*, ed by CB MacPherson, Harmondsworth, Middlesex, England, Pelican [1651], 1968.

Horowitz, Asher, *Rousseau, Nature, and History*, Toronto, Univ. of Toronto Press, 1987.

Howard, John, Prime Minister, 'Towards an Economic Policy for the Family', speech delivered to the Council for the National Interest, Sydney 7 March 1994.

Howe, Renate & Shurlee Swain, 'Saving the Child and Punishing the Mother: Single Mothers and the State 1912-1942' in Howe, Renate, ed, *Women and the State: Australian Perspectives*, Bundoora, La Trobe University Press, 1993; (1993) 37 *Journal of Australian Studies* 31 (a special issue).

HREOC, 'Stretching Flexibility: Enterprise Bargaining, Women Workers and Changes to Working Hours' downloaded on 15 November 1999.

Huggins, Jackie, 'Pretty deadly tidda business' in Gunew, Sneja Marina & Anna Yeatman, eds, *Feminism and the Politics of Difference*, St Leonards, NSW, Allen & Unwin, 1993, 61.

Hunter, Rosemary, 'Part-time work & indirect discrimination' (1996) 21 *Alternative Law Journal* 220.

Hunter, Rosemary, 'Sex Discrimination and Alternative Dispute Resolution: British Proposals in the Light of International Experience' (1997) *Public Law* 298.

Hunter, Rosemary, 'Gender and legal practice' (1999) 24 *Alternative Law Journal* 57.

Hunter, Rosemary & Elaine Shoben 'Disparate Impact Discrimination: American Oddity or Internationally Accepted Concept? (1998) 19 *Berkeley Journal of Employment and Labor Law* 108.

Ikemoto, Lisa C, 'The Code of Perfect Pregnancy: At the Intersection of the Ideology of Motherhood, the Practice of Defaulting to Science, and the Interventionist Mindset of Law' (1992) *53 Ohio St LJ* 1205.

ILO 'World Employment Report 1998-99, Women and Training in the Global Economy' accessed at http://www.ilo.org/ on 14 November 99.

ILO, 'Breaking through the glass ceiling: Women in management' *World of Work* No. 23 February 1988, accessed on 18 November at http://www.ilo.org/.

ILO, 'World Employment Report 1998-99, Women and Training in the Global Economy', Geneva, ILO, 1999.

Independent Women's Forum, 'Statistical Summary' at http://www.iwf.org/ accessed on 7 April 2000.

Jaimes, M Annette (with Theresa Halsey), 'American Indian Women: At the Center of Indigenous Resistance in Contemporary North America' in McClintock, Anne, Aamir Mufti & Ella Shohat, eds, *Dangerous Liaisons: Gender, Nation & Postcolonial Perspectives*, Minneapolis, University of Minnesota Press, 1997.

Jefferson, Thomas, *Notes on the State of Virginia* 1781-1785.

Junior, Anne, 'Permanent part-time work: new family-friendly standard or high intensity cheap skills?' (1998) 8 *Labour & Industry* 77.

Junor, Anne, 'Permanent Part-Time Work: Win-Win or Double Whammy?' in *Current Research in Industrial Relations, Proceedings of the 125th AIRAANZ Conference*, eds Raymond Harbridge, Claire Gadd and Aaron Crawford, Wellington, NZ AIRAANZ, 1998.

Kamir, Orit, *Every Breath You Take*, Ann Arbor, Univ. of Mich Press, 2001.

Kaye, Miranda & Julia Tolmie, 'Fathers' Rights Groups in Australia and Their Engagement with Issues in Family Law' (1998) 12 *Australian Journal of Family Law* 19.

Kaye, Miranda & Julie Tolmie, 'The Discourse of Fathers' Rights Groups' (1998) 22 *Melb Univ. LR* 162.

Kerr, Barbara, 'The Dating Game', The *Australian*, 31 March 1999.

Knowles, Lilian, quoted in Cooper, Graeme S, Robert L Deutsch & Richard E Krever, *Cooper, Krever & Vann's Income Taxation*, 2nd ed, Sydney, LBC, 1993.

Kramar, Robin, 'Equal employment opportunity: An essential and integral part of good human resource management' in O'Neill, Graham L & Robin Kramar, *Australian Human Resources Management: Current Trends in Management Practice*, Melbourne, Pitman Publishing, 1995, 223.

Krautil, Fiona, 'Action News' Issue 40, December 1999, Equal Opportunity for Women in the Workplace Agency.

Kymlicka, Will, *Multicultural citizenship : a liberal theory of minority rights*, Oxford, OUP, 1995.

Lake, Marilyn, 'Childbearers as Rights-bearers: feminist discourse on the rights of Aboriginal and non-aboriginal mothers in Australia, 1920-50' (1999) 8 *Women's History Review* 347.

Lambert, Simon, Gillian Beer & Julie Smith, 'Taxing the Individual or the Couple: A Distributional Analysis' Discussion Paper 15, National Centre for Social and Economic Modelling, University of Canberra, 1996.

Lee, Julie and Glenda Strachan, 'Who's Minding the Baby Now? Child Care Under the Howard Government' (1998) 9 (2) *Labour and Industry* 81.

Levit, Nancy, *The Gender Line: Men, Women and the Law*, New York, NYU Press, 1998.

Lewis, Jane, 'The Problem of Lone-Mother Families in Twentieth-Century Britain' (1998) 20(3) *Journal of Social Welfare and Family Law* 251.

López, Ian F Haney, 'The Social Construction of Race' in Delgado, Richard, ed, *Critical Race Theory: The Cutting Edge*, Philadelphia, Temple Univ. Press, 1995, 191.

MacDermott, Kathy, 'Women's Productivity: Productivity Bargaining and Service Workers' (1993) 55(4) *The Journal of Industrial Relations* 538.

MacDermott, Therese, 'Industrial Legislation in 1996: The Reform Agenda' (1997) 39(1) *Journal of Industrial Relations* 52.

MacDermott, Therese, 'Bargaining Under the New Industrial Relations Regime and its Impact on Women' in Cass, Bettina & Rowanne Couch, eds, *Divided Work Divided Society: Employment, Unemployment and the Distribution of Income in 1990s Australia*, Sydney, Research Institute for Humanities and Social Sciences, University of Sydney, 1998.

MacIntyre, Alastair, *Whose Justice? Which Rationality?*, Notre Dame, Univ. of Notre Dame Press, 1988.

Mann, Patricia S, *Micro-Politics: Agency in a Post-Feminist Era*, Minneapolis, Univ. of Minnesota Press, 1994.

Mansbridge, Jane, 'Using Power/Fighting Power: The Polity' in Benhabib, Seyla, ed, *Democracy and Difference: Contesting the Boundaries of the Political*, Princeton, NJ, Princeton University Press, 1996, 46.

Mathias, Malcolm, 'Family Breakdown in Australia: An attempt to get at the truth about the magnitude of the problem' at http://www.netspace.net.au/~lfaavic/html/ accessed 1 February 1999.

Matsuda, Mari J, 'Voices of America: Accent, Anti-Discrimination Law, and a Jurisprudence for the Last Reconstruction', 100 *Yale LJ* 1334, 1405 (1991).

McGregor, Richard, 'Fathers force PM to review child support', The *Australian*, 17 April 1998.

McKenna, Michael & Michelle Hele, 'Women's hard labour, Workforce still discriminates on pregnancy, The *Courier-Mail*, July 14, 1999.

Megalogenis, George, 'Women Win the Jobs Race', The *Australian*, 12 November, 1999.

Mich Comp Laws Ann § 722.23© (Supp. 1981-82).

Minow, Martha, 'Interpreting Rights: An Essay for Robert Cover' (1987) 96 *Yale LJ* 1860.

Minow, Martha, *Making All the Difference: Inclusion, Exclusion, and American Law*, Ithaca, NY, Cornell Univ. Press, 1990.

Mison, Robert B, 'Homophobia in Manslaughter: The Homosexual Advance as Insufficient Provocation' (1992) 80 California Law Review 133.

Mitchell, Deborah, 'Family Policy and the State' in Hancock, Linda, ed, *Women, Public Policy and the State*, South Yarra, Vic, Macmillan Education, 1999.

Monks, Kathy & Patricia Barker, 'The Glass Ceiling: Cracked but not Broken? Evidence from a Study of Chartered Accountants', DCUBS Research Papers 1995-6 No. 1.

Moran, Leslie, *The Homosexuality of Law*, London, Routledge, 1996.

Mossman, Mary Jane & Morag MacLean, 'Family Law and Social Welfare: Toward a New Equality' (1986) 5 *Canadian Journal of Family Law* 79.

Muehlenberg, Bill, 'What is a Family?' (1995) 16 *The Australian Family* 3.

'Myth of the Single Mother Revealed', The *Sunday Telegraph*, 12 December 1999.

National Federation of Australian Women, 'Raising Women's Economic Standing – Breaking Through the 80¢ in the Dollar Barrier', prepared for the Australian Women's Roundtable 1998, Canberra, 19-20 August 1998 accessed on 2 May 2000 at http://www.dpmc.gov.au/osw/.

National Pregnancy and Work Inquiry, 'Pregnant and Productive: It's a right not a privilege to work while pregnant', Canberra, AGPS, 1999.

National Women's Law Centre, 'Report to the Leadership Conference on Civil Rights' accessed on line at http://www.civilrights.org/ on 12 November 1999.

Neallani, Shelina, 'Women of Colour in the Legal Profession: Facing the Familiar Barriers of Race and Sex' (1992) 5 *Canadian Journal of Women & the Law* 148.

Ng, Roxana, 'Sexism, racism & Canadian nationalism' in Gunew, Sneja Marina & Anna Yeatman, eds, *Feminism and the Politics of Difference*, St Leonards, NSW, Allen & Unwin, 1993, 197.

Nicholson, Alastair AO RFD (Chief Justice of the Family Court), 'The Changing Concept of Family – the Significance of Recognition and Protection' (1997) 11 *Australian Journal of Family Law* 13.

Nightengale, Martina, 'Women and a flexible workforce' in Edwards, Anne and Susan Magarey, eds, *Women in a Restructuring Australia*, St Leonards, NSW, Allen & Unwin, 1995, 121.

Norington, Brad, 'Working Mother Tests Family Friendly Hours' The *Sydney Morning Herald*, 2 August 1999.

Note, 'The First Amendment and the American Indian Religious Freedom Act: An Approach to Protecting Native American Religion' 71 *Iowa Law Review* 869 (1986).

Nozari, Fariborz, 'The 1987 Swedish Family Law Reform' (1989) 17 *International Journal of Legal Information* 219.

Olsen, Frances E, 'The Family and the Market: A Study of Ideology and Legal Reform' (1983) 96 *Harvard LR* 1497.

Otlowski, Margaret, 'Shared (Week About) Parenting Arrangements Leads to Neither Parent Qualifying for Sole Parent Pension: Legislative Changes Effective 1 July 1999 May Produce a Different Outcome' (1999) 5 *Current Family Law* 93.

Parliamentary Debates, 1977, House of Representatives, Vol. H of R 107, Canberra, Commonwealth Government Printer, 1977.

Patrick, Vincent & Antonia Feitz, 'Is a mismatch between family choices and government policy hurting children?', presented at the National Social Policy Conference, UNSW, 21-23 July, 1999.

Peetz, David, Margaret Gardner, Kerry Brown & Sandra Berns, 'Gender Equity, Affirmative Action Legislation and the Workplace', Centre for Research in Employment and Work, Griffith University, Report to the Review of the Affirmative Action Act May 1998.

Pocock, B, 'Better the Devil You Know: Prospects for Women under Labor and Coalition Industrial Relations Policies' in Bryce, Marilyn (ed), *Industrial Relations Policy under the Microscope*, ACIRRT Working Paper No. 40, April 1996.

Pocock, Barbara, 'Gender and Australian Industrial Relations Theory' (1997) 8 (1) *Labour & Industry* 1.

Pocock, Barbara, 'Gender and the Labour Market' (1998) 40 *Journal of Industrial Relations* 580.

Pocock, Barbara, 'Equal Pay Thirty Years On: Policy and Practice' in 'Policy Forum: The Equal Pay Case – Thirty Years On' (1999) 32 (2) *Australian Economics Review* 279.

Polikoff, Nancy D, 'Why are Mothers Losing: A Brief Analysis of Criteria Used in Child Custody Determinations' (1992) 14 *Women's Rights Law Reporter* 175.

Probert, Belinda, *Part-time Work and Managerial Strategy: Flexibility in the New Industrial Relations Framework*, Canberra, AGPS, 1995.

Rawls, John, *Political Liberalism*, New York, Columbia Univ. Press, 1993.

Retschlag, Christine 'School's out on low birth rate' The *Courier Mail*, 14 December 1999.

Robson, Ruthann, 'Resisting the Family: Repositioning Lesbians in Legal Theory' (1994) 19 *Signs* 975.

Rousseau, Jean Jacques, *The Social Contract and Discourses*, trans. with an introduction by GDH Cole, London, JM Dent & Sons, 1913.

Russell, Jennifer M, 'On Being a Gorilla in Your Midst, or, The Life of One Blackwoman in the Legal Academy' in Delgado, Richard, ed, *Critical Race Theory: The Cutting Edge*, Philadelphia, Temple Univ. Press, 1995, 498.

Sackville, Ronald, 'Social Security and Family Law in Australia' (1978) 27 *Int & Comp Law Quarterly* 127.

Sandel, Michael, *Liberalism and the Limits of Justice*, Cambridge, Cambridge Univ. Press, 1982.

Saunders, Peter, 'Poverty and Deprivation in Australia', Year Book Australia, 1996, ABS Cat. 1301.0.

Schiratzki, Johanna, 'Custody of Children in Sweden: Recent Developments' in Wahlgren, Peter, ed, *Legal Issues of the Late 1990s*, Scandinavian Studies in Law Volume 38, Stockholm, Stockholm University Law Faculty, 1998, 255.

Schneider, Elizabeth, 'Equal Rights to Trial for Women: Sex Bias in the Law of Self-Defence' 15 *Harv CR-CL LR* 623 (1980).

Scott, Katherine & Clarence Lochhead, 'Are Women Catching up in the Earnings Race?' accessed at http://www.ccsd.ca/insite6.htm on 11 November 1999.

Shaver, Sheila 'Poverty, Gender and Sole Parenthood' in Fincher, Ruth and John Nieuwenhuysen, eds, *Australian Poverty: Then and Now*, Melbourne, Melbourne Univ. Press, 1998.

Shute, Carmel, 'Unequal Partners: Women, Power and the Trade Union Movement' in Grieve, Norma & Ailsa Burns, eds, *Australian Women: Contemporary Feminist Thought'* Melbourne, OUP, 1994, 166.

Siim, Birte, 'The Gendered Scandinavian Welfare States: The Interplay between Women's Roles as Mothers, Workers and Citizens in Denmark' in Lewis, Jane, ed, *Women and Social Policies in Europe: Work, Family and the State*, Aldershot, Edward Elgar, 1993.

Silverstein, Louise B & Carl F Auerbach 'Deconstructing the Essential Father' (1999) 54 (6) *American Psychologist* 397.

Smallwood, Margaret, 'This Violence is Not Our Way: An Aboriginal Perspective on Domestic Violence' in Thorpe, Ros and Jude Irwin, eds, *Women and Violence Working for Change*, Sydney, Hale & Ironmonger, 1996.

Smith, Adam, *Wealth of Nations*, New York, Random House, 1965, 14.

Smith, Meg & Peter Ewer, *The Position of Women in the National Training Reform Agenda and Enterprise Bargaining*, WREIP, Department of Employment and Training, Canberra, AGPS, 1995.

Statistics Canada, Labour Force Participation Rates accessed on 25 March 2000 at http://www.statcan.ca/english/.

Stewart, Miranda, 'Domesticating Tax Reform: The Family in Australian Tax and Transfer Law' (1999) 21 *Sydney Law Review* 453.

Stoltz, Pauline, 'Single Mothers and the Dilemmas of Universal Social Policies' (1997) 26(4) *Jnl Soc Pol* 425.

Swedish Institute, 'Equality Between Men and Women' accessed on http://www.si.se/eng/esverige/equality.html on 22 December 1999.

Tapper, Alan, 'Family Policy and Family Problems in the Australian Welfare State' and Joseph, Gerard, 'Objectives for Family Policy' in Barcan, Alan R and Patrick O'Flaherty, *Family, Education and Society: The Australian Perspective*, A PWPA Australia Publication, Canberra, Academy Press, 1995.

Taxation Review Committee, *Full Report*, Canberra, AGPS, 1975.

Taylor, Janet, 'Issues of Paid Employment for Mothers of Young Children' (1996) 17 *Women and Work* 12.

Thomson, Holly B & Jon M Werner, 'The Family and Medical Leave Act: Assessing the Costs and Benefits of Use', 146 accessed at http://www.kentlaw.edu/ on 10 November 1999.

Thornton, Margaret, 'The Seductive Allure of EEO' in Grieve, Norma & Ailsa Burns, ed, *Australian Women: Contemporary Feminist Thought*, Melbourne, OUP, 1994, 215.

Thornton, Margaret, 'Embodying the Citizen' in Thornton, Margaret, ed, *Public and Private: Feminist Legal Debates*, Melbourne, OUP, 1995, 1998.

Thornton, Margaret, *The Liberal Promise: Anti-discrimination Legislation in Australia*, Melbourne, OUP, 1990.

Trainor, Brian T, 'The Forgotten Children', *IPA Review*, Melbourne, 1995; Woods, Mary Helen, 'Difficulties Faced in Sole Parent Families' (1987) 18 (3) *The Australian Family: Journal of the Family Association* 26.

United Nations, 'Statistics and Indicators on the World's Women' accessed at http://www.un.org/Depts/unsd/gender/intro.htm on 3 December 1999.

US Census Bureau, *Statistical Abstract of the United States*, 'Labor Force, Employment and Earnings' accessed on line at http://www.census.gov/ on 16 March 2000.

US Department of Labor, Women's Bureau, 'Facts on Working Women' accessed on 11 November 1999 at http://www.dol.gov/dol/.

US Department of Labor, 'Monthly Labor Review' at http://stats.bls.gov/ downloaded on 7 April 2000.

Van Gramberg, Bernadine, 'Women, industrial relations and public policy' in Hancock, Linda, *Women, Public Policy and the State*, Macmillan Education, Victoria, 1999, 99.

Vogel, Joachim, 'The European "Welfare Mix": Institutional Configuration and Distributive Outcome in Sweden and the European Union: A Longitudinal and Comparative Perspective' (1999) 48 *Social Indicators Research* 245.

Walzer, Michael, *Spheres of Justice: A Defence of Pluralism and Equality*, Oxford, Martin Robertson, 1983.

Walzer, Michael, 'Liberalism and the Art of Separation' (1984) 12 (3) *Political Theory* 315.

Walzer, Michael, *On Toleration*, Princeton, NJ, Yale Univ. Press, 1997.

West, Robin L, 'Foreword: Taking Freedom Seriously' 104 *Harv LR* 43 (1990).

West, Robin L, *Caring for Justice*, New York, NYU Press, 1997.

Williams, Patricia J, *The Alchemy of Race and Rights*, Cambridge, MA, Harvard Univ. Press, 1991.

Winter, Bronwyn, 'Women, the Law, and Cultural Relativism in France: The Case of Excision' (1994) 19 *Signs* 939.

Women's Action Alliance, 'Family Unit Taxation' accessed on 14 April 2000 at http://users.bigpond.com/jsmitty/waaFamilyUnitTaxation.html.

Yeatman, Anna, 'Voice and representation in the politics of difference' in Gunew, Sneja M & Anna Yeatman, *Feminism and the Politics of Difference*, Sydney, Allen & Unwin, 1993, 228.

Yeo, Stanley, 'Sex, Ethnicity, Power of Self-Control and Provocation Revisited' (1996) 18 *Sydney Law Review* 304.

Young, Claire, 'Taxing Times for Women: Feminism Confronts Tax Policy' (1999) 21 *Sydney Law Review* 487.

Zanetti, Carmen, 'Sole Parents: Trends and Issues' (December 1994) *Social Security Journal* 92.

Index